ENGLISH HOUSES
1200–1800

ROYAL
COMMISSION
ON THE HISTORICAL
MONUMENTS
OF ENGLAND

ENGLISH HOUSES
1200–1800

THE HERTFORDSHIRE EVIDENCE

J T Smith

LONDON : HMSO

© Crown copyright 1992
First published 1992

ISBN 0 11 300037 5

British Library Cataloguing in
Publication Data
A CIP catalogue record for this book
is available from the British Library

Printed in the United Kingdom for HMSO
Dd. 292028 C25 3/92 5673

Contents

Illustrations

The Royal Commission is grateful to the various institutions and individuals who permitted the photographing of topographical material in their care and the reproduction of copyright material.

Sources of illustrations, other than photographs or line drawings prepared by Royal Commission staff, are as follows:

The Bodleian Library, Oxford 86, 94, 95; British Library 82, 85, 92, 193; Hertford Museum 25, 32, 97, 138, 139, 142, 195, 223, 225, 227, 265; Hertfordshire County Record Office 15, 16, 17, 24, 31, 40, 47, 123, 130, 131, 134, 144, 147, 187, 189, 194, 203, 204, 208, 209, 240, 246, 254, 263, 270 (187 and 189 reproduced by permission of the executors of Lady Ravensdale); Hitchin Museum 274; Meynell Collection 212; Public Record Office 103, 105; The Royal Society 2; St Albans Public Library 18; Watford Central Library 10, 250 .

The Royal Commission is indebted to Hertford County Council for permission to use measured drawings by Harold Leach, formerly of the County Planning Department, as a basis for those reproduced as Figure 236.

Every effort has been made to trace copyright holders; the Royal Commission wishes to apologise to any who may have been inadvertently omitted from the above list.

Commissioners

Chairman's Foreword

It is in the nature of a dynamic record of the nation's heritage that the updating and reinterpretation of material should be a continuing process, both to take account of new findings and to present the material in new ways to serve the changing needs of the broad constituency of users.

The Royal Commission's first published inventory, on the historical monuments of Hertfordshire, appeared in 1910. This was followed by a succession of county inventories which over the years grew increasingly long and detailed, whilst respecting the format set by the first. Eventually the value of this format was itself questioned as it became apparent that the availability of individual records of buildings and sites in the National Monuments Record made it unnecessary to publish detailed accounts of all buildings recorded by Royal Commission staff. The information could be better presented as a published synthesis of significant findings, supported by the records held in the archive. This volume on the domestic architecture of Hertfordshire is one of the direct results of this change in attitude towards the way in which information might be presented, a change which the author, Mr J T Smith, did so much to foster.

Mr Smith, for many years the Royal Commission's principal architectural investigator, retired in 1987. This volume, based on many years of detailed investigation of buildings within the county of Hertfordshire, is informed by knowledge gained over nearly forty years of work with the Royal Commission, during which time Mr Smith developed his characteristically rigorous and questioning approach towards the historical evidence presented by buildings. Thus, whilst this volume is devoted to one English county, its findings have a far wider application: it is hoped that the book will stimulate further research into the problems which the buildings raise.

The Commissioners wish to thank Mr Smith for his outstanding service to the Royal Commission and for bringing this synthesis to completion. They also wish to join him in thanking colleagues who assisted in the recording of the individual buildings, particularly the late John Bassham, whose photographs set new levels of excellence in architectural recording.

The greater part of the fieldwork and documentary research for this book was completed by 1982 although some minor updating has been incorporated in the end notes. Factors both internal and external have conspired to delay publication, so we are particularly pleased that we are at last able to make this long-awaited volume available.

Whilst the Commissioners have offered criticism and advice on the text, the views expressed are those of the author. The Commissioners are particularly grateful for the generous co-operation given by the owners of the houses which have been recorded.

The complete archive of material relating to the buildings is available to the public and may be consulted at the National Buildings Record, RCHME, 23 Savile Row, London W1X 2JQ.

PARK OF MONMOUTH

Author's Preface

The genesis of the present work rests with a former Secretary of the Royal Commission, Mr A R Dufty, who, aware of the inadequacies of the 1910 Hertfordshire *Inventory*, and also of the impossibility of revision on the scale of the Dorset volumes appearing in the early 1970s, enquired whether a survey of Hertfordshire might be possible on the lines of that of Breconshire carried out by Mr Stanley Jones and myself: a survey undertaken for Breconshire County Council between 1959 and 1967 and published between 1963 and 1972 in the county journal *Brycheiniog*.

The work thus instigated had three principal aims: to provide information on the houses of a county about which the Royal Commission continually received inquiries; to establish generalisations which might enable houses not reported on to be interpreted; and to draw historical conclusions from the architectural evidence. At that time a target of about 500 buildings was agreed; at least one building in every parish was to be examined. In the event, Mr John Bassham and I, working together, visited nearly twice the number of buildings envisaged at the outset, a major part of the ensuing record being formed by Mr Bassham's photographs. Mr Bassham's understanding of the houses and of the kind of record needed in the unusual circumstances, very different from those of a normal inventory, enabled him frequently to produce a comparatively small body of photographs covering all the evidence crucial to understanding the building in question.

At the outset Sir John Summerson, then a Commissioner, directed attention to Professor Lawrence Stone's important work on Hertfordshire country houses,[1] in which a quantitative assessment of the building done between 1540 and 1879 is attempted. The need, in any such assessment, to take cognisance of long-demolished houses reinforced two points made earlier by Sir John himself with reference to 18th-century country houses: that the study of types of buildings is retarded by comparison with the work devoted to the architects who built them, and that existing buildings have received more attention than those known from records.[2]

The exceptionally large number of engravings, drawings and old photographs available for Hertfordshire revealed that surviving country houses are quite unrepresentative of the county's social history and largely unintelligible out of their vanished architectural context. These considerations governed the presentation of the evidence and accentuated the tendency observable in recent publications of both English and Welsh Royal Commissions to use vanished buildings to amplify the evidence of the surviving ones. But engravings and drawings, clear though they may be to the specialist reader, frequently require interpretation for their significance to be apparent to others, as, equally, does the complicated structural development of many still existing houses. To that end development diagrams and reconstructions of both the ground plan and external appearance of houses have been used here in the hope of bringing successive historical phases more vividly before the reader, specialist or not. Mr Nigel Fradgley began and contributed largely to this aspect of the work, finding a variety of ways to show not only how houses developed, but also the architectural problems created by successive enlargements or alterations; Mr George Wilson and Mr Allan Adams successively built on the foundations he laid. All showed much ingenuity in devising appropriate forms of illustration to present what is often, and inevitably, inadequate evidence. It must be stressed, though, that no attempt was made to cover systematically the same ground as Professor Stone. Some great houses where plentiful graphic evidence did not sufficiently elucidate the plan and development are excluded; Ashridge, Little Gaddesden, is the most notable instance. Nineteenth-century houses are excluded, although the original intention, frustrated by the size of the task, was to carry the story up to at least 1850. A few of the houses included were not visited, even though they survive; Wrotham Park, Potters Bar, burnt out in the 19th century, is one such.

Chance also played a part in the work. My assistant, Mrs Pauline Fenley, drew Dr Clive Rouse's attention to some recently discovered wall paintings, on which he produced reports more expert by far than would otherwise have been possible. Subsequently, Dr Rouse was prevailed upon to consider all wall paintings in Hertfordshire, accompanied by Mrs Fenley. His account of them, originally intended for publication here, will appear in Volume 146 of *The Archaeological Journal* and is the first attempt to survey comprehensively the wall paintings of a whole county.

It has proved impossible, for reasons of cost, to publish here the descriptive list of significant houses recorded. This will be available, at a nominal charge, direct from the RCHME. It contains a brief historical analysis of each house and just sufficient architectural detail to indicate the basis of the conclusions. It is hoped that such detail, viewed in the light of the inferential methods expounded in Chapter 1, will prove adequate for the reader seeking examples of a particular type or anxious to test a generalisation; where no solution to a problem was found, or where elements of doubt remain, that is plainly stated. The complete record for each recorded building is available in the National Buildings Record.

Acknowledgements

It is both a duty and a pleasure to thank the many people other than those already mentioned who have been involved in the preparation of this book. First and foremost I have to thank Commissioners and four successive Secretaries, Mr A R Dufty CBE, Mr R W McDowall OBE, Professor P J Fowler and Mr T G Hassall, first for accepting that a survey of this kind was feasible, then for permitting it to go forward and bearing with the innumerable problems entailed in its writing. Two former members of staff, Mr R F Meades and Mrs L Titmus, prepared drawings at an early stage. Dr Bridgett Jones undertook valuable documentary research in Hertford and other record offices; Mrs Pauline Fenley acted as research assistant to the project for several years and searched out drawings and plans in museums and libraries; Mr Stephen Croad interpreted engravings and drawings; Mrs Ann Irvine, and later Mrs Jean Irving, typed several drafts of the text from what is politely termed a difficult hand.

The research could not have been done without the most generous co-operation of many owners of drawings and manuscripts. The Marquess of Salisbury kindly permitted the use of plans and drawings of Hatfield House in the Hatfield MSS, and the publication of drawings based on them. The Marquess's librarian and archivist, Mr R Harcourt-Williams, gave generously of his time in producing documents and answering queries. Mr Godfrey Meynell kindly permitted the copying and reproduction of certain drawings in his collection, as did Mr David Lewis a book of plans and drawings of Newsells Park, Barkway, then in his possession. The staffs of the British Library and the Ashmolean, Victoria and Albert and Soane Museums were consistently helpful, but special mention must be made of the Society of Antiquaries and its former librarian, Mr John Hopkins.

Mrs Barbara Hutton's generous gift of a copy of the second edition of Chauncy's *Hertfordshire* was of great help. Mr Graham Bailey, Mr Stephen Castle, Mr Philip Coverdale, Mr Adrian Gibson and the late Mr Gordon Moody MBE were generous with information and drawings. Mr Guy Beresford provided information about Ashwell. Mr Peter Walne and his staff at the County Record Office were unfailingly helpful, as were the directors and staffs of the county's principal museums: Hertford (Mr A Gordon Davies); Hitchin (Mr Alan Fleck); St Albans (Mr D Gareth Davies) and Watford (Mrs Helen Poole); also the research librarians at St Albans (Miss Vivienne Prowse) and Watford (Miss Marshall).

Mr John Onslow, County Architect, and members of his staff, as well as the staff of several district councils, were of great assistance, notably Mr Alan Carter, Mr D Russell Craig, Mr William Dodd and Dr Mervyn Miller. Four brewery companies, Greene King, Ind Coope, McMullen and Whitbread, provided plans of the many historically interesting buildings they own. It is impossible to list all the people, especially those in various local history groups, who helped in many ways, notably by lending plans and old photographs. I hope they will accept my general thanks.

Mr Michael Aston, Mr Robert Machin and Professor Lawrence Stone each read portions of the text in draft; for their comments I am grateful, even though it has not been possible to incorporate all their suggestions.

Finally, I thank the many householders who welcomed Mr Bassham and myself into their houses. I hope they will find satisfaction in having assisted in this enterprise.

J T Smith

Notes on Photography

During five years of fieldwork for the survey of Hertfordshire, some 950 buildings were investigated, representing a selection of houses from the biggest to the smallest. Each was visited by an investigator and photographer, working together as a team and usually completing the record without the need for further visits.

The photographs taken form a greater part of the primary investigation than in any of the Royal Commission's previous fieldwork, yet no attempt has been made to provide complete photographic cover of a building's structure or decoration. Rather, they were taken with the aim of presenting the essential evidence on which the historical conclusions are based. Little effort has been put into recording such details as fireplaces, doorcases and panelling except where these features are precisely datable and can be useful for comparative purposes. These subjects are more usually included in an architectural context, but they are of sufficient size on a large-format negative, and of high enough quality to accept enlargement for closer examination, should this be necessary. Furthermore, in part because so little original detail remains in its original position, it was thought undesirable to concentrate on showing the general appearance of individual rooms; instead, whenever possible, photographs were taken to show the relationship of significant features in different rooms. It is hoped in this way to give an impression of what the interior of a building is like and to convey the impression given when standing inside, looking through doors, down passages and including in the view windows and fireplaces.

The exteriors were taken specifically for record purposes. Photographs showing the relationship between the various phases of building have been concentrated upon, with a general absence of straight-on views of elevations. The illustration of relationships between chimney-stacks and entrances has been sought; also, external evidence of staircases where indicated by windows.

Roof spaces were normally photographed rather than drawn, to save time, but, to compensate for this, photographs often included details in addition to general views. When recording the smoke-blackened interior of early roofs the camera is particularly useful because soot deposits can sometimes show up quite spectacularly on the plaster partitions. The recording of roof areas is often the most arduous and time-consuming of all photography, with little or no daylight and cramped working conditions. The frequent absence of electric light makes setting up the camera and focusing a problem, and certain of the essential details may be in recessed or inaccessible corners. This type of photography usually has to be done whilst balanced on narrow rafters, difficult enough with a large-format monorail camera and heavy tripod.

For most of this work, a half-plate 6½" x 4¾" DeVere monorail camera was used because of its large high-quality negative and the movement of the lens plane that allows for correcting vertical distortion. However, during the early stages of the project in eastern and some northern parishes, a 5" x 4" Linhof camera was adapted with a 70 mm roll-film back, capable of taking up to eighty exposures, and was used to carry out a rapid initial survey of all listed buildings from which a choice of buildings to be visited could be made. This proved useful compact equipment for a quick survey as it combined the advantages of a smaller format roll-film camera with the movements of a monorail. A limited choice of available lenses for the camera tended to reduce the quality of some of these photographs, although many were of sufficiently high quality to be used in this volume.

The camera employed for most of the fieldwork used 6½" x 4¾" sheets of flat film, which can be exposed and then processed individually. This has the advantage of allowing the use of normal, high or low contrast developers, but also variation in developing times, to give still further contrast control. A typical example of a low-contrast subject might be a fragment of a wall painting, requiring high-contrast film and developer. Conversely, a black timber-framed building with white plasterwork, all bathed in bright sunshine, is a good example of the opposite, and will require quite different exposure and development to obtain the most satisfactory results.

Considering the quality of the illustrations used here, and, in particular, the exterior views, it has to be remembered that ideal weather conditions did not always prevail when the photographs were taken as this would have lengthened the task unacceptably. But, equally, views were seldom taken when conditions were to any serious degree unsuitable, in order to avoid the dull and lifeless results they would have produced. Sunshine was waited for if thought necessary to enhance the texture and mouldings on a main elevation, but often avoided with jettied timber fronts, if the projecting floors produced detail obscuring shadows.

Interiors were usually illuminated by powerful flashlight, owing to the difficulty of managing highlights such as windows included in or situated uncomfortably near to the edge of the picture area. The type of interior view desired and already described calls for the very careful positioning of lights when more than one room, together with perhaps a staircase, fireplaces and corridors, may be included. One of the few disadvantages posed by the large-format camera is the need to use a very small aperture to obtain a picture sharply in focus from close to the camera to the far distance. Working at such small aperture (f32, or even f45 occasionally), powerful expendable flash bulbs are more suitable than any form of electronic flash yet available. They can be used to light the views described, fired both from the camera position and concealed behind suitable objects within the picture area, and activated by photo-electric cells. Thus the well-lit room, dimly lit passage and dark staircase can appear in the picture all equally and evenly lit, revealing their detail in a way never seen by the naked eye.

John Bassham

Editorial Notes

English Houses 1200–1800: the Hertfordshire evidence is based on the detailed investigation of over 900 houses in Hertfordshire. It does not attempt to repeat the investigative methods and presentation of the Royal Commission's earlier publication on the buildings of that county (RCHME *Hertfordshire*, 1910) but seeks to use the evidence of the buildings, some of which are known to us only through illustrations, supported by documentary research, to draw broad conclusions about the general development of domestic architecture in England.

It is inevitable, given the nature of the material and the present state of knowledge, that many of the conclusions drawn about these houses are speculative. They are designed to contribute to the continuing discussion of a very rich and so far inadequately researched body of historical material. The nature of the evidence and the problems and methods of interpretation and inference are discussed in Chapter 1.

Further information about the houses discussed in this book, and a complete record of houses surveyed, can be found in an inventory of Hertfordshire buildings, available on request from the Royal Commission.

Diagrams

For reasons of space, only a small selection of old drawings and engravings can be reproduced here. For those houses with a very complicated historical development, drawings have been used in conjunction with plans to produce diagrams which, it is hoped, will illustrate the main stages of development more clearly than plans or elevations alone. These diagrams, although in part conjectural, represent a collation of as many sources as were available and are designed not only for purposes of elucidation but also to provide a basis for further work by others. (Illustrations, both line drawings and half-tones, are indicated in the text by means of bold numbers contained within square brackets.)

Interpretation of line drawings

Unless otherwise indicated, plans are of the ground floor of a building and were drawn to a scale of either one-eighth of an inch to one foot (1:96) or one-sixteenth of an inch to one foot (1:192).

Where more than one plan is shown, the lower floors are to the left or below the upper floors. Plans show the state of a building as it was when recorded unless otherwise stated.

Initial letters have been used on certain plans to indicate former or conjectural room use. A key is given opposite:

B	Bedchamber/Bedroom		G	Gallery
Ba	Bakehouse		H	Hall
B Cl	Bed closet		K	Kitchen
Bil	Billiard room		La	Larder
Brew	Brewhouse		LC	Lodging chamber
Br R	Breakfast room		Li	Library
But Py	Butler's pantry		Lo	Lobby
By	Buttery		Ny	Nursery
Ch	Chamber		P	Parlour
Cl	Closet		Pal	Pallet chamber
CP	Common parlour		Py	Pantry
Cu	Cupboard		S	Saloon
Din	Dining room/Dining parlour/Eating room		Sc	Scullery
			SH	Servants' hall
Dr	Dressing room		Sit	Sitting room
Drg	Drawing room		St	Study/Office
Dy	Dairy		WC	Water closet
EC	Earth closet			
EH	Entrance-hall			

(An arrow on a staircase indicates the direction of the upward flight.)

Dating

The terms 'early' and 'late', applied to a century, refer here to the first and second half of that century respectively.

'Late medieval' denotes the 15th and the early 16th centuries and is used primarily with reference to types of plan and structure current at those periods and even persisting into the late 16th century.

The dates 'c.1500' or 'c.1600' are used when the dating can be more precise, with a possible range of c.1470–1530 or c.1570–1630. In those cases where even greater precision is possible, a narrower date range is used.

Parish names

A reference to an individual house consists of its name and parish location, except where this duplicates the house name: for example, Wyddial Hall, Wyddial. This becomes simply 'Wyddial Hall' in the text. A list of Hertfordshire houses mentioned in the text can be found on pp 204–7, arranged alphabetically under their civil parish and each with a unique National Buildings Record archive reference number. The names and boundaries of the parishes are those effective after April 1974.

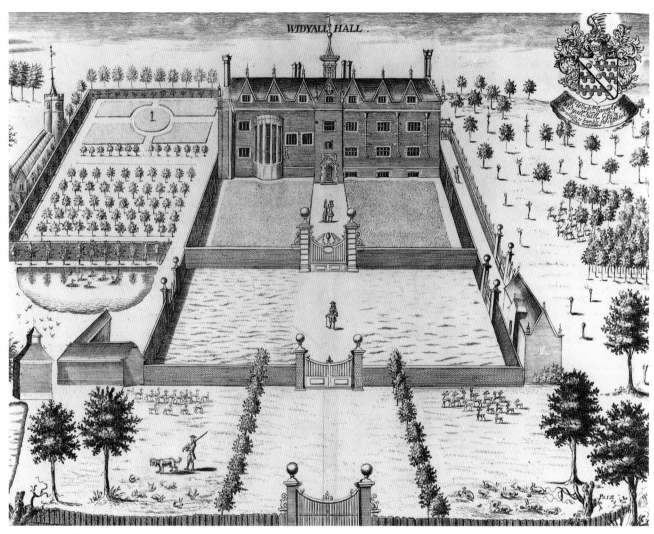

1 *Wyddial Hall: east elevation* (Drapentier)

3 *Wyddial Hall: east elevation*

Chapter 1

The nature of the evidence and
its interpretation

One of the difficulties in writing about buildings, and particularly about the very complicated sort in which Hertfordshire abounds, is to present convincingly the evidence on which the conclusions are based. Houses built before 1914 have inevitably been altered to enable them to survive; houses several centuries old will have undergone even more drastic changes. Over the last hundred years tradition-conscious owners have complicated this process, at first by freely copying old windows, fireplaces and the like, and latterly, in vernacular buildings, by stripping houses of later accretions in an attempt to restore them to their supposed original condition. Both situations create difficulties for the architectural historian. In the first, he is faced with fragmentary evidence needing much conjecture to make it comprehensible; in the second, he finds all too often a house reduced to a barely intelligible framework by the removal of all the subsequent stages of its development. Because the evidence in both cases is slight and hard to illustrate, some recurrent points of difficulty are discussed here and the assumptions made are set out explicitly. Even when some more or less satisfactory solution has been found for problems of an archaeological nature, that is to say those relating to the form of a building and its sequence of development, there are, as in all studies of material culture, difficulties of dating, and both the general approach to such questions and the solutions adopted for particular features are discussed.

Inference from plan: Wyddial Hall

The most important matter of this kind is the extent to which early phases of the history of a building can properly be inferred from its plan or form without the support of any datable evidence. Wyddial Hall provides an instance of such reasoning, which is set out in detail so that it can act as a touchstone for the less fully argued cases. Three pieces of evidence provide the basis of argument: an engraving by Drapentier[1] for Sir Henry Chauncy's *Historical Antiquities of Hertfordshire*, published in 1700 [1]; the record made of an old door-head pulled out after fire damage in 1733 [2]; and the form of the existing building. No reliance has been placed on a report of medieval work surviving in the cellars because there is now nothing which can definitely be

ascribed to so early a date – the dating of brickwork is at present very uncertain – and although some of the roof timbers are 17th-century work everything else about the house is no earlier than the post-fire rebuilding and much of it is a good deal later [3].

Nevertheless, certain features of the plan [4] and structure of Wyddial Hall that are anomalous in a mid 18th-century house can best be explained by postulating the survival of much earlier arrangements, some of which are not documented in any way and which may represent unrecorded changes made between the building of the house and its thorough renovation after 1743. The key to these inferences is the way in which the house is entered: by a doorway set to one side of the large entrance-hall [5] rather than opening into the middle of it as would be usual in Georgian planning. Equally surprising is the placing of the imposing main staircase [6]. This, in its present form, is mid Victorian, sited away from the entrance-hall altogether, so that instead of opening off either the back or one side of the hall in a position which would show it to advantage, as would be expected in a Georgian house, it can be seen only from a corridor. Such failure to exploit the visual possibilities of what was clearly intended to be an impressive architectural feature can be accounted for by the hypothesis that the block within which it stands pre-dates both the existing staircase and the 18th-century work of the entrance-hall. These apparent anomalies are explicable if the early 16th-century house shown in the Drapentier engraving is presumed to have survived in large part [7]: the present front doorway corresponds to one of the opposite doorways customary in a late medieval house [8]; the entrance-hall corresponds in its position to a hall open from the ground to roof, usual in medieval houses; and the semi-octagonal bay window replaces the oriel window at the upper end of the hall. The survival of the oriel suggests that as late as 1700 the hall still

2 *Wyddial Hall: door-head* (Phil Trans Royal Soc **39**, 1735–6, No. 439, Tab. 1, Fig. 1)

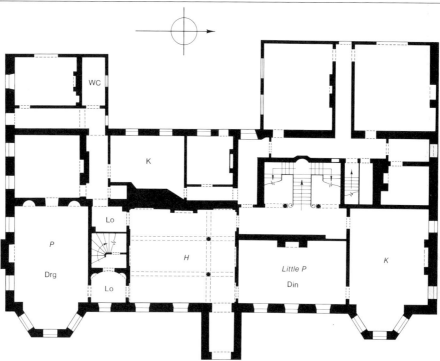

4   *Wyddial Hall: plan*

5   *Wyddial Hall: entrance-hall*

6 *Wyddial Hall: main staircase*

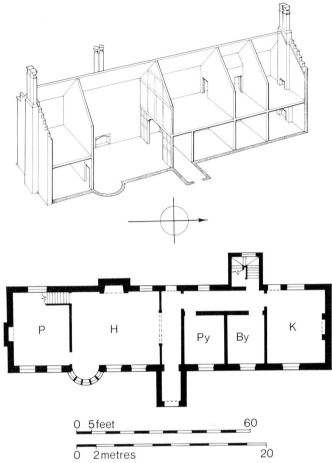

0 5feet   60

0 2metres   20

7 *Wyddial Hall: reconstruction of its 17th-century plan, and perspective cut-away*

extended through two storeys, no longer open to the roof but to a ceiling below the gabled attics, which look as if they were added in the early 17th century. Such an open hall would preclude the kind of staircase favoured in the 17th century, which combined visual effect with the convenience afforded by its central position. Consequently, the main stair was added at the lower end of the open hall to the two-

storeyed part of the house, which was no doubt extended and improved at that time. One of the original staircases was thereby either replaced or relegated to minor uses; the second, needed to approach the first-floor chambers at the upper end, was replaced by the present newel stair, set in a most unusual position between hall and parlour. This staircase is early 19th century but it probably succeeds an older

1516
1662

8 *Wyddial Hall: development perspectives*

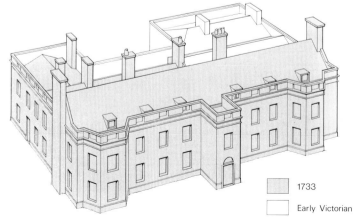

1733
Early Victorian

3

one of the same form going back, perhaps, to the 16th-century house.

On a first visit to Wyddial Hall the striking contrast between the Drapentier engraving and the existing front, coupled with the unlikely date of 1016 which was ascribed to the old door-head, led to the graphic evidence being disregarded, and it was only when the plan suggested a late medieval element in the present house that its significance was realised. Confirmation of the initial hypothesis gives confidence in the scores of similar interpretations which are based solely on the analysis of form and function.

9 *Howell's Farm, Weston: plan showing the former wing, now the north range*

Hall implied from the existence of cross-wings

One of the commonest problems in interpretation is presented by the two-storeyed timber-framed wing which adjoins a range of later date set at right angles to it. An explanation which has found favour in recent years is that the wing was built as an independent structure to which a ground-floor hall was added subsequently. Where the hall and the wing are large, and particularly where both are relatively early and not very different in date, it is not uncommon for the

wing to be explained as a first-floor hall to which a ground floor has been added later, as, for example, at Little Chesterford (Essex) and Middle Farm, Harwell (Berks).[2] Howell's Farm, Weston [9], has a comparable wing, although there a contemporaneous medieval hall is presumed to have existed.

An explanation of the phenomenon in terms of a complete change of building type on the same site, often with family

10 *Old Farm, Great Munden (photograph by A W Anderson, 1896)*

continuity, implies a correspondingly great change in the way of life of the household. This has never been elucidated satisfactorily and, indeed, has been contradicted in a number of instances where excavation has taken place on manorial sites. An alternative explanation, adopted here, has much in common with the concept of 'alternate development' advanced by Fox and Raglan in respect of farmhouses in Monmouthshire,[3] in assuming that the wing was never a complete house but was always closely associated with a hall which stood either on or near to the existing site. Where both hall and cross-wing are of relatively early date, the house is assumed to represent the period of transition from one form of construction to another: from the comparatively short-lived techniques using timbers set in or on the ground which have been called primitive framing[4] to those of fully framed construction capable of lasting for several generations. This assumption has been strengthened by the excavation of Penhallam Manor (Cornwall)[5] where the siting of the cross-wing (or *camera*) in relation to the entrance to the moated enclosure could only be explained by postulating the existence of a hall of which no trace could be found.

A similar problem is common in Hertfordshire. There are cases where a small cross-wing (occasionally with a crown-post roof proclaiming a late medieval origin but usually with the less easily datable clasped-purlin roof) adjoins a loftier block built to a post-medieval plan. Such houses have an outline sufficiently distinctive to permit interpretation. One long-demolished example is Old Farm, Great Munden [10], and at Pirton Grange [11] the inference made from external evidence can be confirmed inside by the survival of the remnant of a crown-post roof in the low south wing, without which the wing would be undatable. The main range adjoining it to the north is of the 17th century, yet, in a way exactly comparable to Penhallam, the wing is set towards a corner of the moated enclosure, whereas the lobby-entrance of the later building stands directly in line with the gatehouse and the bridge over the moat. Where there is no moat the smallness of the wing may itself be regarded as proof that it was never a complete house, and often the lack of any original fireplace means, if the suggestion of braziers is ruled out,[6] that there was no form of heating. Whether in such cases the destroyed hall was contemporary with or earlier than the wing is a problem incapable, in principle, of solution. Since the two parts of such timber-framed houses were not always jointed together and, consequently, either part could be removed without leaving any trace of mutilation in the other, the evidence for such removal is often subjective. The best that can be hoped for is evidence of intercommunication on the ground floor; for instance, the jambs of an original doorway may remain in a position where an external opening is unlikely. Other structural evidence may be provided by the timber framing on the side towards the postulated hall. If the wall of the wing is low enough to preclude a first-floor doorway without cutting through the wall-plate, it shows that there was no contemporary two-storeyed structure on that side; and if, as often happens, the existing building on the site of the presumed hall has a first floor higher than the wing, it may be regarded, firstly, as proof that the two parts of the house are not contemporaneous and, secondly, as arguing strongly that the wing is the earlier. If enough framing is exposed it may be clear that there were windows on only one side of the wing, or only on such parts of the wall as were not masked by a hall.

Weathered and smoke-blackened timbers

Two other kinds of evidence, both open to misinterpretation, have from time to time been used to support the presumed existence of a vanished hall. Firstly, when the framing of the wall of the cross-wing next to the hall lacks the corrugated surface characteristic of timbers which have been exposed to the weather for some time [12], it can be deduced that this side was always protected by some adjoining structure. Occasionally it is possible to distinguish those timbers which were protected by the presumed hall from others which are weathered, such as those above the former roof line of the hall. Secondly, the later range, incorporating a chimney from the outset, may have in its roof some rafters blackened by soot from an open hearth and evidently reused from an older building. It cannot be proved that they come from the immediate predecessor of the building in which they are reused, but it is unlikely that second-hand material was transported far to be used in a building of good quality, so that the more blackened rafters there are, the more likely it is that they come from a hall on that site. Moreover, if the old rafters, by the position of the mortises from which collar and other beams have been removed, appear to have belonged to a building of approximately the same width as the one in which they stand, and if that building would be appropriate to the length and dispositions of the wing, they can be taken as positive evidence of the existence of a medieval hall. Such is the case at Pirton Grange, where three or four couples of blackened rafters stand at the lower end of the main range.

Smoke-blackened roof timbers are usually of an even matt black colour, produced by a deposit of soot which rubs off as fine, almost powdery, granules. Sometimes, though, where the roof timbers have been thoroughly cleaned in the course of repair, the coating of soot may be largely removed except

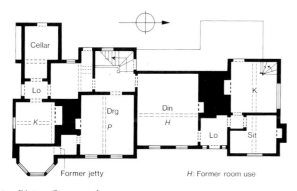

11 *Pirton Grange: plan*

12 *Holt Farm, St Stephen: interior showing weathered timbering at the south end of the larger of the two ranges*

on the inside face of a mortise within which the tenon has shrunk and allowed smoke to penetrate: where the inner surfaces of a mortise are entirely clean, the timber has probably never had an open hearth under it.

Timbers cleaned to allow the roof space to be used as an attic may be of a rather dark brown colour, not unlike that produced by stain or preservative. In some storeyed buildings where there is no question of an open hearth, the roof timbers appear to be smoke-stained, that is to say they are darker than their natural colour without any indication that a preservative has been applied. In such a case the cause may be a leaking chimney-flue, and this is easier to envisage if there is evidence that a timber chimney or a smoke-bay once existed than it is with a brick chimney-stack. Discolouration of this kind is referred to as smoke-staining rather than by the conventional terms smoke-blackening or sooting. That the explanation of leakage is likely to be correct is suggested by the occasional staining observable on roof timbers on the clean side of a partition heavily encrusted with soot. Such staining can also occur from a wide fire-

place (perhaps as a result of blacksmithing): this is apparent at Church Cottage, Brent Pelham, where it occurs on the boarded ceiling of a ground-floor room.

Open-hall or single-storey house?

Many small houses show evidence of having been of only one storey originally. Very few have any sign of smoke-blackening in the roof and all are of one storey with a half storey or semi-attic above. The principal and often only indication that this storey is an insertion is provided by tie-beams which have been cut through to provide doorways between the upstairs rooms. Moor Hall Cottage, Ardeley [13], is a clearer example than most; the west part of the original house has beams applied to the walls to carry the ends of the floorboards, an arch-braced tie-beam has been cut through, and at least one smoke-stained rafter survives in what is now largely a modern roof. These points taken together suggest that Moor Hall Cottage was an unusually small and late house with an open hall. More tenuous evidence exists at High Tree Farm, Ardeley, where a slight outward slope in the upper part of the front wall may be accounted for by supposing that the building has been heightened. When a timber-framed structure received an additional storey it was difficult to provide effective lateral stiffening for the upper part, because the mortises necessary for the diagonal braces required to keep both old and new parts rigid could not be cut into the standing timbers with the required precision; in time, the later work would begin to lean as the timber dried out and the joints weakened. This is evident enough in a sizeable medieval house such as Chells Manor, Aston [14], but is less expected behind the absolutely plain exterior of High Tree Farm; yet in both houses it is confirmed by a tie-beam and wall-plates now boxed in at floor level. The point is nicely confirmed at Cutting Hill Farm, Benington, where housings for the original rafters can be seen in the exposed top of the wall-plate. Sometimes the original wall height permitted the insertion

13 *Moor Hall Cottage, Ardeley: from the south east*

14 *Chells Manor, Aston: the heightened front wall leans outwards above the old wall-plate*

of a floor a foot or more below the old plate, but not sufficiently below it for the upper storey to resemble a half storey or semi-attic. Wherever any of these kinds of evidence occur they may be taken to indicate that the house was originally open from ground to roof, though it did not necessarily have an open hearth.

Difficulties in interpretation

Timber-framed construction

Timber framing is, in principle, so perfectly logical that interpretation of any alterations should present few problems. Each post and stud and brace is affixed at both ends to other timbers by some form of lap (halved) joint or by mortise and tenon, and each joint is secured by a wooden peg driven through it. When a member of such a structure has been removed the peg-holes will remain to testify to its existence and any timber inserted later can be detected by the lack of peg-holes, it being impossible to fit tenons tightly at both ends into corresponding mortises within an already standing frame. In addition, the spacing of timbers in such prefabricated structures is usually regular unless there is

reason for doing otherwise, such as the need to fit in doorways and windows.

However, almost every timber-framed building shows some peg-holes for which it is difficult to account. Sometimes they flatly contradict other evidence. At Hyde Lane Farm, Abbots Langley, one corner of the building is clearly indicated by the characteristic slight tapering of the wall-plate where it projected beyond the end wall to carry a barge-board, yet in the corner-post itself, about 5 ft (1.5 m) lower down, is a peg-hole which suggests that a longitudinal timber extended beyond the apparent gable wall. There can really be no doubt that the house ended at this point, yet if the termination of the plate had been concealed or removed or had decayed, the peg-hole would give rise to a problem of interpretation. How did it get there? Possibly the post has been reused from an earlier building, or perhaps the carpenter may have made a mistake.

The problem of what appears to be a mistake occurs frequently with chamfer stops. The chamfer provides a decorative finish for any exposed timber and is almost invariably applied to bridging joists and bearers. Theoretically, every chamfer is brought back to the square-cut edge of the timber (the arris) by means of a stop, which can be plain or elaborate, and if some aesthetic effect is sought it is logical to put a stop at each end of the chamfer. In all work of quality this is invariably the case, and close examination will reveal that the apparent exceptions result either from the careful continuation of the chamfer by cutting back the stop or from concealment of the stop by later plasterwork or other wall covering. Difficulties arise where no such explanation is possible, as is often the case with comparatively late and humble buildings in which only one end of a chamfered beam may be stopped, and this has usually to be ascribed to poor workmanship or timber. The explanation may be correct but it is unsatisfying.

A more positive mode of interpretation is provided by the way timbers forming internal partitions, which also normally correspond to the principal structural frames and the roof trusses, are made flush on one face. At the ends of such a partition, the corner-posts are of larger scantling than the studs between them, so all are made flush on the side facing the superior room, often the hall; in many mutilated buildings this kind of evidence helps to decide which was hall and which the service end or parlour. The same situation occurs in a wing with more than one room on each floor, where the flush face will be towards the superior room. In end-frames of a building, all the timberwork will be made flush, except for the projection of the wall-plates and purlins to carry barge-boards, in order to prevent rainwater from lodging on surfaces; where other timbers, notably ground sills, do extend even a short distance beyond an otherwise flush wall it is virtually certain that the wall in question was originally internal.

The copying of old styles

In general, past investigations into Hertfordshire buildings have not paid enough attention to the enormous amount of

15 *Rawdon House, Hoddesdon* (Buckler)

copying of old features and the interpolation of new work reproducing old styles which has taken place.

J E Cussans knew that the 4th Earl of Clarendon had made additions to The Grove, Sarratt, 'but so cleverly were they made that it is impossible to designate them'; within forty years even Andrew Whitford Anderson, who was by far the most knowledgeable and competent man ever to have looked at the houses of the county, was deceived at times. He accepted that Rawdon House, Hoddesdon, was built in 1622, the date over the porch and on rain-water heads, yet a Buckler drawing of the front [15] shows no such date nor does an Oldfield drawing of the back where 1622 is also proclaimed. Neither artist is likely to have missed such a point of antiquarian interest; and, in fact, the dates seem to have been added by the architects responsible for the 1880 restoration, Ernest George and Peto. In the same house, the staircase also has been generally and mistakenly accepted as original work. It took less than a generation for such fabrications as the rain-water heads and staircase to be accepted as genuine, no doubt through a misplaced trust that owners and architects were only repairing or revealing original work and not introducing innovations of their own.

In general, reproduction styles of the late 16th and early 17th century present less difficulty now than they did to ear-

lier architectural historians. The existence of large rooms apparently unaltered since the Civil War arouses suspicion, particularly where minor details are inaccurately reproduced. Alertness to the possibility of such copying is more difficult to maintain when later 17th or early 18th-century work is in question. At that period, the forms were simpler and appropriate fielded panelling could be expertly copied on an enormous scale by the Edwardians. After the wear and tear and repainting of seventy years or more, which may include the vicissitudes of military occupation during two World Wars, it is very difficult to distinguish imitation from genuine work of the period.

Discrepancies between different types of evidence

A particular difficulty for the architectural historian is the contradiction sometimes apparent between architectural and documentary evidence.

It is exemplified by Beeches, Brent Pelham, where explicit literary evidence that 'a fair house' was built in 1587 cannot be matched by anything observable in the existing timber-framed building; yet on general grounds that building is unlikely to have been totally replaced by 1662 when its then

8

owner was assessed for seven hearths. In this case, either the framing needs closer examination than has been possible or the confusion arises because of successive campaigns carried out over a comparatively short period, as happened at Brent Pelham Hall. There, early in the present century, the inscribed date 1608 was observed on a door lintel that may either have been reset or have formed part of an earlier house than the present one. The literary evidence begins with the clear statement that Edward Newport built, in 1619, 'a slight but well contrived House in this Mannor' and became Sheriff in 1620. A succeeding owner 'adorned this House' in the mid 17th century and his son refronted it, probably between 1678 and 1686.[7] Of the four building phases thus recorded the first two have left no discernible trace, the principal evidence of the third has been removed in recent years and antiquarian restoration has confused matters still further. It is now impossible to decide whether Edward Newport added a house to an older one or merely incorporated part of the latter, and there are further difficulties in reconciling literary and architectural with graphic evidence.

These two buildings illustrate an important and so far unresolved difficulty in the history of the 17th-century house. During the period c.1630–70 some as yet undefined social change seems to have been translated quite rapidly into architectural form, accompanied by changes in style and building materials. This phenomenon is not confined to Hertfordshire: Sudbury Hall (Derbyshire) has a history of delayed completion; Ham House, Richmond (Surrey), built in the early 17th century, had two phases of alteration and enlargement before 1680; Chevening Park and St Clere, Kemsing, both in Kent,[8] are of comparable complexity, and other examples may be found. The point needs to be stressed that this period of English history is one in which the importance of dating building works to before or after that watershed formed by the Civil War and Commonwealth is especially crucial, and the direction of change is fundamental to historical interpretation.

Many of the arguments in this book are based on graphic evidence as well as the evidence provided by surviving buildings. Hertfordshire is comparatively rich in graphic sources which, by their very abundance, reveal their contra-

16 *Morris Cottage, Much Hadham: Buckler drawing showing a double jetty – an architectural impossibility*

17 *Hadham Hall, Little Hadham* (Buckler)

18 *Hadham Hall, Little Hadham* (Luppino)

dictions and limitations. In cases where an architectural absurdity has been perpetrated, as in the Buckler drawing of Morris Cottage, Much Hadham [16],⁹ which depicts inaccurately a jettied upper storey, the lack of reliability in the evidence is easy to detect. Where drawings show differences of detail in the same building, reliability is harder to judge. Two drawings by Buckler of Hadham Hall, Little Hadham, dated 1832 [17], show all the ground-floor windows in 16th-century form; so does the slightly earlier pencil sketch by Clutterbuck. However, a sketch by Luppino¹⁰ in 1819 [18] indicates that one of the windows had been replaced by a doorway which, in a Wilcox¹¹ sketch of 1842, appears to be of the 18th century, a date confirmed by the antiquary William Minet, who considered it to be *c.*1720. Evidently Buckler's and Clutterbuck's drawings restored the original form of the building, and possibly their antiquarian zeal led them to depart from literal representation in other instances that are harder to detect.¹²

Engravings also must be used with caution. Those by Drapentier and John Oliver,¹³ published in Chauncy's *Hertfordshire* of 1700, are indispensable for reconstructing the original appearance of country houses, but nevertheless they cannot always be taken at face value. Without Chauncy's explicit statement that Balls Park, Hertford, was built round a courtyard, it would hardly be possible to deduce so from the engraving. To Drapentier's deficiencies of perspective must be added the limitations produced by a schematic treatment of detail, so that, for instance, it is difficult to rely on drawings of chimney-stacks which may be merely conventional, or may reflect accurately the long continuance of a standard type.

Drapentier is especially useful in depicting the outbuildings and farmyards connected with country houses that his successors often took pains to exclude from their work. The change in attitude towards such buildings led gradually to their removal from the vicinity of the house and Oldfield¹⁴ took pains to accommodate owners' preferences by a careful choice of viewpoint and by the introduction of discreet planting to screen the stables and service ranges. Goldings, Hertford, and Tewin House are instances of this, and every one of the Buckler drawings is selective in this way.

One other class of graphic evidence used in this survey is that of estate maps. These have provided not only the general outline of houses and their relationship to service wings, but in some cases have provided detailed information about destroyed or altered houses for which other evidence is sparse. A tiny block plan of Bedwell Park, Essendon, when enlarged to a scale of ⅛ inch to 1 foot, was found to have no more than a 2 to 3 per cent error when compared with a modern architect's drawing, and another such block plan of Broxbourne Bury, Hoddesdon, showed external details corresponding so closely in their general disposition to those of other Elizabethan houses as to put its reliability beyond question.

Chapter 2

Medieval manor houses

Hertfordshire is remarkable for the large number of houses built in the hundred years before the Reformation. On present knowledge, only a few other counties, particularly Essex, Suffolk, Sussex and Surrey, are equally rich; Kent is much richer. Research has shown that a few houses are far older than had previously been realised and in this, too, Hertfordshire conforms to the regional pattern of the south east of England. These unusually old houses date from the 12th to the 14th centuries and invariably are manorial halls. It is a situation quite unlike that in central Germany, the only other part of Europe where timber-framed houses of comparable age have been recognised, where the oldest examples are all urban.[1]

The survival of timber manor houses dating from the 12th century is due to the adoption of aisled construction in which two rows of posts divide a large barn-like hall open from ground to roof into nave and aisles. Stability was ensured by the age-old method of setting the posts in the ground, but whereas the outer walls, in contact with perpetually damp soil, rotted within fifty years, the inner posts remained dry and survived. Survival of the outer walls became possible in the early 13th century when their timbers were freed from damp by being set on stone footings.

Aisled halls

The beginning

One of the oldest inhabited houses in England can be found in fragmentary state at Burston Manor, St Stephen, on the outskirts of St Albans. All that can now be seen of the original structure is part of the principal roof truss spanning the middle of the nave, and the rafters on one side of the nave roof. A capital on one of the nave columns is scalloped [19], a form of decoration pointing to a date between 1140 and 1180. How much time elapsed before fashionable church ornament was adopted for domestic buildings is unknown, but Burston Manor is probably datable to no later than the 1170s or 1180s and in quality, though not in size, is comparable with the late 12th-century timber hall of the Bishop's Palace at Hereford.[2] A manor house of about the same period at Brome (Suffolk) combined earthfast arcade-posts supporting the nave roof with aisle walls raised clear of the

ground on slightly built ground sills,[3] as did the 12th-century east hall of the royal palace at Cheddar (Somerset).[4] A recent discovery at Fyfield Hall (Essex) showed that one well-preserved arcade-post of the aisled hall extended some 3 ft (1 m) below floor level, and it is possible that Burston Manor, too, had earthfast arcade-posts, although this cannot be proved. By the early 14th century, Nurstead Court (Kent), a manor house of unusually high quality, with outer walls of flint, had the arcade-posts and no doubt all other internal timbers set on stone footings; this provides an approximate upper limit for the abandonment of earthfast construction at this social level.[5]

In the 13th and 14th centuries

The impetus to rebuild manor houses in an enduring form seems to have originated around the middle of the 13th century and to have been maintained over much of England for about a hundred years.[6] Almshoe Bury, Ippollitts, had a more articulated hall of two and a half bays, the half being to

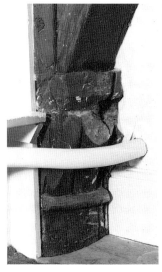

19   (left) Burston Manor, St Stephen: scalloped capital of south post of open truss

20   (right) Almshoe Bury, Ippollitts: arch-brace showing moulded capital and dog-tooth ornament facing the upper end of the hall

21 *Thorley Hall: the surviving hall bay (with high roof) can be seen to the left of the chimney-stack, with the cross-wing at the right of the picture*

accommodate the cross-passage. Both its date and high quality are attested by the fragment of an arch-brace forming part of the open truss, on one side of which is carved dogtooth ornament of about the middle of the 13th century [**20**]. This ornament makes explicit the social distinction between the upper end, where the owner of the house had his seat, and the lower end nearer the entrance, towards which the brace is merely moulded.

At each end of the hall the structure appears to have continued to form a further bay, as seems to have been the case at Burston Manor and probably at Thorley Hall, a house of *c.*1300 where now even the length and width of the hall are uncertain [**21**]. By the early 14th century, when the manor house of Ware (now Place House) was built, a more developed plan had evolved. A bay at the lower end of the hall incorporated service rooms – pantry and buttery – with a chamber on the upper floor, but at the upper end was a two-storey cross-wing. A somewhat later and smaller house, Sutes, Standon, has a cross-wing at the upper end, of identical plan, but again, whatever originally stood below the pas-

sage has been removed. The most fragmentary of Hertfordshire's aisled halls is at Beech Hyde, Redbourn, where only one smoke-blackened bay of the nave roof remains. It is likely to be of 14th-century or possibly 15th-century date.

Besides the six aisled halls surviving or definitely recorded in Hertfordshire – Hertford Castle hall is the seventh – the existence of two more can be inferred. All that remains of Pirton Old Hall, now called Docwra Manor, is an early 17th-century cross-wing of stone evidently added to a timber hall now demolished. Between the ends of the stone walls which abutted the earlier building is a gap of 34 ft (10 m), as if the hall had been so wide that it must have been aisled – as wide, indeed, as the hall of Hertford Castle. Still more tenuous is the evidence at Howell's Farm, Weston, where a large cross-wing, comparable to that at Sutes in the heaviness of its timbering, must formerly have been linked to a correspondingly large hall; the length of the wing suggests the possibility that the hall was about the same width as Almshoe Bury and therefore aisled.

13

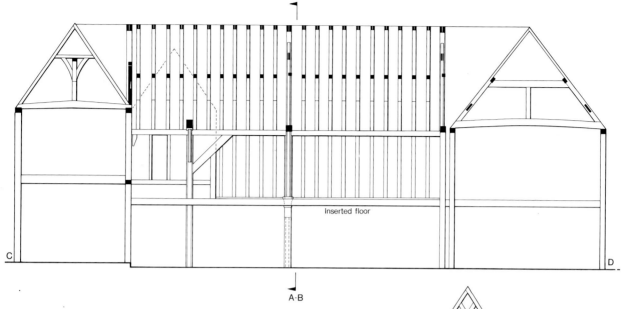

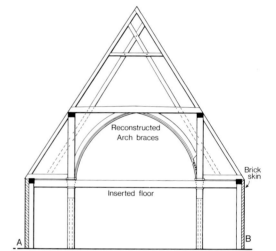

22 *Almshoe Bury, Ippollitts: long section depicting two hall bays and short screen bay between later cross-wings (above) and cross-section (below)*

Their development

The principal development in the hall proper is the structural separation of the space between the opposed doorways, used purely for circulation, from the remaining space, used for daily life. No such division is observable in the hall of Hertford Castle, merely three equal bays, in one of which were opposed doors. At Almshoe Bury, Ippollitts, the entrance was in a half bay screened from two bays of equal length by an aisled truss of normal construction in which the aisles were blocked by screens known as speres – hence a spere-truss [22]; at Place House, Ware, the spere-truss was located within the lower end bay to separate the entrance, now reduced to passage width, from a roughly square living-space. The middle part of the hall was further shielded from draughts coming from the passage by a movable screen partly blocking the space between the posts. Place House has one such, a very rare survival (see [67]). That was to remain the norm for as long as open halls were built, whether aisled or not.

What happened at the ends of the hall is not so clear. Burston Manor, Almshoe Bury and Thorley Hall probably had end bays, the uses of which may be indicated by an early 14th-century house, Nurstead Court (Kent), where the upper end bay, previously assumed to have been always of two storeys, has been proved to have been open to the roof originally. This room has long been a parlour (a more private room than the hall), as the quality of its ornament suggests; the projection back of the customary use of this room implies the same possibility at the other end, and argues for service rooms there.[7] These are the uses conventionally assigned to end bays by analogy with those carried on in the wings which superseded them; however, the bays bear a formal resemblance to the rather narrow rooms partitioned off at each end of some earlier, excavated, halls, the use of which is uncertain.

The earliest wing of which evidence has survived was the upper end of Place House, Ware [23]. Although now

destroyed, its length can be estimated at about 28 ft (8.5 m), so that whatever its width – probably about 15–16 ft (4.7 m) – it provided for loftier and grander accommodation upstairs than was possible with a bay in series with the hall. Whether either storey was divided into two rooms, or provided with a fireplace, is unknown. This architectural change corresponds to one observed at a number of high-status manor houses and often dated to the 13th century: the addition of a two-storeyed chamber block or *camera*, commonly of stone, to an earlier hall.[8] It is a stage in the long process of bringing together functions once performed in separate buildings and of creating extra rooms instead of using the hall for several purposes.

Their builders

Aisled halls provide the first illustration of a recurrent theme in the following pages, that of the diffusion through the

23 *Place House, Ware: the filled mortise (arrowed) shows the former position of a removed tie-beam of the demolished cross-wing*

social system of techniques first observable in magnates' houses. The royal hall of the 12th century differed from manorial halls in function as well as in scale because it was intended for official and ceremonial acts rather than primarily for domestic occasions. To what degree the formal functions predominated will only be learned through the complete excavation of a palace site, although all that is known already of royal castles and palaces shows that such a hall was a major building surrounded by several lesser ones. One such was a chapel. Almshoe Bury is the only surviving manor house known to have had a chapel, but other examples can be found; the oratory at The Hoo, St Paul's Walden, recorded in the early 13th century, must have been built near an important house, probably an aisled hall. At Almshoe Bury the chapel and the quality of enrichment of the hall were appropriate to the residence of a man who, though not a magnate, was someone to be reckoned with in the feudal hierarchy, for this, with the exception of Hertford Castle, is the only aisled hall in the county known to have been visited by royalty. In 1358, Isabella, wife of Edward II, and her daughter, Joan, wife of David Bruce, King of Scotland, were 'in the Park of Almshoe', no doubt for the

hunting, and the amounts paid suggest they spent a night at the house. While we cannot be sure that Simon Fitz Adam, who was a sub-tenant, not a tenant-in-chief under the king, built the aisled hall, it was he who settled the house on his wife at their marriage in 1241, and it may not be coincidental that his family henceforth adopted Fitz Simon as a surname. Almshoe Bury thus raises the possibility of a link between architectural and name studies.

Chauncy, indeed, noted that Simon's son John, 'who was knighted, received his surname from his Father'. This invites comparison with the situation in Wales in the 16th and 17th centuries, where a significant conjunction of architectural and social changes was remarked on by at least one historian. Theophilus Jones, writing of Breconshire, occasionally mentions a family as abandoning partible inheritance (which he refers to as gavelkind), adopting a surname in place of a three-generation name of the type of John ap Morgan ap Evan, and building a house, by which is implied one more durable than its predecessors and capable, by virtue of its superior building techniques, of long outlasting its builder.* Only two of these events are recorded for Almshoe Bury, where nothing is known about inheritance customs, and the

15

same appears to be true of Aspenden Hall. A third instance is possibly to be found at Furneux Pelham in the late 12th and early 13th centuries. There, Ralph de Furnevill or Furneus was succeeded by Simon son of Ralph de Furneus whose son and heir, Simon de Furneux, adopted a surname; the manor house has disappeared but it was important enough for the last-named Simon to be granted licence to build a chapel in 1237–41. Possibly the hundred years after 1180, which is the time when the earliest houses appear, also sees the general adoption of surnames among the class that built them.

Simon Fitz Adam's position as a landowner establishes the social level of Almshoe Bury and helps to explain why aisled, rather than single-span, construction was adopted. By providing a wide hall, aisled construction allowed for large-scale entertaining on those occasions when a reciprocal pattern of obligation required the lord of the manor to feast his dependants. It also provided a more impressive architectural setting, underlining the rank and social position of the owner, than anything else then available, for the moulded capitals and bases of the arcade-posts and the braces rising above them were superior aesthetically as well as structurally to the tie-beam construction which was then the only alternative.

One of the uses of the resulting large square room was as a manorial court, the seat of private justice; it is not certain whether it was also in daily use to feed the body of dependants known collectively as the *familia*. The grandest aisled halls – at Almshoe Bury and Hertford Castle – may have had a second, smaller hall for the daily use of the staff as distinct from the retinue, much like the small preceptory of the Knights Templar at South Witham (Lincs), which had separate halls for the greater personages and the labourers.[10] Separate provision of this kind can perhaps be inferred in the 15th century at Rye House, Stanstead Abbots (see p 21).

No other aisled hall can be assigned to a likely builder with the same confidence as Almshoe Bury. It is particularly unfortunate that the name of the tenant of the abbey of St Albans who built Burston Manor is not known; it may have been Hamo, the father of Robert Fitz Hamo who endowed the abbey with land in 1225. As for other aisled halls, the sub-tenant and likely builder of Place House – the manor house of Ware – was the Thomas Wake who founded a Franciscan friary in the town in 1338. Thorley Hall belonged, apparently, to a fairly minor landowning family, no individual member of which can be credited with the existing hall, and Sutes takes its name from the family of Robert Swote, who was of sufficient standing to appear in a lay subsidy roll of 1330. The builder of Beech Hyde, which was a property of the monastery of St Albans, is not known.

Building materials

Classification of buildings by the materials used in their construction is often unsatisfactory because it creates artificial divisions between houses of similar plan and, historically, the plan is the most fundamental consideration. In Hertfordshire, this objection has less force than usual

because different types of early manor house correspond broadly to the different materials employed, so that aisled halls are of timber, aisleless ground-floor halls are of stone, and halls built above an undercroft are of brick.

Stone

The background to the use of stone for house building lies in the decline of the castles which, with the exception of Hertford itself, fell into disuse. Although the dates of their abandonment are known only in very general terms, their decline corresponds broadly to the building of a number of important houses which superseded the castle halls as residences of the ruling class. These new houses were not fortified, although often licensed to be so. By the late 14th century, fortification of houses was often more apparent than real, and must have been little more than an indication of social status and of conformity to fashion. The earliest of these undefended stone houses was Aspenden Hall, built in the late 13th century. Until it was razed in the middle of the 19th century, the medieval hall endured with little change; its tall window was drawn by Oldfield [24] and carefully hidden by Buckler. It is the only house of the kind known to have been built by a layman.

Nyn Hall, Northaw [25], a property of St Albans Abbey until the Dissolution and demolished in 1774, incorporated a hall range of five bays, each with a tall traceried window which rose up into a gable, much like the hall windows of Stokesay Castle (Shropshire).[11] Depicted variously as being of three or four lights, the windows of Nyn Hall date it to the early part of the 14th century. A six-year lease for the sum of £60, granted in the time of Hugh, Abbot from 1308 to 1326, supports this.

Stone suitable for building was hard to come by in Hertfordshire except in the border with Bedfordshire where the kind of chalk called Totternhoe stone could be quarried.[12] On the northern edges of the county clunch was available. Elsewhere, flint was the sole material for mass walls, with worked stone used only for the openings and quoins; Nyn Hall and Aspenden Hall were probably like this. It is indica-

24 *Aspenden Hall* (Oldfield)

25 *Nyn Hall, Northaw: engraving of the early 19th century*

tive of their expense and the labour needed that these prestige materials are usually associated with great ecclesiastical estates. Like Nyn Hall, Redbournbury [26] belonged to the abbey of St Albans, which built there in the 15th century a large hall of flint and stone dressings, distinguished from purely domestic buildings by its length relative to its width and by the lack of any equally impressive subsidiary rooms – again like Nyn Hall. It was three bays in length, some 36 ft (11 m) internally, and shows no sign of a spere-truss or other subdivision [27]. At the lower end is a timber-framed cross-

26 *Redbournbury: front elevation*

27 *Redbournbury: plan*

wing, and though the evidence is less clear, there appears to have been another one in series at the opposite end. It is the emphasis thus given to the hall, an emphasis in contrast to its declining importance relative to other rooms in contemporary lay houses, which suggests that Redbournbury was built for the official purposes of the monastery rather than as the hall of a bailiff or steward. Nyn Hall was perhaps similar in this respect.

Ecclesiastical manor houses differed from lay ones in other ways. The Old Rectory, Therfield, until the Dissolution a property of Ramsey Abbey, is now no more than a fragment of a building of considerable size and high quality [28]. What survives is a two-storey wing, long in comparison to its modest width of 11 ft (3.3 m), which incorporated on each floor a large room heated by a lateral fireplace and smaller rooms in separate projections. No architectural details remain to show the purpose of these rooms, although a tall east-facing pointed window suggests that one of the upper rooms may have been a chapel or oratory. Such a wing and its appendages cannot have formed a complete house and it may be presumed that a hall adjoined the wing on the west with perhaps another bay or wing beyond that [29]. Despite the destruction of so much, it is evident that this house was of greater complexity than most and it may be that the existing wing was in effect a private suite of rooms, lacking only a kitchen to make it a self-contained domestic unit. The degree of separation may be due to the rector's need for both private accommodation and a manorial hall. Research in

28 *The Old Rectory, Therfield: the medieval wing flanks an 18th-century block that replaced the hall*

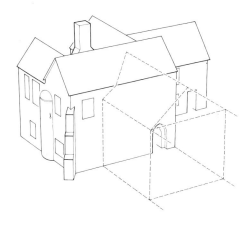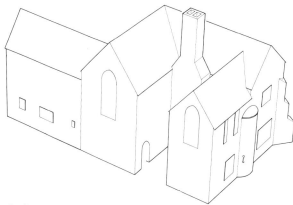

29 *The Old Rectory, Therfield: development perspectives of the medieval wing from the north east (left) and the south west (right)*

recent years has brought to light a class of such large rectories built in the late Middle Ages by wealthy clerics. Garston House, a manor that once belonged to St Albans Abbey, incorporated a wing very similar to the one at The Old Rectory, Therfield, even to the extent of having a smaller wing projecting from it. A fragment of what may have been a comparable building appears in Oldfield's drawing of the parsonage at Ickleford, which is depicted as an 18th-century house abutting what is evidently part of a medieval stone structure with a pointed-arch doorway.

A fourth stone house, this time of lay origin, survives as Hinxworth Place [30] and, if it is identified correctly with the manor formerly known as Pulters, it was probably built by an owner of that name who lived in the reign of Edward IV and who sold it in 1485. A date in the third quarter of the 15th century, while according satisfactorily with the mouldings, presents some difficulties for the plan and form of the house, which was unlike any other so far discussed in being of two storeys throughout. Its plan is discussed below in conjunction with comparable timber-framed houses.

30 *Hinxworth Place: the remains of a timber-framed wing can be seen to the left*

Brick

Very few laymen built in stone. They were deterred by the lack of material of the right quality as much as by cost, so that when, in the 15th century, brick first began to be used on any considerable scale in eastern England, its possibilities were soon exploited in Hertfordshire.

At first the new material was used as a facing to walls of chalk or flint rubble, or for quoins and the dressings – jambs, mullions, arched heads – of doors and windows, while in the more costly buildings it could be carved and moulded for cornices, corbels and the like; used, that is, simply as a substitute for the hard, workable stone so scarce in the county. Archaeological excavation at The More, Rickmansworth, a house for which a licence to crenellate was granted in 1426, revealed walls 2 ft 6 in (0.75 m) thick, built of chalk, rubble faced outside, and often inside as well, with brick which was generally yellow in colour.[13] Such brick, reminiscent of the late 13th-century work at Little

31 *Rye House, Stanstead Abbots* (Buckler)

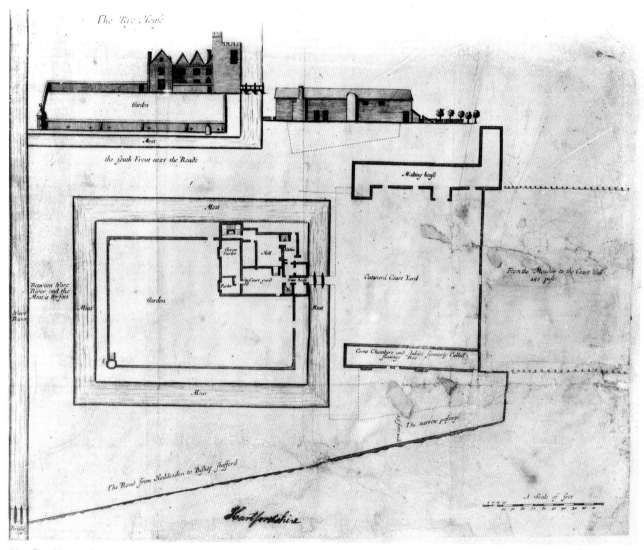

32 *Rye House, Stanstead Abbots: plan of 1683*

Wenham Hall in Suffolk,[14] seems not to exist in any standing building in Hertfordshire, and may, as some orange-coloured bricks at The More suggest, have been used only briefly before different clays were found or new firing methods used which produced the warm reds found in all other early brick buildings of the county.

At Rye House, Stanstead Abbots [31], the now roofless gatehouse has some of the earliest domestic brickwork to be seen in the county. It is dated by the licence to crenellate granted to Sir Andrew Ogard and others in 1443 and, although most of the work of that date has been pulled down, the plan and drawings of the house, made after a later owner's involvement in the Rye House Plot, throw some light on late medieval houses generally. The 15th-century traveller William Worcester was sufficiently impressed to remark that 'the building of the Inner Court with brick and the rooms with the cloister cost, including repairs, a total of 2 [2000?] marks and more'. Yet, as drawn in 1683 [32], the hall was of relatively modest size, no more than about 32 ft (9.8 m) long and 26 ft (7.9 m) wide, or, in William Worcester's pacing, 34 ft (10 m) by 24 ft (7.3 m). These dimensions, which would be unusually large in an Elizabethan or later house of the size depicted in the engraving, confirm that the hall was still, in 1685, basically a medieval structure, however much altered.

The house was certainly defensible insofar as the inner court within which it stood lay inside a large outer court surrounded by a moat and a brick wall 'provided with turrets, battlements and machicolations',[15] all affording sufficient protection against predatory feudal magnates. The kind of assault the defences were built to resist is illustrated by the seizure of Ramerick manor house (now Old Ramerick Manor), Ickleford, on 22 February 1530 by Lord Cobham who, at about 3 o'clock in the morning 'intending by his great power utterly to destroy the premises', led armed men (who behaved like retainers even if they were no longer so called) to the house. Then, 'the door...being locked and barred and the windows being shut', the men at Cobham's command 'took a ladder and climbed xvii or xviii fete high and there did break a bay of the walls of the same house . . . and so continuously ever since have kept the house'.[16] This was what the battlements and the rest at Rye House were primarily intended to stop, for the large oriel windows and elaborate detail of the gatehouse make it clear that the building was intended to impress more by its quality and material than as a serious military work.

One of the three men whose names are associated with Ogard's in the licence to crenellate Rye House was Sir William Oldhall who, according to William Worcester, built the manor house of Hunsdon c.1447–8. This large and expensive building, with its hundred-foot tower in which was the upper storey 'called an oriel', had an unorthodox plan, approximately 80 ft square, according to William Worcester; the principal room in every storey appears to have extended the full width of the building and to have been flanked by subsidiary rooms on both sides. The house must have been comparable in size and impressiveness to Tattershall Castle (Lincs) and Layer Marney Tower (Essex).[17]

33 *Bushey Hall (Drapentier): details from the 'east and west prospect'*

Another great house now quite destroyed that may well belong to this group is the house known as Bushey Hall or Bushey Bury, begun by Thomas, Earl of Salisbury, in 1428 [33]; for, although its building material is nowhere specified, it is likely, in this county and at that date, to have been brick, not stone. Three engravings made for Sir Henry Chauncy's *Historical Antiquities of Hertfordshire* suggest that something of it survived until as late as 1700; they depict a large, rambling building approximating to a T-plan with a hall and cross-wing above an undercroft.

Bushey Hall, Hunsdon House and their like were built by aristocrats or their associates among the important gentry. Towards the end of the Middle Ages, brick was taken up by people of somewhat lower standing, gentry whose lands and influence were more localised than those of men such as Ogard. Two houses come into this category: one of them is Wyddial Hall (pp 1–4); the other, Cheshunt Great House, now demolished, consisted of an open hall between a short parlour wing at one end and a service wing or, more likely, a bay at the other [34]. It was unusual in standing over an undercroft (perhaps a badge of status), part of which was vaulted. Why the vaulting beneath the hall should have been of two types is not clear, although the thick transverse wall separating them, which was somewhat nearer the upper end, would have been well placed to support an open hearth; but if one were ever intended, it was either not built or was soon replaced by a lateral fireplace. It is interesting that the vaulting did not extend beneath the parlour, the floor of which was supported by brick columns and beams. Possibly this was because wood was kinder to the feet than brick, or warmer, and therefore appropriate to a more private apartment, but, whatever the reason, this example is the precursor of a long line of wood-floored parlours. The Great House was notable also for its detail; the head and angel corbels and the capitals of the undercroft piers, although by no means of the highest quality, represent kinds of ornament once common in buildings at this social level.

It is hard to tell how widespread the use of brick was by the early 16th century. Pendley Manor, Tring, as engraved by John Oliver for Chauncy's *History* [35], has what looks

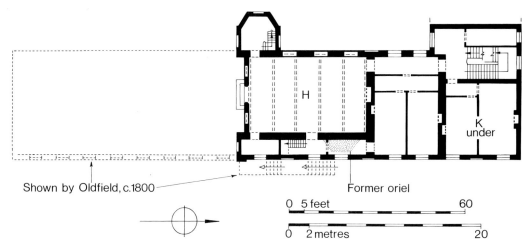

34 *Cheshunt Great House: plan showing the hall above a vaulted cellar and the parlour to the north of the hall*

To the Honourable
this Plate of the Mannor
Humbly Dedicated

Sʳ Richard Anderſon Barᵗ
Houſe of Penley is
by John Oliver

35 *Pendley Manor, Tring (Oliver in Chauncy): the vaulted cloister is visible through the entrance*

36   *Salisbury Hall, Shenley: from the south east; the lower part to the left is modern, replacing the service end of Sir John Cutte's house*

like late medieval details. More significantly perhaps, a Drapentier engraving *c.*1700 of Bedwell Park, Essendon, shows an outbuilding, in all probability a kitchen, with a Gothic window, and since that part of the county has no good stone, this building is likely to have been of brick. If a minor structure were so built, the same material may well have been used in the house.

During the first half of the 16th century, brick came into use for additions to good but much less important houses such as Clintons, Little Hadham, so probably the owners of the greater manor houses used nothing else. Sir John Cutte's rebuilding of Salisbury Hall, Shenley [36], is known only from Leland's mention of it and a drawing of *c.*1800 shows the only part of his house then surviving, the service end, built in brick.

Timber buildings of a single span

The handful of known brick and stone buildings represent the highest achievements of late medieval house building in the county. Contemporary with them are a number of apparently modest timber-framed buildings which, in their day, before the development of the country house market in

Hertfordshire in the 16th century, belonged to men of some importance locally and had an architectural quality which can only be appreciated by comparing them with the kind of building they replaced. Such comparison relates to another major theme in the history of domestic architecture already mentioned in connection with aisled halls: the replacement of comparatively short-lived structures, incapable by the manner of their construction of lasting more than one or two generations, by buildings which could endure for centuries. This is illustrated by the excavation of The More, Rickmansworth [37], where, prior to the erection of the stone and brick house in the 1420s, there stood the principal messuage of a small manor. By the standards of surviving 14th and 15th-century buildings, its setting-out is poor and the use of an earthfast post at one point would have ensured its decay within perhaps a generation or fifty years at most. The form of construction used for the building is not clear and may have varied somewhat from one part to another, but in general shows a combination of timber with stone or tile which, while it was undoubtedly superior to earlier techniques in which all structural timbers were in contact with the soil, nevertheless lacked the precise carpentry and consequent stability of the houses described below.

23

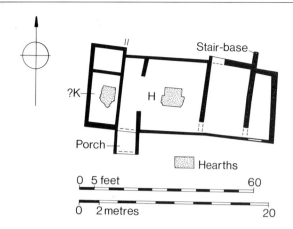

37 *The More, Rickmansworth: plan of medieval house as excavated (after* Biddle *et al 1959)*

Among the small number of timber-framed mono-span halls which represent the best of their kind prior to the Reformation, only Wymondley Bury can be dated with reasonable certainty to before 1400. One of the paradoxes of timber-framed buildings is that the best of them have been so altered by successive prosperous owners that they have lost much of the decorative detail by which they might have been dated. In one or two houses, the survival of a medieval open hall in greatly disguised form can be inferred, and the descent of the property and the size of the buildings make a late 14th-century date perfectly possible; in this situation it

may be legitimate to augment the very thin evidence of date by supposing that a man who became Sheriff commonly built or enlarged his house at about the time he held office. This may be the case at Old Ramerick Manor, Ickleford, where an older house was refronted and transformed inside in the late 17th century. Although not a single original detail of the earlier timber-framed building is now visible, the low eaves at the back and certain deviations from orthodox late 17th-century planning establish the existence of a single-storey house with a hall some 22 ft (6.7 m) long and 27 ft (8.2 m) wide; in effect, a square hall with the addition of a cross-passage. Since this order of size generally seems to denote an owner of importance, it is possible that this hall was built by the Gerard Braybrook in whose family it was for many years and who became Sheriff in 1405; but, whatever doubts surround its precise date and form, Old Ramerick Manor belongs to a small group of houses which were larger, earlier and originally better finished than the majority of open-hall houses.

One of the best of these is Clintons, Little Hadham [**38**]. All that survives of the 15th-century house is a two-storey cross-wing and an open hall truncated at one end [**39**]. What remains of the hall is about 20 ft (6.1 m) square and is likely to have formed the living-space, the cross-passage having been destroyed along with the service room. Clintons has some indications that it may be earlier than the one precisely dated house of this group, Stebbing Farm, Stevenage, built in 1442–3. At Chells Manor, Aston, an open hall can be

38 *Clintons, Little Hadham: the hall (centre) is flanked on the right by an early 16th-century building*

Phase 1. Early 15th cent.

Cross wing stack. Phase 3

Phase 2. Early 16th cent.
Phase 3. 1588-1612

Phase 4. 1660-1670

Phase 5. 18th cent.

39 *Clintons, Little Hadham: development perspectives*

inferred from the same tenuous evidence of plan and cross-section as at Old Ramerick Manor, and this is confirmed by an original tie-beam now encased in a first-floor partition. By a different process of alteration, the hall of Letchworth Hall has been reduced to a mere shell, only its dimensions linking it with the slightly superior class of house under discussion. Two others both belonging to the second rather than the first half of the 15th century have preserved the quality of detail otherwise found only at Clintons; they are Ayot Place, Ayot St Peter, which can be ascribed to the 15th century by tracery in the spandrels of the principal roof truss, and The Lordship, Cottered, where a quite different kind of carved and moulded detail can be assigned to much the same period.

Plan developments

The houses so far discussed have a bearing on the history of house plans and building construction in England generally. From the 12th to the 16th centuries, houses steadily increased in complexity. Structures formerly separate were grouped together, thereby bringing the functions they performed into a closer relationship. In the highest reaches of society, for example, there is a change from the late Saxon or Norman palace which comprised a scatter of separate buildings to a more coherent but still rather rambling group of interconnected structures. Change at this level arose from the greater size and complexity of the household, which corresponded to the elaboration of government, but the same process is observable to a lesser extent in all ranks of the feudal hierarchy. At a lower level, the most obvious architectural change over this period is a decline in the importance of the hall. Even at the highest level of society, this process of change has not been properly documented and lower down the social scale the evidence from different periods is often not closely comparable. At present, little is known about the lesser buildings grouped around such a hall as Almshoe Bury, Ippollitts, yet the administration of the manor and possibly of outlying lands, too, no doubt necessitated accommodation for a steward, and there must have been detached buildings for the chapel and kitchen and perhaps a bower or separate house for the women of the family. No late medieval house in Hertfordshire has preserved enough of its structure to show such accommodation at that period.

By comparison with developments elsewhere in Europe there is a surprising persistence of the type of hall open to the roof and heated by a hearth without any kind of hood or chimney over it. Why such an archaic mode of heating survived so long in England has yet to be explained adequately. Similarly, the fact that the hall windows were often not fully glazed, with the consequent need for cross-lighting to enable shutters to be closed at need on the windward side, meant that the only practical place to add rooms was at either end. Freestanding halls like the one at Wasperton (Warwickshire)[18] are unknown in Hertfordshire. When additional rooms were needed there seems to have been some uncertainty about where to put them and which end was the more important, although the upper and lower ends of the hall were clearly defined. At the stage of development represented by Almshoe Bury, the ends will have been of more or less equal importance. In Place House, Ware, the cross-wing was at the upper end of the hall; at the other end there was only a two-storey service bay. At Wymondley Bury [40], which cannot be so very different in date, the situation is reversed; the cross-wing with a large first-floor room over the service rooms is at the lower end, whereas the upper end has only a two-storey bay with a hipped roof in series with the hall, so that the conventionally superior part has an altogether humbler aspect and a less commodious upper chamber than the lower end.

Where the lower end has been mutilated and there is a well-timbered cross-wing at the upper end, as at Clintons, Little Hadham, and Sutes, Standon, it is reasonable to sup-

40 *Wymondley Bury* (Oldfield)

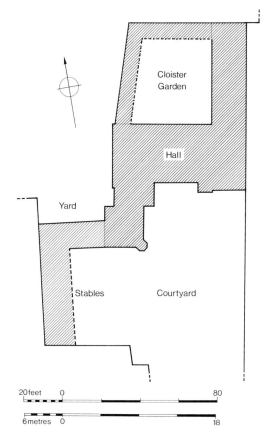

42 *Place House, Ware: block plan*

pose that a service bay has been removed. Conversely, Letchworth Hall must have been like Wymondley Bury, with a cross-wing of some importance at the lower end and a further bay at the other end of the hall if it was not built simply as an end-hall – that is, with subsidiary rooms at only one end of the house. The Lordship, Cottered, also has a cross-wing at the lower end, the upper room being imposing and dignified and in every way superior to its counterpart at Letchworth Hall, whereas Stebbing Farm, Stevenage, has no more than a two-storey bay with the usual hipped roof [**41**]. From these few instances it is difficult to suppose that first-floor rooms at the upper end of the hall were invariably regarded in the Middle Ages, as they usually are today, as being superior in status to those at the lower end, or that where there were two wings the principal rooms were necessarily at the upper end.

41 *Stebbing Farm, Stevenage: the two-storey bay is to the left and the hall, with later dormer window, to the right*

The grouping of buildings together

The plan of Rye House, Stanstead Abbots, made in the late 17th century, although useful, does not altogether show what the house was like in the 1440s. A cloister mentioned by William Worcester had been removed, no doubt to enlarge the garden, and another known to have existed at The Old Rectory, Therfield, has also disappeared without trace. Only for Place House, Ware, do a plan and description survive to show how, in the late Middle Ages, the various household functions were grouped together much as they might have been in a small monastic house, though less formally. Above the cloister was a long gallery and within it a small garden [**42**]. The gallery, like the house, was divided into two occupancies; at one end it adjoined the buttery in the west wing, and at the other end possibly the kitchen in the east wing, although this is not specifically stated; this duality is not necessarily medieval. No mention is made of any division of the cloister, from which it may be inferred that there was common access to certain service rooms or buildings: 'a little room with a cellar in the backyard', a 'backhouse', a woodhouse in the courtyard and a chamber over it, and a double stable and one other stable, each with haylofts.

What little is known about other cloisters reinforces the impression given by Place House. Comparison with surviving examples is not very fruitful since the only published cloister is at Ockwells, Bray (Berks), of the mid 15th century;[19] there, pantry, buttery and kitchen are grouped together opposite the hall and outside the cloister. This cloister is rather small for one important function of such buildings, that of providing a covered space for exercise; the one at The Old Rectory, Therfield, was described as 'a little walking cloister', just as the later term 'long gallery' implies the same purpose.

Most domestic cloisters were of timber, like those in small monastic houses. Few can have equalled the splendour of that at Pendley Manor, Tring, where an engraving (see [35]) shows what was very probably a vaulted walk visible through the open door of what was presumably the hall range. Cloisters in the late Middle Ages certainly had the secondary functions of screening off and giving access to outbuildings, such as the 'other kitchen' at Therfield, as well as the buildings recorded at Place House, and in this respect they mark a first stage in the grouping and formalising of subsidiary buildings which was a continuing preoccupation of the owners of large houses. Earlier references to cloisters such as those at Ardeley Bury in the 12th century may signify no more than covered walks or pentices connecting an irregular scatter of buildings, like those at Clarendon Palace.[20]

The abandonment of the open hall

In the three or four decades prior to the Dissolution, houses were built that retained the hall open to the roof but broke with the past in abandoning the open hearth, thereby taking the first step towards the fully storeyed house. This innovation first appeared in Hertfordshire at the highest social levels, probably not much before 1450. The earliest surviving hall to incorporate a lateral wall fireplace from the first is at Morton's palace, Hatfield, built during his tenure of the Bishopric of Ely from 1478 to 1486 (see [90]). For the Bishop and his retinue, a building of impressive quality and dimensions was provided, about 100 ft (30.5 m) long, originally with a clear internal span of 30 ft (9.1 m) and incorporating a hall some 45 ft (13.7 m) long, excluding the screens passage. The only other episcopal palace in the county, that of the Bishops of London at Much Hadham, is much less pretentious. Its only distinguishable features are a hall heated by a lateral fireplace and of much the same size as might be found in important contemporary lay manors, and also a cross-wing rather bigger than was usual. Wyddial Hall and Cheshunt Great House, both with an open hall heated by a lateral fireplace, are comparable.

During the same period as chimney-stacks were appearing the first houses of two storeys throughout occur. One of them, Hinxworth Place, has already been mentioned as exceptional in being of stone. Others, not manors but comparable in size and quality, are timber-framed but are exceptional in a different way; they incorporate on two or three of the four sides the overhanging upper storey called a jetty, a structural feature which was undoubtedly prized for its visual impact and conveyed a certain prestige. All the houses in this little group are of rectangular plan. Hinxworth

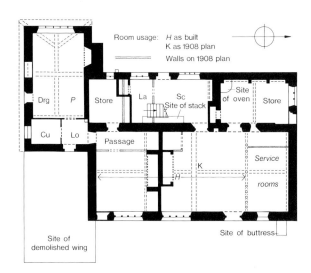

43 *Hinxworth Place: plan*

Place [43] has two rooms on each floor, one small, one large. The large room on the ground floor is the hall and above it is a great chamber of the same size; both have a fireplace discharging into a lateral chimney-stack. The great chamber appears to have been reached by a staircase opening off the upper end of the hall. At the lower end are the two service rooms customary by then, and there was formerly a staircase leading to a small upstairs chamber, completely separate from the adjoining chamber.

A timber-framed and jettied house of much the same overall size is Redcoats, Wymondley [44]. It is the only house of its kind where the original fireplaces remain, and it is their moulded and carved jambs and depressed pointed heads which indicate a date in the late 15th century. The house has a more developed plan than Hinxworth Place, with a quite unusual provision of heated rooms for its size (hall and parlour on the ground floor with two chambers above) as well as a service room and an unheated room [45]. The timbering matched the fireplaces in quality, with close-studding and four-centred heads to all the doorways and window lights. Even with the amount of detail that remains, it is difficult to assess the relative importance of the upstairs and downstairs rooms. The ornament of the largest upstairs room gives the impression of a first-floor chamber equal in importance to anything on the ground floor – so good that it could be thought of as a first-floor hall – yet the suite of mouldings remaining on the fireplace jambs in the former parlour is more elaborate than anything of the kind upstairs and may well be proof that hall and parlour were better finished than the chambers. Presumably the existing house was originally served by a number of ancillary structures for household staff and guests, as well as kitchen and service rooms. It can be envisaged as the highly finished centrepiece of a group of buildings, the one in which were concentrated the important rooms equivalent to those in the cross-wings of a large open-hall house, as well as the hall itself, reduced to one storey in height. It was usual for one such room to have a fireplace; to have two or more so heated was a mark

44 *Redcoats, Wymondley: isometric drawing showing fireplaces in the parlour and the chamber over the parlour*

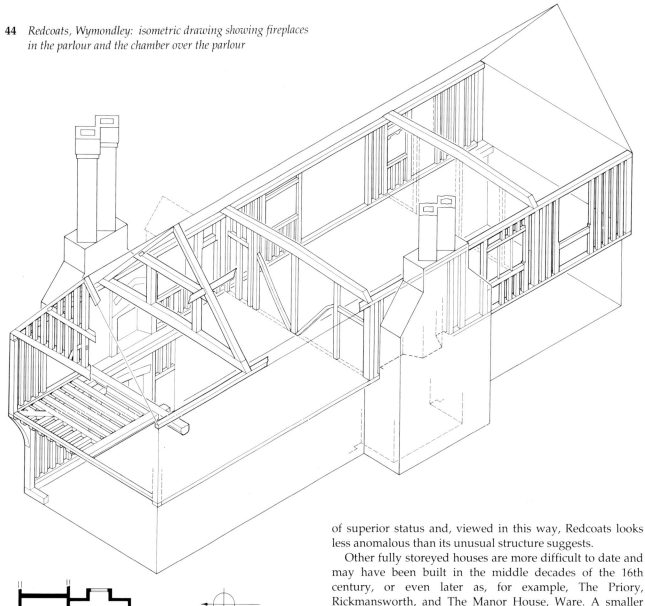

45 *Redcoats, Wymondley: plan*

of superior status and, viewed in this way, Redcoats looks less anomalous than its unusual structure suggests.

Other fully storeyed houses are more difficult to date and may have been built in the middle decades of the 16th century, or even later as, for example, The Priory, Rickmansworth, and The Manor House, Ware. A smaller building, King John's Farm, Chorleywood, appears by its quality and date to be related to Redcoats and Hinxworth Place, though it can hardly be said to be of the same type. At King John's Farm, the larger of the two ground-floor rooms has the better-finished timbering, as if it were the hall, and there are two chambers on the first-floor, but the building must be later than the others and could well be of the 1530s.

Little is known of the men who abandoned the usual late medieval open hall in favour of storeyed construction. If Hinxworth Place is correctly identified with Pulters, it was built either by the John Pulter of Hitchin who figures in the late 15th-century list of gentlemen worth £10 per annum, or William Pulter who was Sheriff in 1496. The family seems to have made its money in cloth. A John Pulter who died in 1421[21] is styled esquire, whereas later members of the family appear as gentlemen. There is no reason to suppose that Hinxworth Place was the only seat of the Pulters, nor that the nearly contemporary Redcoats was the only seat of the

Sturgeon family who may have built it. Sir John Sturgeon, of whom Chauncy says that he 'was Sheriff of this County and a Man of Great Account at that time', enjoined in his will of 1492, 'my place called Redcotes to be sold'. A Sturgeon of Hitchin who appears in the 1433 list may have been his father and, although nothing is known of the family or the source of their wealth, his place of origin suggests that his background was similar to the Pulters'.

The concept of the elevation

The long period which begins with Burston Manor and ends with Redcoats not only saw the planning of houses transformed, but also the growth of a concern for their external appearance. In the 11th and 12th centuries, when even the greatest houses and palaces were groups of buildings, the very idea of an elevation hardly existed in secular architecture, and it was only with the largest Norman halls that a truly monumental treatment of any part of the exterior became possible. At that stage of development the gabled end of a hall which had a principal entrance there, like Westminster, was the natural focus of architectural interest; aesthetically, little could be done with the low side walls of the average aisled hall. When the hall acquired separate end bays and the entrance had necessarily to be in one of the long walls, it must have been thought essential to give the flank of the building some visual emphasis. At Nyn Hall, Northaw, tall gabled windows met this need and also let in more light (see [25]), but it was not a common solution to the problem, and for a long time the importance of the hall was made plain principally by its being larger than any of the ancillary buildings. Only in the early 14th century, when two-storeyed wings began to be built instead of storeyed end bays, did a true elevational treatment become possible for timber-framed halls; Place House, Ware, and Wymondley Bury, each with a gabled cross-wing, must have had an air of novelty when they were built that is now hard to imagine. Whatever circumstances gave rise to the jetty, the wings of aisled halls provided an early application for it,

and even now its powerful effect can be felt in the wing added to Thorley Hall. By the late 14th century such a house might have two wings, though the Hertfordshire examples are later and arose by conversion, as at Almshoe Bury (see also [22]) and Chells Manor [46]. In such a house the exterior appearance is almost symmetrical, apart from differences in the braces of the framing to the wings. This suggests that aesthetic effect was by this time a factor in house design in a way it had not been earlier; that symmetry, albeit of a general rather than an exact kind, was preferred to an appearance which reflected more precisely any functional and social differences between the two wings. This seems to have been true of timber-framed houses of comparatively modest size. In brick-built houses with a more imposing hall – Wyddial Hall, for example – the large bay window, which seems to have provided both a semi-private space and the light which the hall needed, precluded even a general symmetry of bulk unless balanced by a porch.

The house of two storeys throughout presented new aesthetic problems. A stone building such as Hinxworth Place made no concession to symmetry. Like Wyddial Hall it had a bay window at the upper end of the hall, and in Oldfield's drawing the front elevation has a stepped buttress of unclear purpose, near the north-east end of the front wall. At the end of the south-west wall is another shallow buttress, raising the possibility that the Oldfield drawing is not very accurate and that actually there were paired corner buttresses of the usual type. Redcoats, on the other hand, displays concern for appearances on three sides, and since the existing house must have had ancillary buildings it is difficult to see how they can have been set out without either sacrificing convenience or detracting from the visual effect of at least one of the jetties. This house is also unusual in having a large chimney-stack on both the long sides, evidently to provide each of the principal elevations with what was then an impressive and comparatively rare architectural feature. Possibly, as the striking row of upstairs windows suggests, it was the jettied gable end of Redcoats which was intended to be the prime focus of architectural interest.

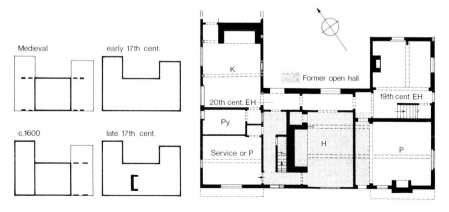

46 *Chells Manor, Aston: development plans*

A representative sample?

How representative of those that once existed are the surviving houses? The loss of buildings is most severe at the highest level. Hunsdon House and Bushey Hall were houses of national importance in their day and whereas a little is known of them, the form of some other major houses is not. Thus the manor house at Bygrave, owned by the Somery family, was good enough for the entertainment of Edward I in 1299 and 1302, and in 1386 Sir John Thorney had licence to crenellate his two houses there; but despite the name 'Palace' accorded to one of these sites, the houses themselves were not necessarily much grander than Aspenden Hall or Rye House.

At a lower level the picture is incomplete in many ways, yet it may give a general impression of what the more important manor houses were like. Some of these houses may be represented by others which survive, for example, Digswell and Ludwick manor houses [47, 48], both now within the bounds of Welwyn Garden City. Both have the taller cross-wing at the upper end and the hall roof terminating at the ridge of the lower wing, and Oldfield's depiction of the storeyed porch at Digswell House suggests that the height of both buildings to the eaves must have been similar. Furthermore, the number and positions of the windows at Digswell House indicate a hall of comparable length to that at Ludwick Hall, so that prior to about 1550 the two houses were probably much alike. The scanty evidence available leads to the conclusion that the smaller manor houses are formally indistinguishable from the better yeomen's houses and often became confused with them; a confusion expressed by the term 'reputed manor'. What is so lacking at

47   *Digswell House, Welwyn Garden City* (Oldfield)

all levels is knowledge of the other buildings that made up the manorial complex.

This applies pre-eminently to the 15th century. In the 13th and 14th centuries there is reason to think there was less difference between houses. Castles, which were comparatively few, represented the highest social stratum. Below this social level, as architectural evidence elsewhere suggests, manor houses were probably more uniform in size and appearance than later, so that Almshoe Bury or Aspenden Hall may represent most of the richer ones.[22] The increasing stratification of the gentry from the later 14th century onwards produces variations of size and plan not easily discernible in the limited sample provided by Hertfordshire.

48   *Ludwick Hall, Welwyn Garden City: front elevation*

Chapter 3

Late medieval vernacular houses in the countryside

The houses discussed here are essentially of a status below the manor house. A distinction between manorial and non-manorial is often difficult to draw in a county like Hertfordshire, where nucleated villages were not the rule and one parish might be divided into several manors. Since the houses definitely associated with these estates are often comparatively small, it is natural to enquire whether other vernacular houses may correspond to the many manors. Sometimes it has been possible to link them, but where, as is often the case, no manorial connection can be established, the explanation may lie in the existence of a class of substantial freeholders able to build as well as the man to whom they owed nominal homage.[1]

Some of these larger vernacular houses are associated with reputed manors whose existence may only be attested for a short period, often in the 16th century. An example is Hawkins Hall Farm, Datchworth, which must have been important long before its mention in 1564 as a reputed manor. It may be thought that this is no more than a formal link without much relation to the income which ultimately decided what an owner was able to build, yet it is virtually certain that then, as later, unwritten conventions governed closely the kind of house built by a person of a given social rank. A comparison between standing buildings and the considerable number of manorial halls found by archaeological excavation reveals a measure of uniformity from the late 12th to the 14th centuries, as if there were a conventional size appropriate to the class of person who built them. Something similar might be expected for later and smaller houses.

The problem is difficult to resolve because so little is known about how houses were used, especially where one man owned several manors. The impression given by manorial descents is that in the late 15th century some men were building up estates comprising three or four adjacent or nearby manors; John Fray, of Cottered, was one such. He owned a rather superior vernacular house called The Lordship, which was presumably his principal residence when not attending to his duties as Chief Baron of the Exchequer, and acquired the manors of Rushden More (in Sandon parish) and Munden Furnivall (or Great Munden),[2] all within a radius of four miles. Presumably three possibilities were open to Fray. He could sell some or all of the surplus produce of his other manors; he could have it carted to Cottered, or even London, for his own consumption; or he might, while residing in the county, have been peripatetic, as must have been the case with the king's greater subjects who owned and built houses widely separated from one another.

The element of chance in the survival of houses makes it difficult to know if appropriate accommodation existed to enable men like Fray to move between their own properties in the way their social superiors did. Certainly, from the reign of Elizabeth to the mid 18th century, some men owned sizeable houses on neighbouring estates and built or altered both.[3] What difference the occasional presence of an owner might have made to a house he needed only intermittently is not clear; perhaps none, for most of his household would accompany him. A resident steward or bailiff would have needed rooms for himself and a hall for holding manorial courts, accommodation perhaps little different from that required by the lord himself when resident. One manor, at least, may have been bought to provide a measure of independence for an eldest son.

Another problem arises from the replacement of impermanent structures by others of a more durable kind. The gradual descent of this change through the social scale is now generally recognised but it is less often realised that there were also different rates of replacement of the structures that made up the manorial complex. This has to be borne in mind when considering the development of farmhouses, many of which, perhaps even a majority of those built before 1650 in Hertfordshire, are the product of piecemeal rebuilding rather than of the introduction of successive, improved types of plan. In principle, it is impossible to know whether the addition of a wing to an older hall corresponds, on the one hand, to the replacement in an improved form of some earthfast building or, on the other, to a real increase in accommodation providing for some new household function or one hitherto carried on in the hall or a subsidiary building. The dismantling and excavation of a house at Pebringe in Denmark[4] proved how complicated the process of piecemeal replacement could be: the Hertfordshire examples are likely to have been similarly complex.

This fundamental problem is bound up with the matter of house types. What does the term mean when applied to houses, and was it a significant concept to the people who built them? We might seek to answer these questions by asking how many houses conform to a given type, and how many merely approximate to it.

Wealden houses

The Wealden differs from its contemporaries only in structure. In plan it is, like them, a simple rectangle partitioned into a hall and two end bays, but the latter are jettied at the front and the wall-plates are continuous, carried in front of the hall so that they provide a roof of simple rectangular plan rather than the three roofs that the building would otherwise demand. The advantages are obvious. At the cost of some increase in structural complexity the roof is simplified, and valleys, points of potential weakness where weather is most likely to penetrate, are avoided, while in so doing an external appearance of great visual interest is achieved. The type is named from its profusion in Kent and it is only in the last twenty years that their sparser existence outside that county and parts of the adjoining counties has been recognised. Of the several in Hertfordshire, one in particular, Fabdens, Standon [49], is very well preserved and in every respect falls within the range of size and structural

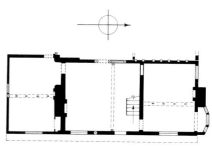

51 *Yew Tree Farm, Much Hadham: plan*

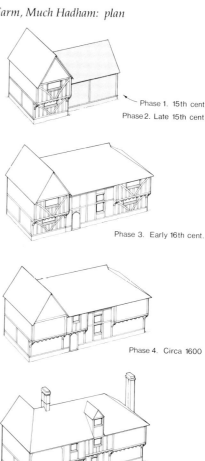

Phase 1. 15th cent.
Phase 2. Late 15th cent.

Phase 3. Early 16th cent.

Phase 4. Circa 1600

Phase 5. 1697

52 *Yew Tree Farm, Much Hadham: development perspectives*

49 *Fabdens, Standon: front elevation*

50 *Yew Tree Farm, Much Hadham: from the south east, incorporating the wing of an earlier house (to the left); the raised part of the jetty is the floor inserted in the hall*

detail found in Kent. Two more, at Barkway and Codicote, conform to Kentish canons, whilst others substitute gables for the hipped roof which is invariable in Kent. In view of their complicated structure, which does not lend itself to building in phases, most Wealdens are of one build, yet there are exceptions to this general rule.

Yew Tree Farm, Much Hadham [50], has preserved its original Wealden appearance despite some alteration at one end, so much so that, until the exterior plastering shown in old photographs was removed, it looked perfectly orthodox. In fact the supposedly altered end bay is a short cross-wing, apparently the service wing, which projects very slightly at the back and is a separate framed structure quite independent of the Wealden hall and end bay [51]. Like most timber-framed buildings it is hard to date precisely and it is unclear whether it is earlier or later than the hall. Yet the wing must be earlier, for had the house been built as a complete Wealden it is hard to imagine what could have prompted the rebuilding of one end so soon, and equally hard to guess why it should have been built in a different form to so little advantage in terms of space, height or appearance.

Other Wealden farmhouses in Hertfordshire could be interpreted in the same way if more were known about their development in the 18th or 19th centuries; Morris Cottage in Much Hadham is one such, Patchetts Green Farm, Bushey, another. That the Patchetts Green house was in some sense double-ended is not to be doubted, since at that end, which now lacks a storeyed bay, the framing and infilling are flush internally towards the hall and therefore cannot also have been flush, and external, on the other face. The conventional assumption, that a jettied bay of normal Wealden type has been demolished, may be correct but is inherently unlikely; and Yew Tree Farm shows that quite another possibility may be envisaged. But the same situation occurs outside the county and wherever it does there is rarely any attempt to explain why demolition or rebuilding should have occurred. A Wealden house at Newport (Essex) has a service bay which is clearly of a different build to the main house, as is also the case at two of the best-known houses of this kind, The Clergy House, Alfriston (East Sussex), and Bayleaf, Chiddingstone (Kent), now in the Weald and Downland Museum (West Sussex). In houses at Headcorn (Kent) and Battle (East Sussex), it is the upper end bay which is of different and allegedly later date than the rest, and isolated single-ended Wealdens are not particularly rare.[5] There is no reason to suppose that these two-phase Wealdens form more than a small proportion of the total, yet they are numerous enough to require some general explanation.

If the sequence at Yew Tree Farm has been correctly determined, the oldest part, the cross-wing, must have been added at the lower end of an existing hall [52]. An alternative possibility, that it was built as a detached two-storey structure, is less likely; its internal divisions are those customary in service wings and there is no sign of the original fireplace such a building would require. The Wealden hall and end bay replaced a hall with earthfast posts or similar structure so markedly inferior that it could not be incorporated in the new work. If this is true of Yew Tree Farm it may also be true of all those cases where the two builds cannot be very different in date.

The explanation here offered has a bearing on the problem of relating house types to social classes, and, if correct, implies a change of mind on the part of the owner. The conventional way of updating a house was by adding a cross-wing; a more conspicuous innovation was to incorporate in rebuilding the hall – something that was an expensive novelty locally – the Wealden structure. Yet the ground plan of Yew Tree Farm is smaller than that of many of its contemporaries built with a hall and cross-wing. Was the decision to change the form of the house made because the owner was attracted by a fashionable type giving a social cachet?

To say so is to risk reducing a number of historical problems to the level of personal whim, yet the scarcity of Wealdens in Hertfordshire suggests that they were the choice of a minority among those who could afford to build houses of equivalent size and quality.

Halls with cross-wings or end bays

Wealden houses formed only a tiny proportion of the total number of vernacular buildings built in the county during the 15th and early 16th centuries. Far commoner was the combination of a cross-wing with a main range (usually a storeyed service bay in addition to the hall wing); that is, a house with all the elements present at Yew Tree Farm, Much Hadham, but lacking the distinctive Wealden structure. As one of the most characteristic features of the Wealden is an open hall considerably higher than that of most other late medieval house types, when the time came to divide it into storeys the change could be accomplished within the existing timber frame, retaining all or part of the roof structure. The same process could not be accommodated inside a hall with lower eaves without sacrificing either amenity or structure. Indeed, complete rebuilding of the hall range might be the easiest way to improve plan and structure simultaneously in this situation. For such reasons, hall and cross-wing houses demonstrably of one build are rarer than might be expected.

Rumbolds in Cottered parish [53] has a hall and a cross-wing at the lower end, and although the evidence is not

53 *Rumbolds, Cottered: the bay to the right of the chimney-stack is a later addition*

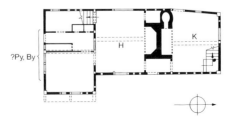

54 *Rumbolds, Cottered: plan*

perfect the two appear to have been built together in the late 15th century [54]. Whatever earlier house the present Rumbolds replaced was destroyed completely; not even the bay added at the upper end of the hall can be regarded as replacing something earlier because the shaped end of one of the old wall-plates is still visible to prove that the first build was complete in itself. Judd's Farm, Hormead [55], which seems to have been begun in the same form at much the same time, shows a more usual course of development. The size of the original hall structure corresponds to that of the rooms now occupying its site; they appear to date wholly from 1724, when whatever adjoined the wing seems to have been completely rebuilt. Such a new start entailed something which was probably contemplated with the greatest reluctance, the demolition rather than the reuse of standing walls, and implies that the original hall was so low or in so poor a condition that it had no further useful life.[6]

The lengths to which a builder would go to preserve parts of an old building still in good enough condition to be incor-

55 *Judd's Farm, Hormead: front elevation*

56 *Bury Green Farm, Little Hadham*

porated in a new one can be demonstrated many times over, not only in houses of some importance, such as Chells Manor, Aston, but also in such smaller houses as Cutting Hill Farm, Benington, and High Tree Farm, Ardeley. Wherever surface irregularities are apparent in the upper part of the long walls the same process of heightening the walls may be suspected. Sometimes evidence that an older structure has been swallowed up by a new one takes another form. Bury Green Farm, Little Hadham [56], is the kind of house where the general external appearance and low proportions of rooms conflict with its ostensibly late 17th-century date. In the roof a single smoke-blackened truss remains as definite evidence that the house is much older than it looks; a process of gradual replacement and renewal accounts for the apparent clash between proportions and datable features. This kind of evidence strengthens the notion that some hall ranges are the direct replacement of earthfast structures.

Rebuilding in whatever shape or sequence has produced the curious result that much evidence for late medieval building activity is derived from parts of houses, usually jettied cross-wings. Where a surviving wing is rather large it is sometimes incorrectly interpreted as an independent house. Interpretation of the adjoining later building will usually reveal this error. Between forty and fifty of these isolated wings have been noted and no doubt many more remain to be found. Any estimate of the amount of building done in late medieval Hertfordshire must depend to a considerable extent on this most important class of fragmentary evidence.[7] Conversely, rural Wealdens, which have long tended to attract notice by their picturesqueness, number less than a dozen.

Hall and parlour ranges 'in series'

Most late medieval houses which comprise two distinct structures have one of them roofed as a cross-wing. A few are arranged differently, the two-storeyed block equivalent to the wing being in series with the hall but with a higher roof and often jettied. Nos 61/63 Park Street, St Albans [57], appears to have been of this kind. Small though it was, the close-studding and paired tension braces in the wing indicated carpentry of some quality, and the same is true of a building of more imposing appearance, Corner Cottage, Nettleden. In these instances the form of the hall is uncertain. Fortunately, Green Street Cottage, Little Hadham, retains enough of the original roof to establish definitely that the hall had an open hearth and that there was a service bay beyond it, although in this case the storeyed parlour block is post-medieval, probably *c*.1600. Indeed, with the present uncertainties about dating, it must be doubtful how many jettied blocks of this kind are pre-1550.

This 'in-series' type may once have been commoner than now appears. A number of small two-storey buildings are jettied on one of the long walls and have an air of incompleteness which is generally confirmed on examination by, for instance, the lack of an original fireplace. In villages or

57   *Nos 61/63 Park Street, St Albans: 'in-series' wing with exposed framing (centre); the hall is to the left*

hamlets they tend to face the street, presenting the best elevation, the jettied one, to the passer-by. Some may be shops with an upper floor for storage, but where there is any suggestion of an adjoining structure a domestic explanation is more likely. Here, incompleteness postulates the existence, when such a house was built, of a hall range which could either have been at right angles to the jettied block – a not very common type[x] – or in series with it, and although there are not many of the second type, they appear more frequently in the late 15th and 16th centuries, and so some at least of these jettied relics are likely to have been of the 'in-series' type. Patchetts, Aldenham [**58**], and 40 Stocks Road, Aldbury, both demonstrably incomplete as they stand, may once have been of this kind, as also The Old Rectory at Welwyn.[u] All are of the late 15th or 16th centuries.

Choice of this mode in preference to a cross-wing may, as has already been hinted, have been dictated wholly by the siting of the house. The jetty was a prized display feature and could be shown off in a variety of ways. A storeyed block in series with the hall presented the longest possible jetty to the side from which the house was approached and, where only one room was required on each floor, the inconvenience of a passage room did not arise; when it did, a cross-wing was no doubt preferred. Owners may have perceived an aesthetic choice between, on the one hand, the cross-wing, providing a roof shape contrasting with the hall and ornamented with barge-boards, and, on the other, the 'in-series' parlour block impressing principally by an appearance of greater bulk in relation to the hall; in both forms the jetty and windows were of roughly equal importance.

58   *Patchetts, Aldenham*

A variant of this serial plan in which the parlour block is jettied at the end gable – the end-jetty house – is not a particularly common type in Hertfordshire. The house now called the Social Club, Aldenham, is one such, Red House Farm, Tring Rural, another, and in the east of the county are Lower Farm, Barley, and a cottage at Blackhall, Brent Pelham. This form could arise by alteration or addition. Rigery's Farm, Standon [59, 60], embodies part of a small, low, late medieval hall to which was added *c*.1600 a taller two-storeyed block of much the same size as its counterpart at Green Street Cottage; it was possibly but not definitely a

59 *Rigery's Farm, Standon: the hall range is in the foreground and the added parlour block to the left*

60 *Rigery's Farm, Standon: plan*

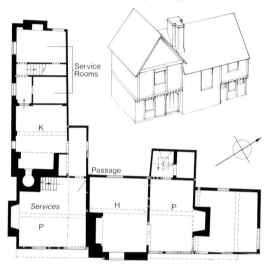

62 *The Old Manor House, Aldbury: plan and perspective drawing*

61 *The Old Manor House, Aldbury*

63 *Glebe House, Great Gaddesden*

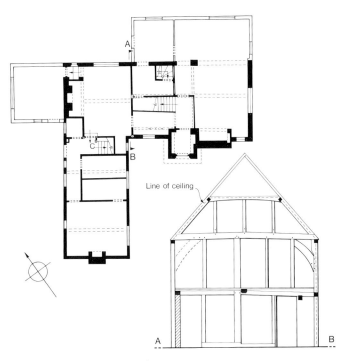

Line of ceiling

64 *Glebe House, Great Gaddesden: plan and section*

parlour block, with a jettied gable end. The two parts present something of the same contrast as the Park Street house mentioned earlier, but the aesthetic emphasis was different. Inferences from the siting of a particular house without detailed study of its landscape history are hazardous, but Rigery's Farm seems to have been designed to face the present, and by inference original, approach road.

The advanced-hall type

The aesthetic appeal of the Wealden house is strong today and no doubt always was. It came as a surprise to find houses which combine the same accommodation as a single-ended Wealden with a totally different aesthetic, so that they might almost be called inverted Wealdens: the relative prominence given to the planes of the walls is reversed, so that instead of the hall being recessed behind a jettied upper storey it is flush with it, and only the ground floor of the single-storeyed bay is recessed. At first sight it was scarcely believable, and The Old Manor House, Aldbury [61, 62], had a large question mark beside it until it became clear at Glebe House, Great Gaddesden [63, 64], that the two parts, jettied bay and advanced hall, were coeval; the first-floor bressumer is jointed to the framing of the hall. As far as can now

37

be seen, the two houses each comprised a squarish hall open to the roof, an undivided ground-floor room adjoining it and a large upstairs chamber. Both houses have been enlarged and much internal evidence has been concealed or removed, but their general form is established by Glebe House; the fact that there are two such houses quite close together suggests that more may be found. The advantages of this minor type appear to be essentially those of a Wealden, in providing a lofty hall, a simple roof and a striking external appearance.

Determinants of vernacular form

Houses with only one end bay, and that open to the roof, like the hall – Green Street Cottage, Little Hadham, is an example – are clearly so because they belonged to people of a comparatively lowly social position among those who could afford to build at all. Those houses with a storeyed bay at one end and an open service bay in series with the hall provided for economically superior people for whom more varied accommodation was needed. But the Wealden type did more than this: it provided two first-floor chambers more or less equal in importance but quite unconnected. It has been suggested that this arrangement would be suitable for members of a kin group, and, indeed, the Wealden type is, on present evidence, as likely to house a small kin group as an economically superior nuclear family and its dependants. It is difficult to see any structural or technical advantage in the different forms of parlour block at Rigery's Farm and Green Street Cottage and so the choice between the two must be accounted an aesthetic one.

The rooms necessary in a late medieval farmhouse could be provided in several ways. They comprised the hall; a service room or rooms, usually referred to as buttery and pantry; a room at the upper end of the hall, often used partly for storage and called a parlour; and a chamber over this. It was possible to put the storeyed block at the lower end and either dispense with a room at the upper end of the hall or, though this was rare, have a bay open to the roof. In the late Middle Ages few houses below manorial level appear to have had two two-storey ends; the hall with two cross-wings, once thought to be the classic late 15th-century type,[10] seems to have been comparatively rare.

So a single two-storey block was the usual requirement in a late medieval house, and there were three ways of providing it. Where this arrangement was envisaged from the first, the cross-wing seems to have been the invariable choice, partly on grounds of cost, since the framing of one of its long walls could be combined with that of the end of the hall. Where the parlour block was to be added to an existing hall, the gabled cross-wing had no very obvious advantages over the type with a second block in series. The only exception to this was when problems of access would have arisen where the ground floor was to provide two rooms; but where a house already had one gabled cross-wing, whether at the upper or lower end of the hall, it was likely that enlargement would take the form of a matching wing. Yew Tree Farm,

Much Hadham, is an instructive exception to the rule, indicating the superior status, at least in aesthetic terms, of the Wealden to other house types. For at Yew Tree Farm one of the prime advantages of the Wealden, the simplicity of its roof, was foregone because the rear gable of the older wing had to be retained.

The types of plan

The range of plan types in use in the later Middle Ages is bewilderingly diverse. No vernacular example of the simplest possible plan, a hall standing alone without any integral ancillary rooms, has yet been found, and it may be that, by the time timber-framed construction as opposed to earthfast framing[11] came into use below manorial level, a second room of some kind was an invariable requirement and was always placed at the lower end. In discussing this point 'hall' is an inadequate term, with connotations deriving from its original usage in connection with royal, noble and manorial halls; the term is not altogether appropriate to simple rooms with an open hearth, and perhaps it was only among the higher feudality that a hall standing alone was ever considered. Westminster Hall is the earliest and most famous instance and the one farthest removed from the present context; a few are known from the 12th to early 14th centuries, but even some of them may have had a small chamber at one end.[12] Possibly small open-hearth houses whose owners did not need a representational hall always had some kind of inner room, and the supposed basic type may never have existed at vernacular level. A second room might be provided, either in a bay at one end of the main range or in a wing; such a room could be open to the roof or of two storeys. There is the possibility that a hall with a jettied block in series might correspond to a two-cell plan.

Three-cell houses come in great variety. The simplest form, with a bay open to the roof at each end of the hall, has not been shown definitely to exist, and it may be that at social levels below the manor house two ancillary rooms as simple as this were rarely thought useful. One possible example is a house at Collier's End, Standon, published fully by the RCHME in *English Vernacular Houses* (1975), which can be interpreted as having a late cross-wing replacing the cross-passage and a narrow end bay. Nor have any houses with an open bay at the upper end and a two-storeyed bay or wing at the lower end of the hall been found, although sometimes the evidence is ambiguous. The same combination in reverse, with the storeyed bay at the upper end, is not uncommon. The most developed form of three-cell house, in which both ends have an upper storey, is found in conjunction with end bays as well as cross-wings. One or two quite large houses have a storeyed bay at the upper end and a cross-wing at the lower end, or the other way round.

Finally, there is one instance of a four-cell type, which has at the lower end, beyond the service rooms, an integral kitchen open to the roof; this is Bramfield Bury [65, 66], which, architecturally, must mark the very end of the Middle Ages.[13]

65 *Bramfield Bury*

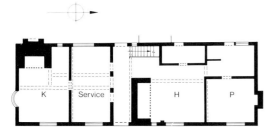

66 *Bramfield Bury: plan*

Excluding types which are only theoretical, nine or possibly ten varieties of late medieval houses are left, some represented by additions or piecemeal rebuilding. The number of potential variations is so large that it is impossible to equate one type or even group of types with any social class or socio-economic group at present definable. In this difficulty one way forward may be to analyse the use of rooms.

Elements in the plan

The hall

In vernacular buildings, as in many of higher standing, the hall appears to have been governed by a convention that it should be of approximately square plan, excluding the space answering to a cross-passage between the two outside doors and irrespective of whether that space was defined struc-

turally or not. The house at Collier's End (see above) is interpreted in the light of this rule.

Structural division, where it occurs, takes the form of a spere-truss to screen the hall from the draughts of the cross-passage. This is not a common feature in Hertfordshire and occurs only in large halls such as Place House, Ware [**67**]; but the notion of screening off the passage from the hall, which is found in a few vernacular houses, may be regarded as a descendant. Bear House, Ashwell [**68**], verges on manor-house size and it is not surprising that it has a simple derived form of spere-truss; so has Bramfield Bury. At a lower social level the same form of structure appears in The Gatehouse, Braughing. In these houses the entrance-passage is within a storeyed bay or jettied wing and rises only to the height of one storey; the spere-truss has been reduced to short screens adjoining the entrance.

Usually the only symbolic division within the hall was provided by the open truss. This was invariably the one which had the best of whatever ornament might be provided and its position corresponded more or less to that of the open hearth, if a little nearer the doors. This correspondence evidently governed what would otherwise appear to be the irrational bay division of the hall, for one of the most constant features of open halls is that the bays are of different length, the upper being slightly the larger of the two. Parenthetically, it may be noted that timber-framed construction based on the repetition of uniform bays, although characteristic of barns everywhere and of houses in some

68 *Bear House, Ashwell: interior view*

67 *Place House, Ware: an early 16th-century movable screen, flanked by added partitions*

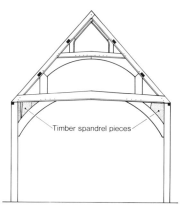

Timber spandrel pieces

69 *Betlow Farm, Tring Rural: section through hall*

parts of England, is quite atypical of Hertfordshire, Kent and the south east generally. No structural advantage was gained by placing the open truss off-centre. It is sometimes supposed that the structure of the louvre above the fire gained support from being next to the open truss, rather than relying on the common rafters for strength; but unequal bays occur in houses such as Nicoll Farm, Elstree, which had no louvre. Evidently, the placing of the open truss was influenced by other than practical considerations, notably the desire to give emphasis to one of the socially most significant points within the hall and, equally important, to provide an architecturally impressive focal point. The crown-post roof with its complex structure and, in many cases, moulded cap and base served a similar aesthetic purpose. A few open trusses with large curved braces beneath the tie-beam have spandrels filled with blocks of wood to give the appearance of a solid arch. This feature is familiar in some of the earliest and largest aisled halls, such as the Bishop's Palace at Hereford and Nurstead Court, Kent, but it persisted in quite modest hall-houses such as Betlow Farm, Tring Rural [69], or Tenements Farm, St Stephen. Careful examination of open trusses might reveal other traces of this kind such as holes for wattle and daub infilling.

At the upper end of the hall there was a fixed bench. None has survived in Hertfordshire but traces of their existence often remain. They usually comprise a line of large holes at an appropriate height in the posts and studs into which, and into a solid oak bench, were driven wooden pegs. Occasionally, other methods of fixing a bench seem to be used, such as the groups of three peg-holes at Turners Hall Farm, Wheathampstead. Wherever a parlour wing or bay existed, it was reached by a doorway at the farthest point of the hall from the front entrance and the bench stopped just short of it; on the inner jamb of the doorway can sometimes be seen the mortises for a decorative bench-end. This kind of evidence is frequently complicated by the existence, often in profusion, of other large peg-holes scattered at varying heights on the studs at the upper end of the hall, and for which there is no satisfactory explanation. One conjecture is that they held pegs from which wall hangings depended; another is that they are the points at which the heavy structure of a loom was secured, and were the latter really so it would negate the idea of a bench.

Light for the hall commonly came from two tall windows on each side, the larger of which was in the middle of the upper bay while the smaller one had to be crowded in between the open truss and the entrance door. They were unglazed, closed by shutters and sometimes divided by a middle rail of framing. These arrangements are unusually well preserved at Yew Tree Farm, Much Hadham.

Wings and bays at the lower end of the hall

Architectural historians tend to think of the rooms at the upper and lower ends of the hall as corresponding in importance and function to their position, those behind the seat of honour being superior to those below the cross-passage. In fact, the situation is in many cases not very clear and the most that can be said with confidence is that by the 16th century a new house of any size was likely to have the best rooms at the upper end of the hall. So confused is the picture that in some houses, especially those where the site of the cross-passage is uncertain, it is difficult to determine which was the upper and which the lower end. At an important house like Burston Manor, St Stephen, the passage end was the first to be improved in the mid 15th century, by rebuilding it as a large cross-wing with two rooms on each floor, and not for another two hundred years did the upper end become more important architecturally, with the addition of a smart brick staircase turret. The continuing importance of the lower or screens end of the house is attested by several late medieval houses such as The Old Manor House, Aldbury (see [61, 62]), where the wing at the lower end is quite clearly the showpiece of the front elevation. That it is the lower end is established by the presence of the well-finished doorway. The unusual feature of such wings is that they have no evidence of subdivision either structurally or by a light screen.

The service end, whether a wing or a bay, was often divided by a structural partition into two equal-sized rooms, entered from the hall by adjoining doors in the middle of the lower end wall. In some houses independent access to the first-floor chamber is provided by a third doorway behind which is, or was, a straight flight of stairs. This pattern varied according to the number of upstairs rooms; where there was only one, as at The Maltings, Kelshall, and Tenements Farm, St Stephen, the door and staircase adjoin the rear wall, but in larger houses where there were two rooms, the stair was between them. Examples of this second arrangement are more frequent in manor houses such as Burston Manor and The Lordship, Cottered [70], although some can be found among the better vernacular buildings which are on the bot-

70 *The Lordship, Cottered: doors at the lower end of the hall; the nearest one is blocked*

tom rung of the manorial ladder, such as Turk's Cottage, Braughing. The Lordship is unusual in having the middle doorway of three treated differently from the others, with a high lintel, or shaped head. Such a middle door is often regarded as giving access by a passage to an outside kitchen, but where it is more important than the others it is more likely to have led to an important upstairs chamber, even if the stair has now gone, than to the most menial of workaday rooms.

The provision of a third door in a vernacular building removed any necessity for entering a service room in order to get upstairs, a point that may have been of particular importance in providing a suitable approach to a single large and dignified room; and placing the staircase against the back wall left the maximum amount of space free for use and enabled the small landing at the stairhead to be lit by a window near the corner of the room. Traces of such a window are not uncommon, as in Nos 3/5 Sun Street, Baldock; the window itself survives as rarely as the staircase, one of these exceptional instances being another house in Baldock, Church Cottages. Even in quite small houses, as, for example, Rumbolds, Cottered, it was usual to separate the stairs from the service rooms in this way. Where the staircase was placed between two service rooms it seems to have emerged at the top, not, as might be expected, into a lobby from which the two upstairs rooms were reached, but into the larger of the two rooms. That is the inference drawn from The Lordship, where one of the two walls now enclosing the stair is later than the other. This arrangement suggests that the two rooms may have been functionally linked in some way, rather like the two rooms forming a lodging or, in a later period, an apartment, and it is probably significant that such a feature is found in a house with the name The Lordship and rarely in genuinely vernacular houses.

But there were other houses no less well built than Rumbolds, of which Nicoll Farm, Elstree, may serve as an example, which had as their only other room a further bay open to the roof. This room must have been a general-purpose store, perhaps partitioned off in some way. It would be interesting to know where people slept in a very simple house like this; the hall seems the most likely place, not least because it housed the only source of heat. A possible alternative can be found in houses where one of the two subsidiary ground-floor rooms is larger than the other, suggesting that the reason for its greater size was not to provide space for a staircase as well as a service function but that it was more like the general-purpose parlour described in 16th and 17th-century probate inventories. Whether that is so or not, the principal upstairs room of a cross-wing was rarely provided with a chimney-stack and fireplace when built; such an amenity is almost always an addition. Where the cross-passage was incorporated in the end bay or wing this might mean either a marked reduction in the space available for the ground-floor service rooms or an equally marked increase in the size of the first-floor chamber.

Wings and bays at the upper end of the hall

It is usually difficult to discover traces of doorways from the hall to the room or rooms beyond the high table and seat of honour. Often the position of the staircase serving the chamber over the parlour gives a clue to the location of one doorway; for even where the original staircase has disappeared, a later stair may occupy its customary position in the far corner from the front entrance. Thus when only one wing of a medieval house survives it is sometimes possible to determine by this criterion at which end of the hall the wing stood, as with No. 40 Stocks Road, Aldbury [71]. The position of the staircase within the room, not originally reached directly from the hall, is significant of the greater privacy at

Site of original stair

71 *No. 40 Stocks Road, Aldbury: plan – hall and storeyed bay 'in-series'*

72 *Bull and Campden Cottages, Much Hadham: the cross-wing has a similar jetty at the rear*

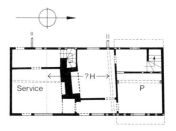

73 *Bull and Campden Cottages, Much Hadham: plan*

this end of the house and reinforces the general view that the ground-floor room was a parlour, though usually, in a vernacular house, without a fireplace. In those rare houses with a jetty at the back as well as the front, the staircase seems to have been placed parallel to the gable end wall of the wing and to have risen to a narrow landing formed by the jetty. Quite small houses were treated thus; one at Much Hadham (now Bull and Campden Cottages [72, 73]) is simple enough in every other respect except for this feature, normally intended for display, which here is and always was hidden from the street. Nos 59/61 Collier's End, Standon [74, 75], also has one of its wings jettied back and front. Perhaps the idea was to combine a modest show at the front with extra space for the first-floor chamber.

Occasionally, the upper end wing or bay had an outside staircase. Evidence of an early example can be found at Clintons, Little Hadham, and is likely to be of the first half of the 15th century; probably a doorway at the rear of the hall, facing the end of the bench, opened to a straight flight of solid wooden stairs which was protected by a pentice roof.[14]

Longhouses

Analysis of the rooms at the ends of open halls showed that a number of houses do not conform to the forms of plan typical of Hertfordshire, and that these peculiarities manifested themselves well into the 17th century. In such houses the confusion between what are conventionally the upper and lower ends is greater than usual; this and other plan features are reminiscent of a class of house familiar in highland

74 *Nos 59/61 Collier's End, Standon: front elevation*

76 *Oak Cottage, Flaunden: front elevation*

77 *Oak Cottage, Flaunden: plan – the parlour is on the site of a presumed byre*

75 *Nos 59/61 Collier's End, Standon: rear elevation*

78 *Ballingdon Cottage, Great Gaddesden: the nearest bay replaces the presumptive byre*

England and Wales but rarely considered in the context of the Midland counties, much less Hertfordshire, that is, the longhouse – with house and byre under one roof – and its derivative forms.[15]

The term 'longhouse derivative' is used of houses which have lost their original dual function of sheltering both family and cattle through the removal of the cattle. The consequent destruction or rebuilding of the byre usually produced houses of two builds and forms of plan, most of which are readily distinguishable from those resulting from the alteration of open-hall houses. A characteristic feature of the longhouse which is often perpetuated in its descendants is the narrow inner service room or pair of rooms – service and parlour – reached only through the hall; demolition or conversion of the byre and the building of a new, larger parlour at the lower end of the hall produces a plan which may bear a formal resemblance to the lobby-entrance house but is distinguishable in detail from it.

Several Hertfordshire houses, among which Oak Cottage, Flaunden [**76**, **77**], is remarkable, conform to these criteria. This house, built in the late 15th century, combines a roof of high quality with a plan resembling the primitive form called the 'long hall'[16] in which the internal partitions were no more than *c*.6 ft (1 m) high. In so far as the known links of this type, as of longhouses, lie with western England and Wales, it may be no coincidence that the long-hall plan has so far been recorded principally in Devon and adjacent counties.[17] Ballingdon Cottage, Great Gaddesden [**78**], which probably had no upper floor originally, may have been simi-

79 *Arne Cottage, Northchurch: the nearest bay replaces the presumptive byre*

lar, although it may have had a low internal partition. Oak Cottage has an open roof of two and a half bays, blackened from end to end by smoke, and the present featureless plaster partition on the ground floor probably perpetuates an earlier, slighter one. At the lower end a roof truss demarcated the cross-passage from the hall. Whatever lay beyond the passage was not separated from it by a partition of full height of the kind usual elsewhere in Hertfordshire. Both features appear in counties such as the former Breconshire and Glamorganshire where longhouses are the medieval norm.[18]

Uncertainties attach to Oak Cottage and much depends on the typological inference. Several other late medieval houses can be interpreted in the same general way, and whether the partition between hall and inner room is original or not, or the inner room was open or had a chamber over it, the most significant fact is that the third room, the one below the cross-passage, has in all cases been either

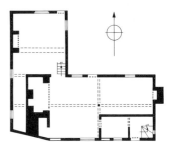

80 *Arne Cottage, Northchurch: plan*

rebuilt or destroyed, leaving no indication that it ever formed a pair of conventional service rooms. Arne Cottage, Northchurch [**79**, **80**], Ballingdon Cottage, Great Gaddesden, Nos 1, 2 and 3 Frithsden Gardens, Nettleden with Potten End, and Water Lane Cottage, Bovingdon, all have this in common.

44

The dating of medieval vernacular houses

The earliest unequivocally vernacular houses to survive date from the middle of the 15th century. Few of them have any closely datable detail and typology of plan, and structure is a very unsafe guide to chronology, so they have been described in the inventory to this volume simply as 'late medieval' or 'late 15th–early 16th century'. This, from an historical standpoint, is unsatisfactory, because evidence of building on a large scale is relevant to the debate on whether the 15th century was a time of economic advance or decline, and greater precision is needed before it can be properly exploited. Despite the acknowledged difficulties, typology has been used in default of anything better, and in this as in other cases the problem is not so much to know when a sequence begins as when it ends. Probably most of the small houses dated late medieval belonged to manorial tenants: copyholders who prospered and were sufficiently sure of passing on their holding to an heir to build in a better way than many others could afford. In addition to these, a few small open-hall houses have been found which are either of yet later date or belonged to people of smaller means.

The problem is to know when the open hearth ceased to be used. In better manor houses the lateral chimney-stack was introduced by about 1500. Timber chimney-stacks appear in vernacular buildings of some size and quality by the third quarter of the 16th century, for example in the former inn now No. 27 Leyton Road, Harpenden (see [306]), and Tudor Cottage, Albury, so that for the best vernacular houses the open hearth had gone out of use by then. How much earlier this had happened depends on the dating of continuous-jetty houses, some of which are ascribed to the second quarter of the 16th century. Putting this evidence together suggests that by the middle of the 16th century a well-built three-cell house was likely to be of two storeys throughout, with a timber chimney-stack; the open hearth had been abandoned. But a large section of the population could not build like this, and there is at present no reason to suppose that the majority abandoned the open hearth; indeed, some early 16th-century houses appear to have continued in use with an open hearth for a hundred years or more. The small farmhouse called Peartrees, Ardeley, was built with an open hall and has in the small upper room the cross-wing braces which by their reverse curvature may be mid or late 16th century.

It is with the smallest type of house, the straight range divided into two or three cells, that the problem of the long persistence of the open hall is most acute. Nicoll Farm, Elstree, has already been mentioned as having been open originally from ground to roof throughout: Yew Tree Cottage, Aston, a three-cell house of simpler construction and lower appearance, was also single-storeyed. Superior to both it and Nicoll Farm, in that one of its three cells had an upper floor, is Acremore Cottage, Little Hadham. What date should be assigned to these three houses? None has any datable original features. The quality of construction, which is rather higher at Nicoll Farm than in the other two, is commonly thought in such circumstances to favour an earlier date. Yet on examination this argument cannot be sustained; for the timber used in the east of the county seems not to have been of as good quality as that in the west and the scantlings are generally smaller, so that on this basis there need be no difference in date between these three houses. Perhaps, then, the differences of quality and even of size may reflect a difference not in date but in the economic and social position of the various owner-builders.

By the 16th century the techniques of permanent building had been dispersed throughout the property-owning classes, and were used with such variety in the south east of England that it is hazardous to place much reliance on them for grouping houses according to the presumed social class of their owners. The available documentary evidence does not clarify the matter. Whatever difficulty there may be in finding like houses to group together is paralleled by the unreliability of information regarding occupation and social status, culled from probate inventories; in these, 'yeoman', 'husbandman' and 'labourers' can cover a quite wide and overlapping range of condition and wealth.[19]

Chapter 4

Country and manor houses from the Dissolution to the Civil War

The dissolution of the monasteries in the 1530s opened a new era in the history of Hertfordshire houses. The transfer of land to lay ownership on a huge scale, coupled with the accessibility of the county for Court and legal officials requiring an estate near London, encouraged a brisk property market. A further stimulus was added from 1567, when Hertfordshire began to provide its own sheriff instead of sharing one with Essex, since it seems to have been customary for a man keen to hold office to build a new house or embellish his existing one. That this might sometimes be as much a matter of necessity as of pride is suggested by John Evelyn's account of his father's shrievalty of Surrey and Sussex in 1633: 'He had 116 servants in liveries [and] divers gentlemen and persons of quality waited on him . . . which at that time (when thirty or forty was the usual retinue of the High Sheriff) was esteemed a great matter'.[1] These circumstances produced many new houses, which were generally larger than their medieval predecessors and, with few exceptions, built of brick, a comparatively unfamiliar material, so that between the Dissolution and the Civil War the architectural landscape underwent a dramatic change.

Today, little is left of the buildings themselves. As social change and continuing architectural ambition gradually destroyed them, two developments in the 19th century combined to reduce still further the historical value of what remained. The first was the growth of antiquarian taste, which eliminated whole phases in the history of some houses of this period in an endeavour to recreate, often with a mistaken confidence, the unity of the original conception; the second, arising from the improvement of communications, was the country house party, which made large rooms and ample provision for servants necessary. To compensate for the loss of evidence, which is especially severe in the large houses, there is, firstly, the interest in architecture shown by historians of the county and, secondly, the large body of work produced by Drapentier, Oldfield, Buckler and other artists. From their evidence and from old estate maps a more intelligible account of an important period of house building can be written than the surviving remains alone would permit.

Some architectural information is to be had for about thirty country or manor houses built between 1540 and 1640. They vary in size from the huge Theobalds Manor, Cheshunt, to Queen Hoo Hall, Tewin, a reputed manor not

very much larger than a big yeoman's house, but despite this disparity they have a few features in common. All retain the crucial relationship between entrance and principal room found in medieval houses, so that whether the hall was of the new kind, only one storey in height, or rose through two storeys in the medieval way (though no longer open to the roof), it had a cross-passage at the lower end separating it from the buttery. Other rooms might be added to these to form the main range of the house but limits to linear extension were imposed by convenience: better to enlarge the house at right angles at each end, a practice which led naturally to the creation of a partly enclosed courtyard. A perpetuation of the late medieval fashion for a grand gatehouse and the need to incorporate this into a unified whole led to the principal court being completely enclosed by buildings, usually leaving the lesser court or courts partly open. Given the medieval ancestry of the two principal elements, hall range and gatehouse, the development of courtyards in houses in which corridors were inconvenient because of the lighting difficulties they created can be regarded as a natural one. Until well into the 17th century, important houses tended to develop around a courtyard, whether large or small, and in fact one of the very last of the kind, Beechwood Park, Flamstead, was not completed until 1702. In that respect it is no doubt something of a freak, yet the continued adaptation of the much older courtyard houses suggests that this kind of plan was for a long time capable of meeting needs very different from those of the generations that built them.

Courtyard houses: a story of gradual growth

Knebworth House illustrates more clearly than any other in Hertfordshire how the courtyard house developed from its late medieval beginnings. Drapentier drew a lofty gatehouse [81], an imposing building devoid of ornament in the face it presented to the world and giving the impression of defensive strength. The builder is likely to have been William Lytton, Governor of Boulogne Castle and Sheriff of Hertfordshire and Essex in 1511. A plan reveals quite clearly that it was built for effect rather than for any real defensive

81   *Knebworth House: gatehouse* (Drapentier)

purpose; this is confirmed by a large storeyed oriel window on its courtyard side, facing the hall [82]. Only the gatehouse has a medieval look about it, the rest being all of the 1560s. It was probably erected to emulate the gatehouse built in the 1460s at the royal castle of Hertford, which itself was perhaps intended more as a show of strength and a demonstration of the royal presence rather than for serious military purposes.

The presence of a gatehouse implies the existence of a hall, and a wall or palisade forming an enclosure around which lay subsidiary buildings. Since a brick hall would probably have survived, Knebworth is likely to have been timber-framed, and the relation between the hall and the gatehouse, before the three brick ranges were built, was no doubt much like that between the timber-framed Lostock Hall (Lancs), built in 1563, and its large stone gatehouse, built in 1591.[2] However, the Lancashire house never underwent the change that took place at Knebworth in the early 1560s, when everything except the gatehouse was swept away to make a large courtyard house of two storeys save for a lofty hall rising to a coved ceiling [83]. The new work

was evidently in the height of fashion, with mullion and transom windows of two lights crowned by classical pediments,[3] yet the house still faced inwards to the courtyard in

82   *Knebworth House: rear of gatehouse* (Skinner. *By permission of the British Library)*

47

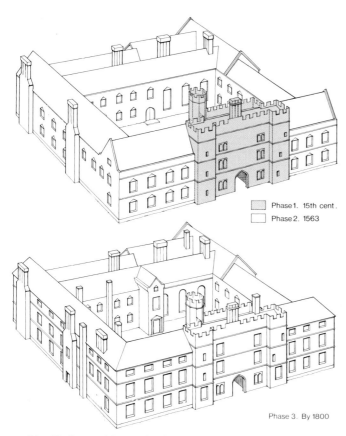

Phase 1. 15th cent.
Phase 2. 1563

Phase 3. By 1800

83 Knebworth House: development perspectives

85 Knebworth House: courtyard with hall beyond. This engraving shows work of 1567 and the early 18th-century refronting of the hall (Skinner. By permission of the British Library)

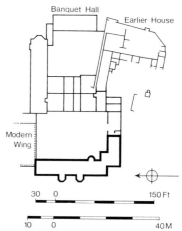

Banquet Hall

Earlier House

Modern Wing

30 0   150 Ft

10 0   40 M

84 Hadham Hall, Little Hadham: plan after Minet – the new house of brick stood to the east of the gatehouse range

work of William Minet early in the 20th century. His conclusion, that a new house of brick replaced the late medieval hall and, together with ancillary buildings, formed the nucleus which developed into a large double-courtyard house, may well be correct but needs corroboration by modern archaeological methods. A generation earlier, within a decade of the dissolution of St Albans Abbey, the first complete courtyard house in the county was built by Sir Richard Lee on the site of the small convent of Sopwell. It is known only through an unpublished archaeological excavation. The house was unusual in following the lines of the old cloister without actually incorporating any of the existing buildings; the hall range appears to have been built on the site of the church. It had a remarkably short life. Hardly thirty years later its builder pulled it down prior to building a bigger house on a different plan – a striking example of competitive building among Elizabethan courtiers seeking royal favour. Five other courtyard houses – Broxbourne Bury, Hatfield Palace, Standon Lordship, Theobalds and Watton Woodhall – were all manifestly the outcome of gradual growth, although the stages by which they developed are now beyond recovery. To these can probably be added Aspenden Hall, which developed around a 13th-century hall, and possibly Pendley Manor, Tring, which appears to have been mostly late medieval. This leaves Berkhamsted Place and probably Gorhambury, St Michael, as the only courtyard houses conceived as such and built on unencumbered sites; for although information is lacking about the medieval Gorhambury, the scanty remains, small-scale excavation and records do not suggest that anything of it was incorporated in the late 16th-century house.

The planning of courtyard houses

The approach to the hall

Usually the gatehouse stood opposite the cross-passage which gave entry to the hall, the principal room of the house

the medieval way, unlike its contemporary, the great Wiltshire house of Longleat.

No other house in Hertfordshire has a gatehouse as imposing as that at Knebworth, nor did any develop in quite the same way. Hadham Hall, Little Hadham [84], survives only as a fragment, no more than the entrance range of a very large house, and the rest is known only through the

48

86 *Gorhambury, St Michael: the old house* (Gough Maps 11, fo. 36ᵃ, item d)

and generally advertised as such by its tall windows. At Knebworth House the drawings made by the Revd John Skinnerᶦ in 1805 convey the marked contrast intended in the early 1560s between the tall windows of the hall and the smaller windows lighting the two-storeyed ranges [**85**]. Hatfield Palace does not present the same contrast but, significantly, throughout its time as a royal residence, the lofty hall remained unchanged. At Gorhambury [**86**], built in the late 1560s, the hall was clearly marked by tall windows, as was the somewhat earlier Standon Lordship; and since Sopwell was complete by the late 1540s it may have had a high hall too. It is difficult to be sure what the halls of Berkhamsted Place and Broxbourne Bury, Hoddesdon, were like originally; the Parliamentary Survey in 1650 mentions 'a living chamber . . . over the hall' at Berkhamsted, which might, however, have been inserted later, and the building sequence and dates are now so hard to determine at Broxbourne Bury that we cannot be certain whether the hall was of one or two storeys.

Another way of emphasising the hall was by the porch; although Hatfield Palace was so provided, and Knebworth House had one of the 17th century (no doubt replacing the original), only at Gorhambury is the sought-after effect still visible in the Renaissance porch, which combines two orders – Doric columns beside the entrance and Ionic above – with an exceptionally elaborate finish achieved by variety of stone [**87**].

Although it was the general rule to locate the hall opposite the gateway into the courtyard, there were exceptions, like The Lordship, Standon [**88**], where an alternative position, to the right of the entrance and at right angles to it, was chosen. Why this should be is unclear. At Standon it may have arisen through the gradual completion of the full courtyard plan whose shape shows that it was not designed as a

87 *Gorhambury, St Michael: late 16th-century porch*

49

88 *The Lordship, Standon* (Drapentier)

whole [**89**]. In so far as the plan permits deductions about its complicated history, Standon may have originated as two parallel ranges like Cokenach, Barkway (see p 64).

Why was a high hall retained for so long? In so far as all large courtyard houses were designed for the reception of royalty, the provision of a large and lofty room for ceremonial occasions appears natural enough. The same consideration applies to the huge Nyn Hall, Northaw (see [**25**]), though not of courtyard plan; the much rarer elongated plan was preferred here. Why the owners of some much smaller houses chose to follow the fashion for a lofty hall while others did not is unclear. In Hertfordshire, almost any part of which might be traversed on the Court's journeys, the hope of entertaining Queen Elizabeth on one of her earlier and less elaborate progresses can plausibly account for virtually all houses of the kind. If Robert Chester's houses at Royston and Cokenach could have been considered (and rejected) for royal entertainment (p 63), Leonard Hyde, knighted in 1603, might well have built Hyde Hall, Sandon, with that hope in mind; indeed, his spacious hall was just

50

what Chester's houses both lacked. Not far away, the rather earlier Wyddial Hall kept its open hall into the early 18th century.[5]

One difference between a late medieval magnate's house and an ordinary manor house was the proportion of length to width shown in the hall; instead of a more or less square manorial hall, the magnate required for his retinue one about twice as long as it was wide. This was how a late 15th-century Bishop of Ely built his hall at Hatfield Palace – only one of his residences – and these are the proportions perpetuated in the hall of every courtyard house in Hertfordshire up to the Civil War.

The superior end of the house

Next to the hall at the upper end of a medieval house was the parlour, with the great chamber over it. In the late 16th century, as the parlour came to be the room where meals were taken, it became customary to have a second important room near it: a withdrawing room. In the grander houses the

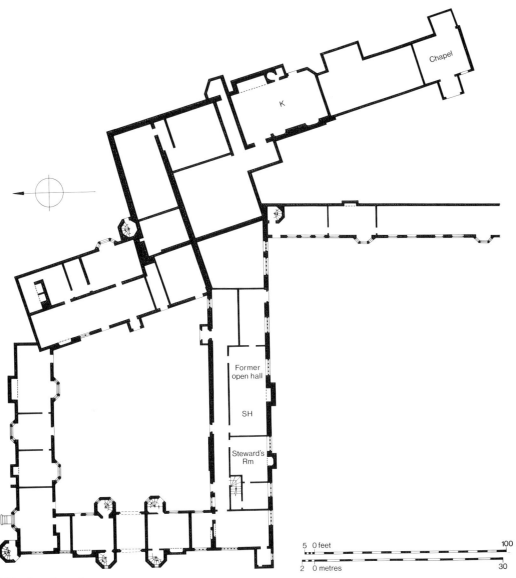

89 *The Lordship, Standon: plan*

function of the parlour was transferred upstairs to the great chamber, which then required a correspondingly dignified approach: a wide staircase with a gentle ascent. Added to an existing house this principal staircase could be put in the angle of the courtyard, as at Hatfield Palace [**90**], and in a new build it might be sited at one end of the parlour, as at Knebworth House. Whatever its exact position, it would be placed as near the upper end of the hall as possible, the model of convenience in this respect being the somewhat later Hatfield House.

The development of the parlour wing in a late 16th-century courtyard house was bound up with the courtier's wish to entertain the monarch, whatever the cost, in hopes of commensurate reward. Consequently, instead of leading simply to a large withdrawing room, the great staircase provided the approach to several rooms intended primarily for the use of the monarch and her personal attendants. Two architectural possibilities were available. One was an enclosed long gallery above a colonnaded ground-floor walk, intended primarily to permit exercise in bad weather and, secondly, the display of pictures. Generally, the stronger the wish to entertain the Queen, the longer the gallery. (Galleries were common in 16th-century houses, but gentlemen lacking a courtier's ambition built less grandly.) The second possibility was to enlarge the great chamber and withdrawing room into the sumptuous suite of rooms needed for a royal visit.

At Knebworth House the withdrawing room was known until the early 18th century as Queen Elizabeth's Room, although the date of any visit she made has not been traced. The gallery opened off it, as, no doubt, the colonnade did off the great or dining parlour originally; the parlour fireplace

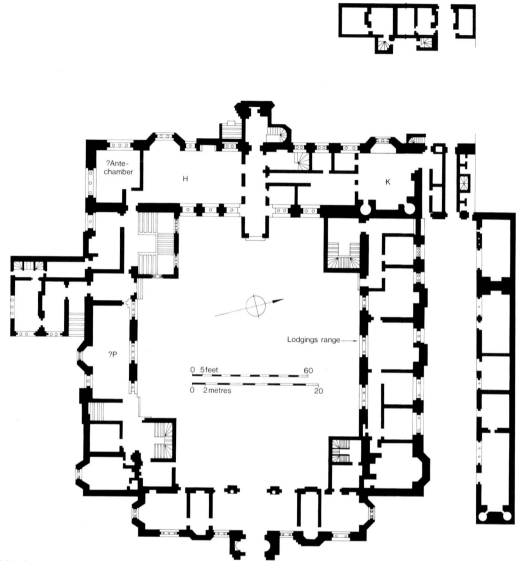

90 *Hatfield Palace: plan by P F Robinson, 1833*

as drawn in a plan of *c*.1800 is nearer the doorway into the hall than to the colonnade, perhaps to allow for a small lobby through which the colonnade was reached. The difficulty with this arrangement in conjunction with a high hall is that it precluded the creation of a suite of royal rooms in the right sequence: great chamber, withdrawing chamber, bedchamber, inner chamber.[6] At Knebworth, the complement of rooms may have been made up by using those on the far side of the staircase from the withdrawing room. Such a solution may well have been found unsatisfactory and was certainly not adopted at Gorhambury where priority was clearly given to the royal suite. That can be inferred from the way Sir Nicholas Bacon responded to Queen Elizabeth's comment that his house was too small, by adding just the feature so conspicuous at Knebworth, a long gallery over a colonnaded walk, looking like a smaller ver-

sion of the three-storey gallery block projecting from the south side of the middle court at Theobalds.[7]

How these two features, royal suite and gallery, were combined elsewhere in Hertfordshire is not known. At Hadham Hall, Little Hadham, the colonnade (and therefore a gallery, too) was on the south side of the main courtyard, which one might expect to correspond to the parlour end of the hall range, yet the evidence of the excavated walls suggests it was the service end. Although Broxbourne Bury throws little light on the point under discussion, interpretations already made permit conjecture about its early form [**91**]. The south range was remodelled at the end of the 18th century with a stuccoed façade and a row of windows in tall round-headed recesses which, with Knebworth [**92**] and Hadham Hall in mind, suggest that a colonnaded gallery range had been easily altered according to the very latest

52

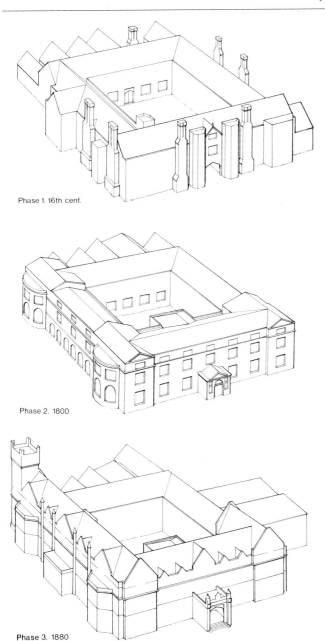

Phase 1. 16th cent.

Phase 2. 1800

Phase 3. 1880

91 *Broxbourne Bury, Hoddesdon: development perspectives*

with an ante-room at each end, occupying all the south range between the two principal staircases, may have been a very grand parlour. This was in contrast to the smaller rooms on the opposite side of the courtyard, which look like lodgings for visitors or for the most important gentlemen of the household and probably formed three two-room apartments; in the apartment at the east end, and possibly at the west end too, the larger room appears to have been reached through a lobby. It is a reminder that many of the rooms in these great houses were entered in a seemingly awkward and inconvenient way, sometimes to keep out draughts, often to ensure access from one room to another without the problems created by passages.

Service rooms and cellars

As late as the reign of James I, Hatfield Palace preserved largely intact the medieval arrangement of a passage from hall to kitchen placed between two smaller rooms, the pantry on one side and the buttery, with a staircase down to the cellar, on the other; other service rooms came between them and the kitchen. Somewhere away from these rooms, which probably included a steward's room, was the 'surveying place' that recurs in nearly all Elizabethan and Jacobean plans where room uses are named. This was where the functionary whose duty it was to oversee the preparation and serving of food performed his task, his station being somewhere between pantry, kitchen and hall.[8] How closely these Elizabethan arrangements at Hatfield (recorded in an early 17th-century plan) preserved those of Cardinal Morton's day is impossible to say, but it is reasonable to suppose that they had been modified to meet Elizabethan practice. Gorhambury, for which there is a painstaking reconstruction based on documents and recollections of its plan by a member of the family, shows what became for a long time the standard arrangement of a corridor leading behind two service rooms to the room beyond. In some houses that was the kitchen, as in the newly built Hatfield House of 1612, and at Knebworth for as long as it remained a courtyard house, but at Gorhambury we cannot be so certain for, by the late 18th century, the room in question was a dining room.

Households of the order of size of the courtyard houses needed food and drink to be stored and prepared on a scale which presented considerable planning problems. There are no strong reasons for thinking that the south wing at Knebworth House was originally devoted to service purposes as it was in the 18th century; it is much more likely to have provided a series of lodgings for which there is otherwise hardly any evidence except in the gatehouse range. But if this is so, Knebworth must have had, outside the courtyard block, a building incorporating the pantry, brewhouse and associated rooms, and in consequence the house presents a different facet of the same problem as Standon Lordship. There, the long ranges extending away from the courtyard must certainly have antedated Drapentier's engraving; no doubt he tidied them up for his engraving of

fashion. If these two colonnades were indeed at the lower ends of the respective houses, it implies concern to provide a larger suite of rooms at the upper end of the hall than was possible at Knebworth.

In houses as large as these it is surprising, not so much that some had a private chapel, as that many apparently did not. Theobalds had a chapel, Gorhambury too, in an equivalent position (in continuation of the hall range and as close to the upper end of the hall as possible). Elsewhere there is no evidence.

A royal suite of three rooms, perhaps a chapel, and a gallery over a colonnade occupied a considerable part of the two courtyard ranges abutting the hall range. What else was there? At Hatfield Palace, a very large bay-windowed room

92 *Knebworth House: view with colonnade* (Skinner. *By permission of the British Library*)

c.1700 in the same spirit that, a hundred years later, Skinner chose his viewpoint of Knebworth House (see [92]) to conceal as far as possible what was presumably a service range running off at an angle at the south-east corner. If these suppositions are correct, they make the irregularity of the plan of Hadham Hall more intelligible; indeed, it may be that such irregularity was a deliberate choice, an aesthetic device to distance the inferior parts of the house from the rest in the eye of the contemporary beholder, whose perception was expected to embrace only what he was expected to admire.

One other service element of the plan was of considerable importance in many houses: the cellars. Where undercrofts or extensive cellars existed they probably provided some accommodation for servants, as was certainly the case at Hatfield House. There, evidence for the multifarious uses to which cellars were put is provided by an 18th-century plan, and it has to be remembered that most such uses had to be met somewhere, even in houses with little cellarage. Surviving cellars are for the most part uninformative, and nearly all have been altered beyond any possibility of close dating. Hadham Hall certainly had cellars which, unusually, were under the colonnade or cloister range, and Gorhambury has some, revealed by excavation, under the hall range. A few houses were raised above what was virtually an undercroft, including the 16th-century Cheshunt Great House, as was Little Court, Buntingford [93], probably built in the 1570s. Here, two doors at the front of the wings

proclaimed the existence of an undercroft, and so there was no question of concealing it in any way or of regarding its everyday use as something to be tucked out of sight in a service court. At Royston Priory (see [103]), where the undercroft was probably a relic of the monastery, it was more than a half-underground cellar, as is demonstrated by the labelling of one of its rooms as 'a bad roome' and another as a 'bad parlour'; and the presence of a 'seller' next to the latter indicated that the term was being used in the older sense of a storeroom which was as likely to be at ground level as below it. The grandest house of all to have had its principal rooms over undercrofts, Watton Woodhall, Watton-at-Stone [94], which was in part pre-Elizabethan, is the one about which least is known.

Some of our uncertainties about the use of storage space in gentry houses may be dispelled when more is known of changing tastes in food and the consequent changes in domestic regimes. It is clear that a horticultural 'revolution' took place on gentlemen's estates in the 16th and 17th centuries. Chauncy mentions individuals whose discerning taste for fruits and vegetables led them to lay out gardens for the purpose; this interest in a better and more varied diet produced new demands for long-term storage and preservation of these products. One instance of such provision is at Hatfield House, where, in 1629, the 'sweetmeat house' was on the ground floor of the west wing; but here and in many another house, service rooms and cellars must have been

93 *Little Court, Buntingford* (Drapentier)

94 *Watton Woodhall, Watton-at-Stone* (Gough Maps 11, fo. 42, item e)

adapted or enlarged to store apples and pears, cider and perry as well as the traditional ale. A growing interest in the produce of the kitchen garden and orchard in the 16th century was matched by greater attention to herbs, both for cooking and for medicinal purposes. All had to be dried, some were infused to make distillations, and all required

some specialised space. More varied meat and fish supplies reached the kitchen as a result of the gentry's increasing interest in keeping dovecotes, fishponds, rabbit warrens and deer parks in the 17th century. Again, the consequences of all this for the layout of the domestic quarters of a gentry house have yet to be investigated.[9]

The gatehouse and lodgings ranges

If the Knebworth gatehouse was not defensive, then what was its purpose? The handsome oriel window overlooking the courtyard lit an important chamber whose only known use is the one it had throughout the 18th century, when it was the billiards room. It might earlier have been a great chamber for an important guest, approached from the courtyard by a newel stair in a tall turret. Though it might be rather unexpected to suggest that such handsome provision for guests might have been at the point farthest from the host, in a block that was at first isolated and later on had little if any intercommunication with the adjoining range, the situation could possibly have arisen through the practical

55

95 *Gorhambury, St Michael* (Gough Maps 11, fo. 36ᵃ, item a)

difficulties, in a large household, of putting guest chambers either near the host's own private chambers at the parlour end of the hall, or at the lower end in a wing; it may have been easier to keep them separate at the far side of the courtyard. A comparable function is implied at Standon Lordship by the staircase turrets flanking the entrance and a large window above it. Even where no more emphasis is given to the entrance than upstairs bay windows, as at Hadham Hall, this again implies the presence of important chambers above the gateway, reached much like the chambers in one kind of inn plan, or in a college. A second kind of entrance range, with an arcaded ground floor like the famous one at Kirby Hall (Northants) of 1575,[10] occurs at Hatfield Palace and Theobalds and apparently at Gorhambury, too [95]. Nothing definite is known about the use of the upper rooms in this arrangement.

Other lodgings for gentlemen, and especially for officers of the royal household, will have been provided elsewhere around the main courtyard, and the inferior servants were put wherever space could be found for them, many probably being lodged in the buildings of the base or kitchen court. No lodgings are now identifiable in any of the large Elizabethan or Jacobean houses in Hertfordshire, but from one chance survival it is possible to see what they were like in smaller gentry houses. The building that is now called Oxhey Hall, Watford Rural [96], is in fact only a lodgings range, the house itself having disappeared. It is timber-framed and provided on each storey two apartments or lodgings, each comprising a pair of rooms reached from a gallery. What the manor house was like, and how big the whole complex was, are quite unknown, but the closeness of the surviving part to the former moat suggests that, in the late 16th century, Oxhey Hall was not very large, though probably it had an outer courtyard as well as an inner. Indeed, it is conceivable that what remains was a detached block quite separate from the house. The lodgings on both floors were reached by a gallery rather than by two separate staircases, an arrangement reminiscent of a sizeable contemporary inn rather than anything found in the larger manor

houses; it was probably a simpler and cheaper way of achieving the desired amount of accommodation in an unpretentious house, even though it entailed some loss of light in the rooms. A gallery along which people passed to get to the superior lodging at the end implies that this small range incorporated the suites corresponding to 'officers' lodgings'. An interesting question is how common such ranges were. Reference in 1679 to 'one parcel of Houseing' at Ardeley Bury implies that this not very large manor house had lodgings like those at Oxhey Hall, and accommodation of such a kind may have been the rule among the gentry.

The contrast between the arrangements at Oxhey Hall and the lodgings ranges of larger houses is striking. In the latter, to ensure the greater privacy to which dignitaries were entitled, each lodging either had its own separate staircase or was reached without passing another set of rooms. This was achieved in a variety of ways. The gatehouse at Knebworth had external doors at the foot of the newel staircase, suggesting that the upper rooms could be reached only from the courtyard and not from the ground-floor rooms: an early, unsophisticated arrangement. At Broxbourne Bury and Cassiobury Park, Watford, the placing of the stair vices [97]

96 *Oxhey Hall, Watford Rural: first-floor gallery in the lodgings range*

97 *Cassiobury Park, Watford: engraving, dated 1800, of the west front*

on the outer wall of the lodgings range establishes that there was internal access to them, possibly by a transverse passage direct from the courtyard (see also [**138**]). Hatfield Palace, the only one of these large Elizabethan houses for which a contemporary plan exists, shows how complex the provision of staircases could be. In earlier houses a series of winding stairs, each in its own turret, ensured a degree of privacy in reaching each lodging suite but was architecturally unimpressive except in external effect, whereas at the Palace the provision of well staircases in the re-entrant angles of the courtyard, each one carefully graded in size according to the importance of the rooms it served, was an effective means of architectural display (see [**90**]). It is very difficult to be sure how many sets of rooms were reached from each stair; probably two or more lodgings on each floor were approached from all but the most important staircase, the one in the south-west corner that clearly gave access to the principal chambers. For the minor rooms upstairs, presumably occupied by members of the household of not very high status, the older fashion of stair persisted, so that a chamber over the kitchen or one of the adjoining rooms still had a winding staircase with an outside door; and there are other not much grander stairs elsewhere.

Secondary courtyards

Broxbourne Bury is the only courtyard house in Hertfordshire to survive complete; not intact by any means, but with evidence of its Elizabethan origin in all four ranges. The service court on the north side, entirely surrounded by Victorian buildings, reinforces the self-contained impression conveyed by the (originally) inward-looking main courtyard. This is exactly the impression Drapentier sought to convey in his engraving of Standon Lordship and is just as misleading as the Victorian restoration of Broxbourne Bury, for in both, as indeed in all other such houses, many sub-

sidiary functions necessary to a great household were performed away from the house itself, either around regularly set-out courtyards or in some less orderly groupings of buildings. The plan of Hatfield Palace made in 1607 is unusual in showing a row of purely functional buildings lying parallel to the north range and forming a narrow secondary court hidden from those rooms used by the principal residents or visitors.

The original outer court at Broxbourne Bury has vanished and if Drapentier's engraving alone had come down to us it might be supposed that Standon Lordship was equally bare of outbuildings in 1700, yet the plan and fragmentary remains show that this was not the case. Minet's plan of Hadham Hall and 18th-century drawings of Knebworth House both show extensive buildings beyond the main court, but only at Gorhambury have the various kinds of evidence been combined to show how the service (or office) court abutted the hall range, whereas the dairy (and stables, presumably) lay quite detached a short distance away. Although the evidence is sparse, it is likely that courts like these were to be found adjoining all large houses. All the houses so far discussed had large courtyards, but only one of this group of perhaps thirteen houses, Brocket Hall, Hatfield, had an elongated courtyard of the kind found at Kirby Hall and Burghley House in Northamptonshire.[11]

Houses with small courtyards

The difference between a large courtyard and a small one is illustrated by the fate of Pishiobury Park, Sawbridgeworth [**98**], where the courtyard was turned into a great central hall, very big for that purpose but only half the size or less of the large courtyards. Pishiobury, built between 1567 and 1590, is the only Elizabethan house of the small courtyard type of which anything survives.

Its plan cannot be reconstructed from internal evidence. Apart from the brick shell, not a scrap of Elizabethan work survived a fire in 1782 and the subsequent reconstruction. Fortunately, an inventory of 1662 can plausibly be related to the plan as James Wyatt left it soon after 1782, and the position of significant features such as windows and chimney-stacks can be checked against Drapentier's engraving: the result is comparable with several small courtyard plans among the Thorpe drawings.[12] With due reservations for changes which may have occurred in the eighty years that had elapsed since the house was built, it is still possible to recognise certain traditional ideas of how rooms should be disposed [**99**]. On the ground floor, the medieval sequence of hall, cross-passage and buttery was followed immediately by the little or winter parlour. This accorded with the underlying principle that the most important rooms on both floors occupied the corners. Importance here is used in a functional as well as a social sense to include the kitchen, which was sited diagonally opposite the hall, rather than in what might appear the more logical place, adjoining the little parlour. There are probably two reasons for putting it here: first, the corner rooms are better lit than the others; second, and prob-

98 *Pishiobury Park, Sawbridgeworth* (Drapentier)

ably more important, outhouses of various kinds, some of
which had to be near the kitchen, will have adjoined the
house, and if the kitchen were placed as far away from the
entrance front as possible without obtruding too much into
the view from the garden and park, so much the better. In
following this planning principle, the remaining corner
room had to be, functionally, some kind of parlour.
Curiously enough, it appears not to have been called the
great parlour, although its designation 'wrought parlour' is
suggestive of highly wrought ornamentation or rich embel-
lishment. That leaves five rooms to locate: two of consequence – the great parlour and the drawing room, which can
only have occupied the east range between the corner
rooms; also, the 'room within the wrought chamber', which
was a kind of closet; and two closets on the opposite side of
the house, the more important of them being Sir Thomas
Hewett's own. This arrangement probably corresponds
quite closely to that current during the Elizabethan era.

99 *Pishiobury Park, Sawbridgeworth: plan showing conjectural
room use in 1662*

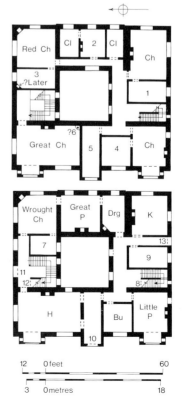

58

100 *Pishiobury Park, Sawbridgeworth: the Elizabethan brickwork survives at the corners, to the top of the first-floor windows; between them it runs at window-sill level*

The front of the house hardly needed any significant change, so much so that even Wyatt, who had a fairly free hand after the fire, did not alter the basic divisions [**100**]; and for the rest of the house, the small-courtyard house plans among the Thorpe drawings confirm that Elizabethan or early Jacobean houses were laid out on almost identical lines. Only on the east side do the position of the great parlour, which was presumably a dining room, and the apparent smallness of the drawing room arouse doubts, there being no such division into two rooms on the old plans. Perhaps an extra room had been created later. The one important element which may have been added to the Elizabethan plan is the corridor on the south or back stairs side, although, in view of the difficulty of bypassing the kitchen, some kind of passage must have been provided there from the first.

On the first floor the same principle obtained, that the corner rooms were the important ones. The great chamber is in the only place possible at that period, over the hall; 'the hole within this room' is a privy. The chambers over the little parlour and kitchen occupy two more corners, leaving the red chamber, conformably to its order in the inventory, at the fourth. Again it is the east side which gives rise to doubt, through the confusing way the rooms around the chamber over the kitchen are described.

Small-courtyard houses, though never very common in Hertfordshire, continued to be built for over a hundred years. For Hamels, Braughing, there is only Chauncy's description of it as 'a neat and uniform Pile of Brick . . . with four Turrets in the four corners thereof' and a Drapentier engraving. The house itself was reconstructed, first early in the 18th century and then a second time to make it something like it was originally. New Place, Gilston, was almost certainly another small-courtyard house; Great Hyde Hall, Sawbridgeworth, may have approximated to this type by the early 17th century through gradual development, and what little is known about Cantlow Bury, Hinxworth, hints at a small-courtyard house. Balls Park, Hertford, is an example in advanced style begun in 1640; The Hoo, St Paul's Walden, was built in 1661; and Beechwood Park, Flamstead, was enlarged to a small-courtyard plan as late as 1702. All these houses are interesting in themselves but none adds greatly to our understanding of this type of plan.

The significance of small-courtyard plans

The small-courtyard house differed from the large in its lack of provision for a suite of guest rooms. Pishiobury, for example, lacks a great parlour of the size and importance of those in the courtyard houses, even though one room bears the name; and the sequence is one room short. Nor is there a long gallery, there being no apparent provision of any indoor place of exercise. Such differences are clear enough and have been explained by the exclusion of their owners, whether willingly or not, from royal progresses and other less formal visits.[13]

This explains why some houses are much smaller than their contemporaries but does not clarify the needs they were built to meet. Why, in a not very large house, were there two staircases, both of considerable pretension? At Pishiobury the back stair was not necessarily for the sole use of servants, for it provided the only way to the two lesser chambers of the four, those over the little parlour and kitchen, and the location of Sir Thomas Hewett's own closet somewhere near it shows that the south range was not simply service quarters. Furthermore, all the plans drawn by Thorpe[14] demonstrate that the back stair was secondary in size but not at all mean, a description which might apply more to the cramped garret stair and to the dark straight flights into the cellars. On the first floor the rooms interconnected to provide a circuit which excluded only the closets and the minor rooms within major rooms. The two staircases, it may be conjectured, were intended to serve two separate suites of rooms on the circuit rather in the way that the far greater staircases of Hatfield Palace must have served separate apartments.

From purely architectural evidence, Pishiobury and its analogues might have been designed with some social custom or convention in mind which involved the entertainment of some person of superior rank to whom the owner assigned the best rooms, himself retiring to the rooms between buttery and kitchen; that is to say, in the way Hatfield House was intended to be used. Any such visitor was accompanied only by personal servants for whom there is no sign of any special provision, since they would have been accommodated in the pallet chambers or rooms 'within' other rooms. Whether or not the social behaviour underlying it has been correctly divined, the need for two not quite equal staircases persisted almost to the end of the 17th century in houses of very different plan and must represent some quite fundamental trait of social life. If that is accepted, the examination of other houses of different plan types may help to define the extent to which this custom operated in society, beginning with a rather amorphous group of plans related to the classic H and half-H types.

Houses with one or two wings

A big house requiring ranges of lodgings did not have to be built round a courtyard. Cassiobury Park, Watford, combined a main range and two long cross-wings in what may perhaps be described as a three-quarters H-plan (see [139]). Having been largely rebuilt after the Restoration it was rebuilt again before being demolished in 1927, and, to add to the difficulties, Chauncy records that it was built in two stages which are now impossible to distinguish. The 16th-century house appears to have had one long and one short wing, the latter comprising a series of lodgings which are clearly shown as such in early 19th-century engravings. The adoption of such a winged plan where an enclosed courtyard would have provided the same accommodation might be attributed to the interruption of the original building programme, when its owner went into exile in 1553 following Mary's accession to the throne, were it not for the fact that Chauncy specifically says that he 'had prepared Matrices for the finishing thereof'. It is interesting that such a plan should have been begun at the very time when Standon Lordship

101 *Hatfield House: view from the south*

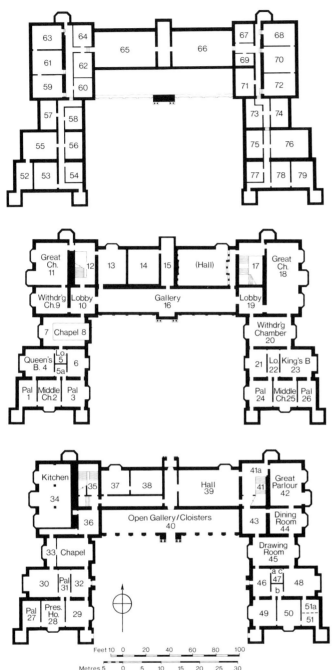

102 *Hatfield House: reconstructed plans of 1612; ground floor (above); first floor (middle); second floor (top)*

H-plan, although others considerably lower down the social scale approximated to it.

The two half-H plan houses, Hatfield House of 1607–12 [**101**, **102**], and the slightly inferior North Mymms Park of about 1599, are among the best known in Hertfordshire. Neither house as it now stands is of much help in the study of Elizabethan or Jacobean plans because of the extraordinarily thorough restoration each underwent during the 19th century, although in the case of Hatfield House the loss is counterbalanced by its rich documentation. Hatfield House is remarkable for combining so compactly the elements needed for the entertainment of the King and Queen; two suites of important rooms and others for attendants, a long gallery above a colonnade, and a main range in which all the traditional elements are enlarged to a truly royal scale. Two innovations greatly reduced the length of the wings that would otherwise have been necessary. One was to make the colonnade and gallery serve also as the frontispiece of the house. Comparison with Knebworth House or the sprawling Gorhambury shows the advantage Hatfield had, with a gallery accessible from both private suites instead of one, and reveals why there was either no way through at all from the end lobbies to the colonnade, or none of any importance, before the early 19th century. The colonnade was not used to provide a good approach to the Queen's apartments, possibly because notions of order and degree demanded less grandeur on that side than on the King's; to reach the King's rooms in proper sequence necessitated starting from the north end and so the main staircase could not rise from the colonnade side. Given these limitations, the essential elements of late 16th-century planning – hall, screens passage, buttery, parlour (translated into steward's room) and kitchen – were preserved, together with the passage leading to the secondary but still large and handsome staircase.

The second innovation was an entirely new way of planning the wings. Two elements were combined to allow easy circulation within a group of five rooms on each of the two main floors: a dark corridor-like room in the middle, entered from the long sides and receiving only borrowed light, and two staircases at the end of each wing. Had protocol not forbidden it, corridors would have provided an easier solution, but given that two graduated series of rooms were needed for royalty and that attendants had always to be at hand, the result was as convenient as could be before the advent of top-lighting for staircases. This arrangement necessitated a short corridor or lobby at the courtyard end of the two withdrawing rooms in the east or King's wing, one on the ground floor and the other above it; to produce a similar circulation pattern in the west or Queen's wing, both the chapel and its galleries had to double as passage rooms. In an age when men attached sanctity more to religious observance than to the building in which it took place, this idea was less shocking than it may now appear. Robert Cecil had precedent for just such an arrangement in Wimbledon House, begun by his older brother Thomas, Earl of Exeter, in 1588.[16] The loss of one important room on the Queen's side as a result of putting the chapel there merely reflected her smaller requirements compared with the King's, while those

was nearing completion, for there the work of c.1547 was of much the same overall size as Cassiobury Park. Fortunately we have John Evelyn's word for it that the huge house he visited in 1680, when it was new, was a rebuilding of an older one on the same lines. The three-quarters H-plan of The Grove, Sarratt, can only be inferred from the sequence of its 18th-century rebuilding and the analogy of Cassiobury.[15] So far as is known, no important house was built on a true

approaching the chapel, whether of high or somewhat lower degree, would do so at the level appropriate to their rank, via either gallery or ground floor.

Convenience of access between all parts of the house was perhaps Hatfield's predominant characteristic in comparison with its contemporaries. As early as 1609 Lyminge (or Wilson?) could write that 'the carpenters have brought up stairs in six several places from the ground to the top of the house';[17] these must have been the four staircases in the corner turrets on the south front and the two called in the account the 'cant staircases' which are on the north front. These six enabled servants to move about the house without ever being compelled to go through more than one room to reach another; only the middle of the three chambers facing southward on both floors of the wings could not be reached directly from a secondary staircase or corridor, without using the two principal staircases. But the Great Staircase led down to the basement and possibly the Adam and Eve Staircase did so too, originally. In addition, there were staircases linking the lower chapel to its galleries, referred to as the 'upper chapel' in the inventories, and the basement to the buttery. Few houses can have been so well provided. It is the more striking, therefore, that the Hall, in the words of the 2nd Marquess, 'was originally a mere passage room and formed the sole communication between the two ends of the house'.[18]

It is important to remember that to the rear of Hatfield were two courtyards surrounded by all kinds of menial buildings, and there was a third somewhere on the west side. As de Sorbière wrote in 1709, 'It has Three Courts below; the First contains the Stablings and other Conveniences for Poultry, etc',[19] whilst Pepys was less specific, noting simply: 'we . . . walked into the great House through all the Courts'.[20] The accounts mention the inner court with its porters' lodges, which must be the one on the south side, the base court, the north court and, also on the north side of the house, the stable court, one side of which was formed by the Old Palace converted into stables; it had 'a great gate giving out into the park'.[21] The shadowy picture that emerges of a great house surrounded by something like a village is one that was true to a lesser degree of all really big houses in the country.

North Mymms Park (see [212]) adds little to our knowledge of Elizabethan houses. Refronting of the parlour wing in the 18th century and the provision of a new entrance-hall, and probably a staircase, too, must have involved considerable rebuilding, every vestige of which was swept away in the 1890s. At the same time, the hall range was largely gutted to form a gallery for the display of tapestries. Little Court, Buntingford, which is known only from Drapentier's engraving of it, was probably of similar plan.

Royston Priory, the only single-winged gentry house of this period, was built on an unusual plan whose irregularities probably stemmed from the adaptation of monastic buildings. It is known only from plans of the undercroft and principal floor made in 1578 by surveyors seeking stopping-places for the Queen on an impending progress [103]. The principal points of interest are the orthodox sequence of

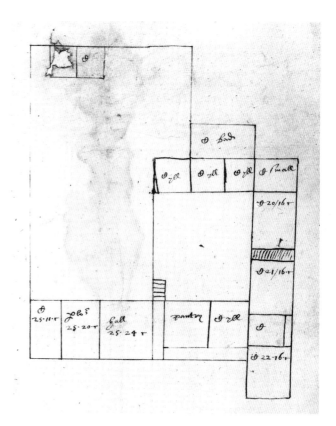

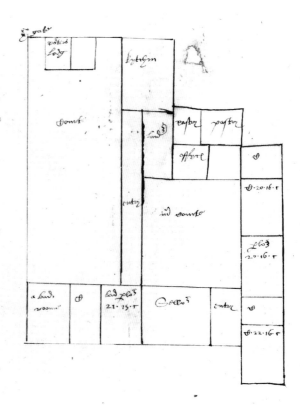

103 *Royston Priory: plans of 1578; ground floor (above); upper or principal floor (top)*

ground-floor rooms, with a corridor running past the pantry and the chamber, which corresponded to the little parlour or steward's room and gave access to rooms in the wing; and the limited number of rooms that met with the surveyor's approval. 'Chamber-yll' occurs five times, and there is a bad room, a bad parlour and one 'chamber-small'. Not surprisingly, it was thought 'A very unnecessary hows for receipt of her Mat.v'.[22]

In this group of houses with wings, Cassiobury Park, North Mymms Park and, especially, Hatfield House all display evidence of the duality of accommodation shown at Pishiobury and in the great courtyard houses.

Two houses for one family

At the higher levels of society, grandees perpetuated the peripatetic life of their medieval predecessors. Of Henry, Lord Berkeley, who carried this way of life to extremes, the historian of his family remarked: 'And thus lived the lord and his wife between London [and] houses in Norfolk, Callowden and Berkeley, never long at one place, the first thirteen years of Queen Elizabeth'.[23] Francis Bacon had a man of that stamp in mind when he advised: ' . . . if he have several Dwellings, that he sort them so, that what he wanteth in the One, he may find in the Other'. Although no Hertfordshire landowner is known to have lived on this scale, some men built or altered two houses in which they apparently lived themselves. Robert Chester converted Royston Priory into a house and built Cokenach less than four miles away, and Francis Bacon himself felt it necessary to build Verulam House only a mile from Gorhambury. His own words, that a man should have one house for summer and another for winter,[24] hardly convey an adequate motive; nor does Lord Burghley's remark that a second home was for use when his great house was a-sweeping.[25] Whatever the explanation, the ownership and use of two houses not far apart may have been commoner than the few instances collected here suggest and probably was done for several reasons: it certainly lasted into the 18th century when Sir

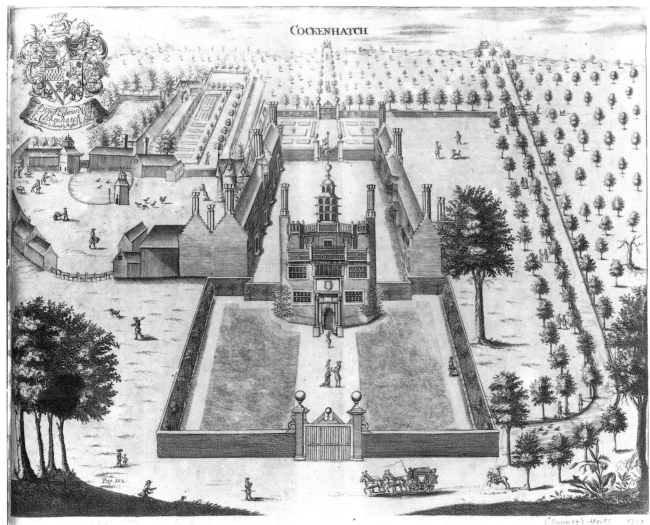

104 *Cokenach, Barkway* (Drapentier)

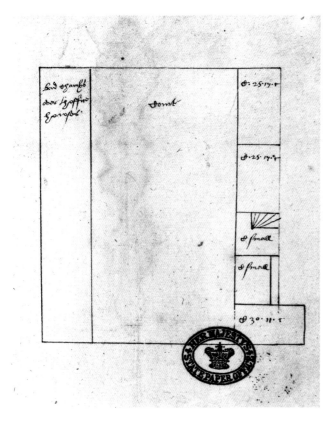

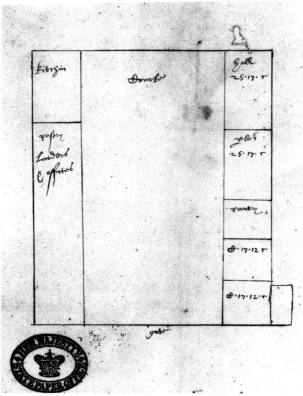

John Jennings was building at the adjoining houses of Newsells Park and Cokenach in Barkway.

An allied and equally obscure phenomenon is the existence at the centre of an estate of two houses where normally one would be expected. Stanstead Bury, Stanstead Abbots, is the only example in Hertfordshire at a high level of society. As a place where Queen Elizabeth stayed, it was of greater importance than the present house might suggest; it developed as two houses, of which one remains, albeit in a remodelled form. Presumably the two houses were occupied by members of the same family, a phenomenon that has been noticed more often at lower social levels (see pp 106 and 111).

Parallel ranges

Cokenach, Barkway [104], provides a caution against overhasty interpretation on the lines of dual occupation. Though it was built as two parallel ranges, one was the house and the other the service quarters, and they were joined at the ends by walls forming an enclosed courtyard. It can be regarded either as a freak or, more instructively, as a hitherto unrecognised type.

Nobody looking at Cokenach today could guess its Elizabethan origins. That knowledge comes from a plan made in 1578 by the same surveyors who visited Royston Priory [105]; continuity with the existing 18th-century house is established by maps and other drawings. Cokenach, one of the many houses built on former monastic property, was unusual in perpetuating a detached kitchen at such a late date, and in doing so in a more formal architectural composition than is found in the Middle Ages, by means of two parallel ranges of buildings [106]. Had the Elizabethan plan come down to us without the names of the rooms, it would be assumed that the hall lay in the normal place between parlour and buttery, whereas the Elizabethan surveyors reversed the usual order and put the parlour between hall and buttery. Hence the hall, where most of the household ate, was conveniently sited in relation to the kitchen at the end of the opposite range; the relation of the hall to the entrance into the courtyard, with the screens at right angles to the line of approach, is exactly the same as at Standon Lordship. This kind of plan was perhaps both more convenient and commoner than its unusual appearance suggests. As well as Cokenach, and, possibly, Standon Lordship, houses can be found elsewhere where no coeval hall range joining the two parallel ranges exists. Cobham Hall in Kent is one such, Trefalun in Denbighshire (now Clwyd) another,[26] and it might be worth considering all such houses as a group to discover what they had in common before the wings were linked.

A representative sample?

The survival rate of the bigger Elizabethan and early Stuart houses in Hertfordshire is low and without the rich docu-

105 *Cokenach, Barkway: plans of 1578 ground floor (above); first floor (top)*

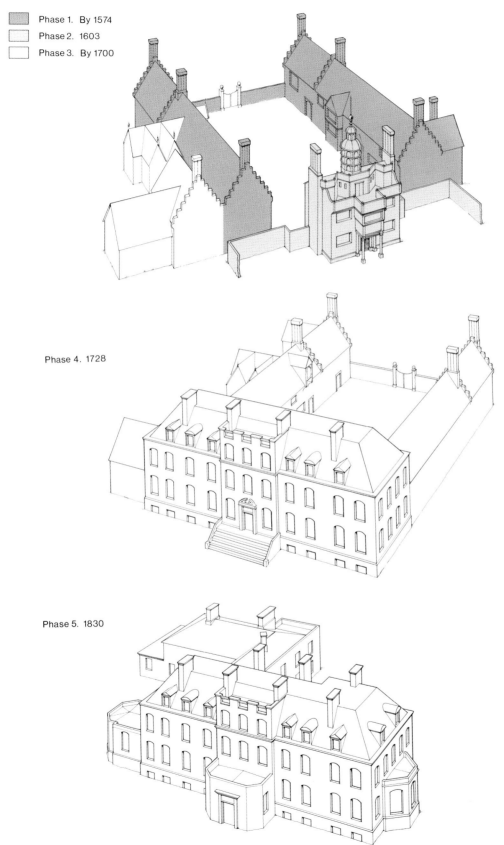

Phase 1. By 1574
Phase 2. 1603
Phase 3. By 1700

Phase 4. 1728

Phase 5. 1830

106 *Cokenach, Barkway: development perspectives*

107 *Quickswood, Clothall: 17th-century fireplace, photographed at Hatfield House where it was later installed*

house of the Cecil family, all that is left is a 17th-century fireplace (now in the Winter Drawing Room of Hatfield House) of a size and quality hinting at a quite sumptuous building [**107**].

It may be that the historian's view is distorted, not so much by the losses among the great Elizabethan and Jacobean houses as by the virtual disappearance of the houses built within a generation after the Dissolution. Several houses were fashioned out of monastic properties at a time when building ambitions were changing rapidly under the impact of the new relationship between the Crown, courtiers and officers, and against a background of new stylistic possibilities. The need to keep pace with these developments, exemplified in the late Elizabethan examples of Theobalds and Gorhambury, had earlier caused Sir Richard Lee to embark on the rebuilding of a house he himself had put up not many years before. Nothing significant is known about the house at Markyate Cell, begun by one courtier and completed by another before Elizabeth came to the throne. The 16th-century house at Tyttenhanger, Ridge, good enough to receive Henry VIII for a fortnight in 1528, and the residence of Sir Thomas Pope, who was twice Sheriff in the 1550s, has disappeared without trace. There is a similar dearth of information about the manor house of The More, Rickmansworth, enlarged by Wolsey and in royal ownership for more than fifty years. These houses represent a phase of architectural history which, in Hertfordshire, is effectively lost, except for an undercroft at Ashridge, divorced from the great house built around it.

Among lay manor houses our total ignorance about Shingey or Shingle Hall, Sawbridgeworth, is perhaps more serious for the medieval than for any later period, for only in the 1590s and 1600s, when John Leventhorpe was Sheriff, knighted and created baronet, did it again become important; and by then the evidence for other houses is comparatively abundant. Five or six more principal residences of sheriffs, among which Putteridge Bury, belonging to the Docwra family, and Cheshunt Nunnery, belonging to the Dennys, are the most important, complete the tally of houses which might modify our view of the architectural history of Hertfordshire between the Reformation and the Civil War.

mentation of Hatfield House and the records made by earlier antiquaries, our knowledge of their relative importance would be even slighter than it is. So many important houses have disappeared, leaving little or nothing to show what they were like. Of Quickswood, Clothall, another

Chapter 5

Country houses of the late 17th century

The second great age of country house building in Hertfordshire began under the Commonwealth and continued into the 18th century. It came immediately after a complete break during the Civil War, which itself followed three decades when very few new houses were begun and the principal activity was the alteration of those houses put up between the Reformation and the death of Queen Elizabeth. Stylistic differences before the Civil War do not form an absolute contrast and are sufficiently well known not to need describing here, whereas little has been written about the changes in internal planning, except for a few of the largest houses.

The best guide to the evolution of internal planning is the recognition of forms unlike those of immediately preceding or subsequent periods. However, by the middle of the 17th century, many manor houses were sufficiently well built and sufficiently large to outlive the social and economic conditions which produced them; and although a late medieval timber-framed house or an Elizabethan house of brick would, by the Restoration, be unsuitable for the needs of an heir or a new owner, its complete replacement by a house of comparable size represented a waste of resources for all but the very richest. Consequently, the tendency was to modify the existing structure or rebuild it piecemeal, and either way the old building enforced a compromise with the new ideas of planning. The limiting effects of incorporating old work in new were well expressed by John Evelyn after seeing how the Earl of Essex had rebuilt Cassiobury Park: '. . . 'tis pitty the house was not situated to more advantage; but it seemes it was built just where the old one was, & which I believe he onely meant to repair at first, which leads men into irremediable errors, & saves but little'.[1] Comparison of new and altered houses will produce many examples of 'irremediable errors' resulting from the inability of owners to follow Evelyn's advice and their own inclinations, simply because of the cost.

The Civil War marked the end of the traditional ground plan which gave the larger Elizabethan houses such a strong family resemblance to their medieval predecessors, although, as with so many of the changes brought about between the reigns of Charles I and Charles II, there was no sharp break. A few houses like Aston Bury Manor perpetuated traditional plan forms under the Commonwealth and these can be glimpsed in attenuated form in some rebuilt

houses of the 1650s and 1670s but, broadly speaking, large houses built after the middle of the century, and to a lesser extent the smaller manor houses, were governed in their planning by two new principles. One was that the first floor was the most important part of a big house, where major rooms or suites of rooms were grouped together. This was not new in the greatest houses such as Hatfield, where the two principal suites were upstairs before 1612; and indeed it may have been more common than the evidence now suggests: for example, a good-sized timber-framed manor house such as Rothamsted Manor, Harpenden Rural, had an upstairs dining room by 1622, and Balls Park, Hertford, seems to have looked forward to Restoration houses as much in this respect as in its outward appearance. The change had the effect of diminishing still further the original function of the hall as the focus of domestic life, reducing it to an entrance-hall where less important visitors might be received. The purpose of this change which, in a middle-sized house, affected both the hall and the parlour adjoining it, was twofold: it increased the owner's dignity by removing him from contact with his inferiors in the hall and provided him and his guests with views of the garden.

The second principle relates to the provision, most clearly observable in middle-sized houses, of large rooms virtually independent of the principal suite and having separate access from the ground floor. Social factors at present unknown must underlie such a rigid division of the household, because the architectural means of organising a house of that overall size into a unified whole were already known. The main staircase led to the most important suite of reception rooms whose occupants, whether family or guests, had the principal bedrooms nearby. Where there was at least one other good room or suite upstairs it was reached by a second staircase of an architectural quality related to the social status of whoever was intended to use it: the secondary staircase was not simply a servants' stair.

The principles applied: Tyttenhanger House

In Hertfordshire the application of these principles is seen most clearly at Tyttenhanger House [108], Ridge, begun

108 *Tyttenhanger House, Ridge: from the south east*

about 1655. It makes a good starting point because it was entirely new. Its form, which is that of a stubby H, and its height, of three storeys and attics above a basement [**109**], were to prove a more enduring model than did the elongated elegance of the celebrated Coleshill, begun approximately two years later.[2] In the middle of the double-pile range between the arms of the H is an entrance positioned to meet the demand for external symmetry while satisfying the need to enter the hall at the lower end in a convenient and conventional way. The rather old-fashioned character of the hall was emphasised by the use of short screens, the successor of the medieval spere-truss, to protect the living space of the room from the draughts at the entrance. At this date the hall was still a large room, though not the most important one, a distinction which seems to have passed to one or other of the rooms in the principal first-floor suite. These are reached by a main stair still placed much as it would have been in earlier houses, in close relation to the upper end of the hall.

Three flights of a gentle ascent give access to the first floor where the visitor is confronted by a blank wall on the other side of the narrow landing, rather than by the important doorway which might be expected. From the landing the visitor passed into a lobby, with two grand doorways to left and right. Such lobbies, like the blind approach from the stair, seem almost to have constituted a design principle in the third quarter of the 17th century, for they, or hints of them, appear elsewhere; two or three are shown in Sir Roger Pratt's plan for Ryston Hall dated 1671.[3]

At this point a problem of interpretation arises. It stems from the difficulty of distinguishing old work from new and bears on the problem of how much intercommunication there was between rooms when the house was built. On the first-floor landing are four pedimented doorcases [**110**], all

110 *Tyttenhanger House, Ridge: pedimented doorcases*

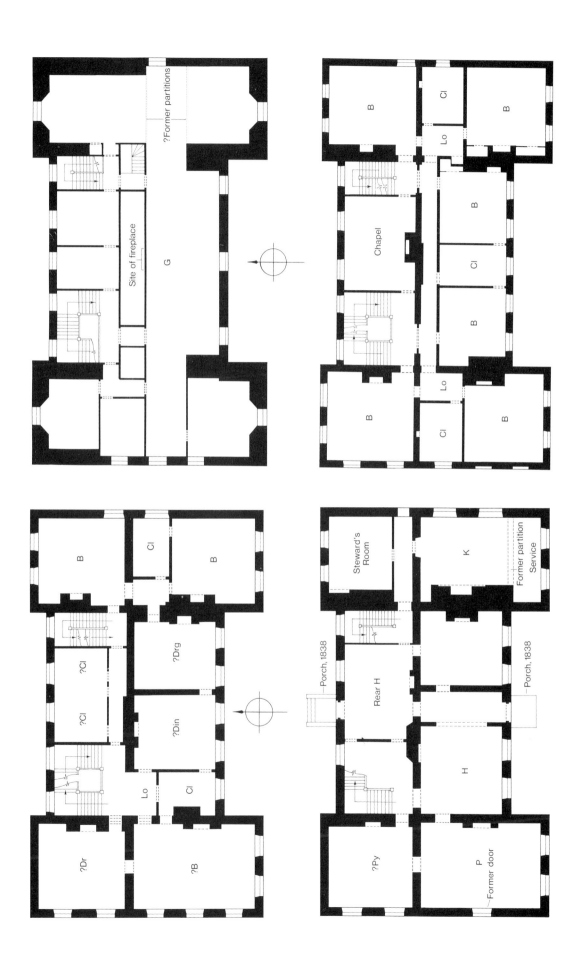

109 *Tyttenhanger House, Ridge: plans; ground floor (above left); first floor (top left); second floor (above right); attic storey (top right)*

Within the plans, the following labels appear:

Ground floor (above left): Steward's Room, K, Former partition, Service, Porch, 1838, Rear H, Porch, 1838, H, ?Py, P, Former door

First floor (top left): ?Dr, B, ?Cl, Cl, Lo, Cl, ?Din, ?Drg, B, ?B

Second floor (above right): B, Cl, Lo, B, B, Cl, B, Chapel, Lo, Cl, B

Attic storey (top right): ?Former partitions, Site of fireplace, G

supposedly of the 1650s. The two facing each other, with triangular pediments, are probably original, but the two with segmental pediments, one of which leads into an unheated closet, have that characteristic late Victorian and Edwardian quality of going one better than the exemplar, so they probably are not. If the two older doors are in their original positions there may not have been another one between them into the antechamber or closet, which was perhaps reached from either or both of the two front rooms. The point is of some importance; the evidence at Tyttenhanger, even if only two doors are allowed to be original, is better than anywhere else in the county.

At the other end of the house was a second and smaller staircase. This one seems to have provided the usual means of access to two bedchambers – an important one at the front of the house and another, less important because lacking an adjoining closet, at the back. The only other possible approach would have been by a corridor from the main stair, an arrangement of which there is little evidence in the 17th century. This means that the secondary staircase was not simply for servants, though it must have been used by them.[1] At its head there is no lobby corresponding to that at the other end of the house, so to reach the south bedchamber it was necessary to go through the adjoining one. At Coleshill, all rooms of any importance, with the exception of the great parlour and the great dining chamber, were entered through a lobby. Applying this example to Tyttenhanger, we might postulate that an internal lobby within the bedchamber may have existed to increase privacy by screening off the door to the landing.

Houses constricted in the middle: Beauchamps and Mackerye End

Tyttenhanger stands alone among late 17th-century country houses in Hertfordshire. Few others were as large or as symmetrical in anything but the front elevation and very few were of three storeys. The most noticeable common characteristic of the dozen or so houses in this group is that, although not divided structurally into two parts, they have two staircases and are narrowed in the middle (the only part not two rooms deep), so effectively creating such a division.

A bipartite or balanced plan of this kind was not new. On a small scale every medieval house with two two-storeyed end bays or cross-wings is so arranged. In Dorset, Cranborne manor house[5] illustrates how readily this arrangement could be adapted to the requirements of the mid 17th century. Given that a continuing need was felt for a hall rising through two storeys, enlargement and improvement tended to be mainly at the ends of the house, even though a third or attic storey might be added, as at Wyddial Hall. The problem is to explain why development took place at the ends rather than in the middle, by means of a T-shaped or any other form of plan which would have created a more centralised and simpler pattern of circula-

tion. Smaller manor houses where a lofty hall was not needed, such as Bride Hall, Wheathampstead, and Albury Lodge House, were built of two storeys throughout but, significantly, instead of having the single main staircase of Queen Hoo Hall, Tewin, they were planned as if the medieval necessity for a staircase at each end still prevailed. This survival may be ascribed to tradition, or alternatively it may suggest a division of social function between the two ends akin to that at Tyttenhanger.

A major change comes when the upstairs rooms rival or surpass the importance of hall and parlour. Beauchamps, Wyddial, a new house of the middle 1650s, shows how the common vernacular plan characterised by an internal chimney-stack and lobby-entrance was adapted to the needs of a small manor house in this new situation. The customary ground plan was enlarged from three rooms to four and divided by the chimney-stack into polite (or family) and service ends, whereas upstairs the rooms were more nearly equal, being differentiated principally by the staircases; at the polite end the wider stair emerged into a large lobby from which the three rooms were reached. On each floor access from one end to the other may have been possible through a closet but would not have been the most important route. That the working of the house corresponded to the bipartite form is demonstrated by the addition, when such a division had become inconvenient during the 19th century, of a passage linking the two ends.

Separation of the household into two parts is apparent elsewhere. A few houses have what is, by the standards of the succeeding period, an unusual siting of the main staircase at the very end, so that in the absence of a first-floor corridor the principal upstairs rooms were even more completely cut off from the rest than was the case at Beauchamps. Mackerye End, Wheathampstead [111, 112], provides the clearest evidence: an imposing staircase at the north-west corner, replacing an earlier, humbler version on the same spot [113], rose to the first-floor landing which was probably arranged rather like Tyttenhanger; in one direction, with an excellent view of the staircase and 'a large

111 *Mackerye End, Wheathampstead: front elevation*

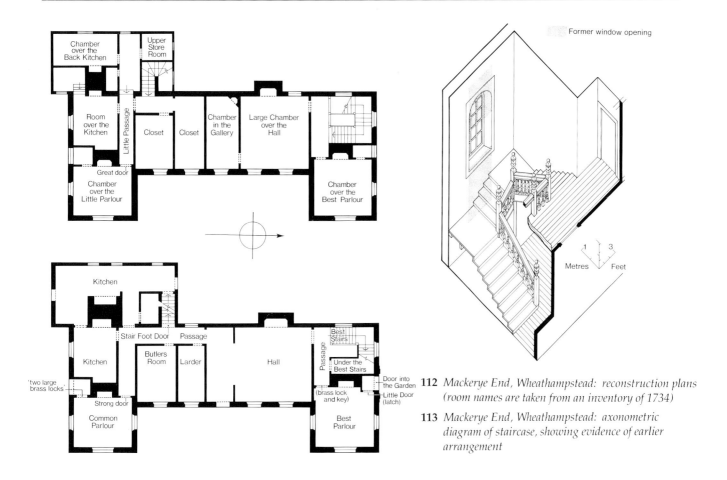

112 *Mackerye End, Wheathampstead: reconstruction plans (room names are taken from an inventory of 1734)*

113 *Mackerye End, Wheathampstead: axonometric diagram of staircase, showing evidence of earlier arrangement*

picture of Juno', lay the great chamber, in the other, a smaller bedchamber. A subsidiary room large enough to be called 'the chamber in the gallery' opened off the great chamber. The smaller bedchamber had only a small square closet beside the chimney-stack, so that the relative importance of this and the great chamber was demonstrated by the size of their respective closets as well as by the comparative dignity of approach. Structural evidence confirms the impression given by the plan; this suite of rooms was completely shut off from the rest of the house by an unbroken, studded partition. Inferior though the other end of the house necessarily was, it contained two bedrooms of importance, the chamber of the little parlour, which had a closet, and the chamber over the kitchen, which did not. As to who slept in these rooms it can only be said that they are far more likely to have been members of the family or guests than servants.

Bipartite houses as a product of rebuilding

At Mackerye End some rather slender evidence suggests it may represent the almost complete rebuilding in 1665 of an earlier house. The same argument can be used with greater confidence to explain Great Nast Hyde, Hatfield, which has a staircase in an identical position; there, the ground plan suggests that a medieval hall-house was rebuilt in the middle of the 17th century with a chimney-stack backing on to the former cross-passage and with a larger staircase giving a grand approach to the new principal rooms upstairs.

A bipartite plan of a different kind was intended, though never finished, at Salisbury Hall, Shenley (see [**36**]), where the unbalanced elevation and the constriction evident at what would have been the middle of the completed house are illustrated in drawings which show that part of an early 16th-century house had been rebuilt when the money ran out. Harpenden Hall, too, owes its appearance to just the same process, first recognised in vernacular architecture under the name 'alternate development';[6] two very much restored and modernised houses, Aldenham House and Upp Hall, Braughing, may be similarly explained; Wyddial Hall too.

Bipartite plans also occur at two houses in Brent Pelham: Brent Pelham Hall, rebuilt in the 1680s, and Beeches, both of which have two good staircases. Lastly, there are two rather unorthodox examples of the type. One is Berkhamsted Place, where a courtyard house was cut down to less than half its size and the 'main' or entrance-hall range, the middle part of the resulting half-H plan, is the narrowest of the three. All the important rooms were concentrated in the

114 *The Palace, Much Hadham: plan*

wings. Oliver's engraving of c.1700 brings this out as clearly as the plan, and the relative importance of the parts is comparable, on a small scale, to that achieved at Hatfield House half a century earlier. The other is The Palace, Much Hadham [**114**], a house intended after the Restoration for dual occupation, yet one which shows in the details of its plan all the features such as lobbies and separate approaches to major rooms which have been remarked upon above.

Approaches to the double-pile

Two major staircases

It might be thought that the duality apparent in so many houses was the inevitable consequence of partial rebuilding and the adaptation of an older plan. True, there were difficulties in adding a room or a passage behind a large external chimney-stack, and the result was usually clumsy by comparison with a new-built house, but it could be done. Little Offley House was well suited to the kind of division favoured for houses with a main range and two cross-wings, each of which must have had a staircase. In the rebuilding they were suppressed in favour of a new staircase added at the middle of the house, thereby producing a more centralised plan than usual [**115**]. A version of the double-depth house was achieved here by the use of passages and corridors, all lit directly by windows at the side or the end, which connected the staircase with the principal rooms.

The difficulty of providing light and access in a house two rooms deep is apparent at Aston Bury Manor [**116**] (see also [**145**]). On the ground floor, a generally conventional plan produced no new problems. Much the most remarkable feature in a house of this modest size is the provision of two staircases, almost identical in appearance and differen-

tiated only slightly in scale and decorative detail. On the first floor, the provision of three pairs of closets to serve the four principal rooms, coupled with the placing of the two middle chimney-stacks on an outside wall, complicated the designer's problem enormously [**117**]. The result was that the two important rooms towards the middle of the house were comparatively long and narrow and because they had end fireplaces they were inefficiently heated; this had to be

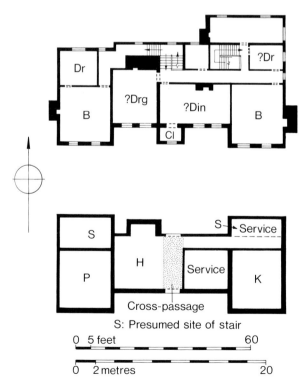

115 *Little Offley House, Offley: plans of c.1695; ground floor (late 16th century) (above); first floor c.1695 (top)*

116 *Aston Bury Manor: a view of the rear of the house*

117 *Aston Bury Manor: cut-away isometric drawing of the house in the 17th century*

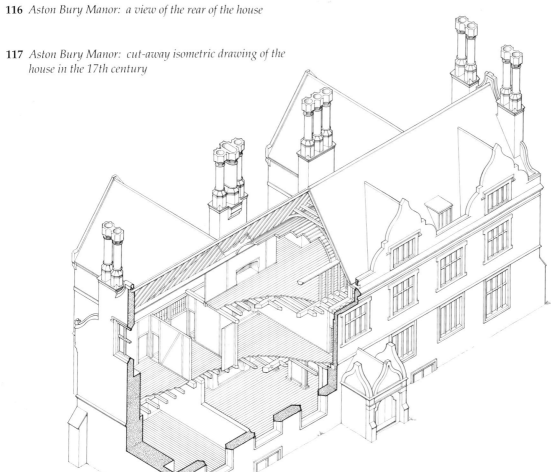

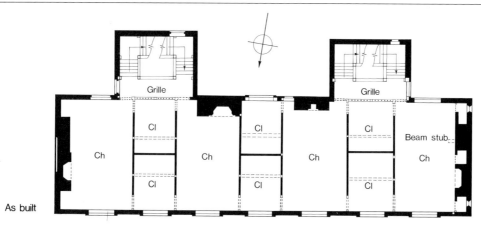

118 *Aston Bury Manor: reconstructed first-floor plan*

so unless the rooms were widened and so made inordinately large. The rear closets received borrowed light through wooden grilles running the length of the partitions which separated them from the staircase. Whether the end room was originally divided up with an ante-room or dressing room next to the staircase is difficult to decide; the proportions require it, but, even using grilles, there would have been great difficulty in lighting any kind of lobby or passage room between stair and bedchamber. The first-floor plan [118] seems designed to permit the flexible use of the six closets: the middle two are approachable from one room only, whereas the others could be entered from either side as convenient. Although Aston Bury Manor could hardly be described as constricted in the middle, it was like Beauchamps, Wyddial, in so far as no way through from end to end was intended upstairs, even if it were physically possible, and the two staircases must correspond to some division of the principal floor. Surprisingly, in a new-built house, the indirect approach to major rooms so evident in all other mid 17th-century houses is here absent, with the possible exception of the room at each end.

Houses with two identical staircases are rare. Strictly speaking, no instance is known in Hertfordshire; even the two staircases at Aston Bury Manor are differentiated slightly, although they are to all intents and purposes identical. A similar difference of size was formerly observable at Markyate Cell and probably the decorative detail also differed slightly. Other virtually identical staircases existed beyond Hertfordshire. In 1645 the negotiations conducted at Uxbridge, Middlesex, for a treaty between Parliamentarians and Royalists took place in 'a good House . . . which was provided for the Treaty, where was a fair Room in the middle of the House . . . for the Commissioners to sit in . . . There were many other Rooms on either side of the great Room . . . and there being good stairs at either end of the House, they never went through each others Quarters; nor met, but in the great Room'.[7] Presumably this was an early instance of a house constricted in the middle – narrow waisted, so to say. Clarendon House, Piccadilly, although it would be absurd to speak of it as constricted in any way, nevertheless had something in common with the type, for

its large, boldly projecting wings were served by two principal staircases, 'My Lord's Staires' or 'The greatt Stayres', and 'My Ladies greatt Stayres'; 'The smaller Stayres' were additional to these.[8] A generation later, the equality of each end of the double-pile Winslow Hall (Bucks)[9] was also expressed by equal staircases. Celia Fiennes' reference to Shuckburgh Hall (Warwickshire) suggests it was like some of the Hertfordshire houses in having 'two good staircases and 3 or 4 good chambers very well furnish'd, tho' not very rich'.[10] Other instances will no doubt appear once they are looked for.

Another unusual and experimental approach to the problems presented by Aston Bury Manor can be found at The Bury, Rickmansworth [119], for this L-shaped house covers as large an area as Tyttenhanger and is much more complicated. Alteration of an older house produced an apparently clumsy ground plan [120], although in fact the rooms of the west range, if their function has been properly interpreted, are remarkably conveniently placed in relation to one another. Planning of the first floor was difficult because there were four or five large bedchambers, to each of which independent access had to be contrived, and a number of closets. The solution was an axial corridor, indirectly lit; some light was borrowed from the staircase at one end, some from wooden grilles set above the doors.

This was not a solution which often found favour because to be satisfactory it required a window at the end of the corridor. Such windows could be provided at a house such as Coleshill because it was very wide, with two ranges of rooms flanking an unusually wide middle corridor, but in houses more modest in size, though still large, the corridor terminated in a room. This was so at The Bury, Rickmansworth [121], and also at Rothamsted Manor, Harpenden Rural, where a group of five chambers and attendant closets were all reached from a corridor which received direct light only at the middle point, the stairwell.

Rothamsted Manor offers an instructive example of the difficulties encountered by an owner who rebuilt a large old house piecemeal while he was living in it (see [143]). On the first floor Sir John Wittewronge needed a suite of four important rooms at the west end of the house, together with

119 *The Bury, Rickmansworth: the original front*

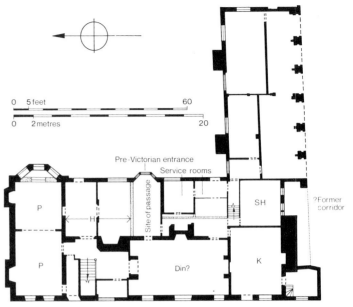

120 *The Bury, Rickmansworth: plan*

121 *The Bury, Rickmansworth: axial corridor. Above the nearest doorway is a panel, originally open and balustraded, to allow light into the corridor*

the necessary closets. Here grandeur precluded a dark corridor and the limitations imposed by the existing structure prevented the placing of these rooms in the middle; but the ultimate reasons for keeping this suite apart from the rest of the house must have been social and were evidently strong enough to necessitate its complete separation. The various requirements were partly met, as at Tyttenhanger, by a lobby at the head of the staircase opening into two

chamber-and-closet units; a third such unit lay beyond the largest chamber from which a gallery or passage may have been partitioned. The resulting plan [**122**] made Rothamsted singularly awkward in comparison with the standards of the centralised plans of a later generation; the long north wing made matters worse and necessitated an awkward approach from the smaller of the two staircases.

Some long-demolished houses may well have belonged to this stage of development preceding the double-pile house. The front elevation of Broadfield, Cottered, looks too early for the house to have been a true double-pile, yet its two great chimney-stacks which bulk so largely in the Buckler drawing [**123**] point to its having had important rooms at both ends. A plan with two staircases is likely. Blakesware Manor, Ware Rural, is less than satisfactorily illustrated, so all that can be said is that its elongated front, punctuated by a two-storey porch and what look like two-storey bay windows, has enough affinity with the front of Rothamsted to suggest that there were important rooms on both sides of the hall. Also, on the still slenderer evidence of their length, Thundridge Bury and Offley Place deserve mention in this context; since their appearance makes it unlikely that they were double-piles, they probably had some kind of elongated bipartite plan with two staircases, whether or not constricted in the middle. Even some timber-framed houses appear to fall into this category. On the grounds of length alone, Woodhall, Hemel Hempstead, is likely to have needed two staircases; one of which occupied a small turret, the other possibly a larger gabled wing, suggesting a staircase within it of the fairly spacious proportions of that at Old Ramerick Manor, Ickleford.

Duality expressed in various forms was no doubt common and tends to go unremarked. Thus Roger North, drawing plans for comparatively small houses, always

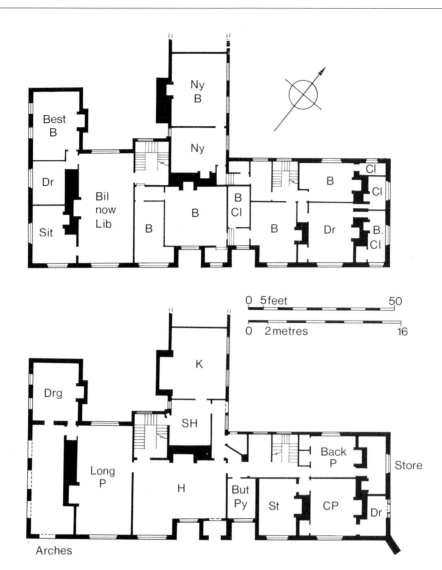

0 5feet 50

0 2metres 16

Arches

122 *Rothamsted Manor, Harpenden Rural: reconstructed ground and first-floor plans as in 1770*

included two good staircases, presumably in pursuance of his precept that 'the chief ground of beauty in uniformity [ie, symmetry] is usefulness'.[11] How far back in time architectural evidence of this kind can be found has yet to be established. Raynham Hall (Norfolk), begun in 1622, was entered by cross-passages at both ends of the hall, each leading to a good staircase.[12] Perhaps Hatfield House was simply a very special form of a quite common principle of planning.

One staircase

In the smallest manor or gentry houses two staircases were unnecessary; even in a house as large as Rothamsted Manor there appears to have been no stair specifically for servants so there was certainly no need for one in houses less than half its size.

Rawdon House, Hoddesdon [**124**], provides more compactly an amount of accommodation comparable to that of a

small Elizabethan or Jacobean manor house such as Bride Hall, Wheathampstead, which had two staircases. The essential change was to set the hall transversely, keeping

123 *Broadfield, Cottered* (Buckler)

124 *Rawdon House, Hoddesdon: front elevation from the south west; the block to the left is modern*

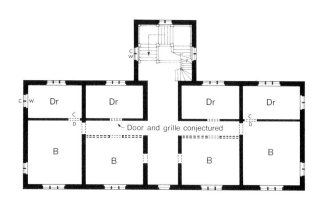

Door and grille conjectured

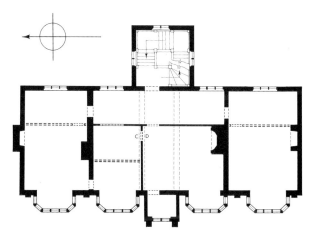

125 *Rawdon House, Hoddesdon: reconstructed first and second-floor plans as in 1650*

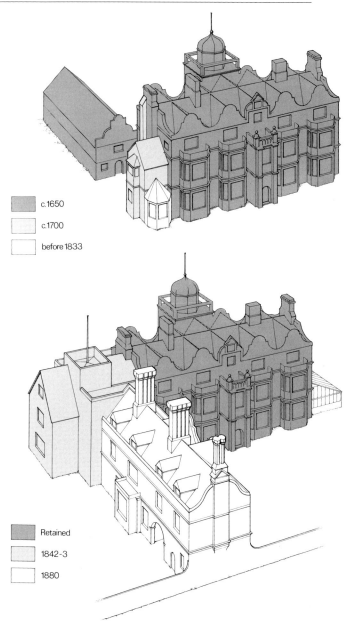

c.1650

c.1700

before 1833

Retained

1842-3

1880

126 *Rawdon House, Hoddesdon: perspective development drawing*

the fireplace in the customary position on one of its long walls; by that means the parlour, instead of projecting as a wing, could be made flush with the hall [**125**, **126**]. At the service end an enclosed corridor gave access to the buttery, pantry or larder, and kitchen, the remaining space being occupied by a little parlour at the front. It was a neat solution which accommodated the old rooms at much their old size, while a porch kept draughts from the hall as effectively as screens did at, say, Tyttenhanger. Upstairs, the original arrangement is less certain. The staircase led to something wider than the words corridor or passage connote – a gallery in Sir Roger Pratt's terminology – from which the three principal bedchambers were reached. Both end chambers were either very large or were subdivided by a parti-

77

tion placed inconveniently near the fireplace – the same problem as at Aston Bury Manor. On the second floor there were corridors and as many as eight rooms.

Two important elements of double-depth planning, the corridor and the gallery, made Rawdon House both compact and roomy, but for smaller houses a different solution was generally found.

The smaller double-pile house

Double-pile houses are not unknown in England before the Civil War but they are rare and none is yet known to have existed in Hertfordshire. A kind of double-pile appeared, probably as early as the Commonwealth period, at The Grange, Hoddesdon, which has two staircases, and, a little later (c.1660), came Codicote Bury [**127**, **128**], the precursor of the medium-sized four-square-looking house which was to become so popular among the lower gentry.

For the gentleman who did not need the large and grand first-floor rooms like those at Rothamsted Manor or The Bury, Rickmansworth, the square double-pile provided all the essentials comparatively cheaply in a moderate compass. At Codicote Bury, what appears to have been the dining room was linked to the kitchen by a lobby through which food could be served without going through the staircase-hall, and a withdrawing room opened off it. Another lobby provided a way through from the withdrawing room to a small parlour at the back, and from both to the garden. Here, as in so many other houses, there is no way of knowing whether the largest upstairs room on the garden side was a reception room or a bedchamber, but whatever its use, the space beside the chimney-stacks provided this and other first-floor rooms with a closet and one, at the south-west corner, with a dressing room. Only in these last two linked rooms was a lobby needed to avoid a passage room; elsewhere in the house lobbies were abandoned. How the roof space was used is uncertain. Probably it was divided into rooms corresponding in plan to those below, though inferior in size and headroom; certainly they were not much inferior in status to the first-floor bedchambers because the staircase by which they were approached is uniform in treatment throughout. Uniformity in this respect may reflect a dual purpose for the topmost rooms comparable to that envisaged by Sir Roger Pratt at a much greater house, Horseheath, when he wrote of ' . . . makeing use of ye Servants chambers for ordinary strangers, when no masters in ye fore chambers . . . '.[13]

As with so many houses, the story told by the existing building is incomplete. Even though the cellar survives, with storage for drink, fuel, etc, somewhere there would have been a pantry, scullery and brewhouse. All may have been accommodated in a lower range, together with servants' bedrooms, on the north side of the house. Houses of this middling size were never designed to embrace all such functions in one monumental composition, and even excluding the brewhouse, which for obvious reasons had to

127 *Codicote Bury: the house from the south west*

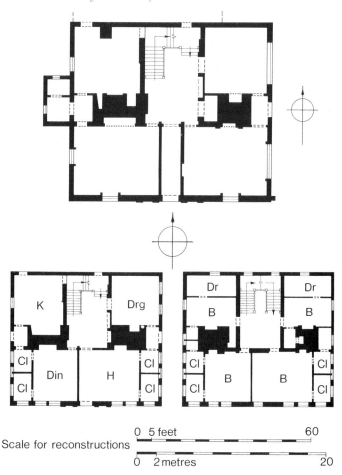

Scale for reconstructions

0 5 feet   60
0 2 metres   20

128 *Codicote Bury: ground-floor plan (above); reconstructed ground and first-floor plans (below)*

be sited away from the living rooms, it was usually better to have a separate range in which to house them.

Subsidiary ranges of this kind could be quite large. Bonningtons, Stanstead Abbots, has a double-depth block which covers nearly as much ground as the handsome house of the 1680s that it adjoins. It is of brick, like the main part, and even though the details of the plan are beyond recovery it is large enough to accommodate every service function required by a minor gentry family. A smaller wing, perhaps of the same period, remains at Furneux Pelham Hall; others, even more drastically altered, exist at Childwick Bury, St Michael, and Westbrook Hay, Bovingdon. The placing of these wings presented difficulties which neither the Caroline builders nor their successors ever solved quite satisfactorily. If the inferior status of such buildings were expressed by an inferior appearance, they had to be as inconspicuous as possible from the front in order not to mar the approach to the main house, yet they could not be sited at the back because that would spoil the layout and view of the garden. In Chauncy's day, even a house as big as Hertingfordbury Park might still have a farmyard on one side and a garden on the other, but houses as large as this, raised above a basement, were able to solve the service-room problem within the framework of four regular elevations.[14]

The development of the smaller double-pile house in Hertfordshire is difficult to trace. Typologically and chronologically, the Manor House, Ayot St Lawrence [129], could be regarded as a precursor of the true double-pile, being one of the smallest houses of its class and one of the least developed. Sandon Bury, built soon after the Restoration, is not much larger but, unlike the Manor House, where the staircase was approached from the hall through a lobby, had what may be regarded as an essential attribute of the double-pile: a staircase so disposed as to reveal its quality to anyone approaching it from the hall. Codicote Bury, Bonningtons, Stanstead Abbots, and probably the very much altered Meesden Hall may be regarded as the classic version of the type.

From this stage onwards, two strands of development can be discerned. One led to a somewhat smaller kind of house, still with the front door opening immediately into the hall. Putting all the chimney-stacks on the outside walls

130 *Childwick Bury, St Michael* (Oldfield)

made possible a freer use of the interior space: Northaw Place, of the 1690s, is like this. This mode of planning produced a good-sized hall in a small house, yet one which had the merit of a well-placed staircase both visually impressive to anyone entering the hall and conveniently placed for circulation. Descendants of this type lasted well into the next century among minor gentry and even longer among farmers.

A second strand led to a somewhat larger house, seven bays wide: Childwick Bury, St Michael [130], and Westbrook Hay, Bovingdon [131], were built by father and son, Joshua and Thomas Lomax, in the 1670s and 1680s respectively. Unfortunately, neither house retains any of its original internal fittings; even such fundamental features as staircases and the sizes of rooms have been altered. What they have in common is the downgrading of the hall from its old function as an important living room to a smaller,

129 *The Manor House, Ayot St Lawrence: from the north east*

131 *Westbrook Hay, Bovingdon* (Oldfield)

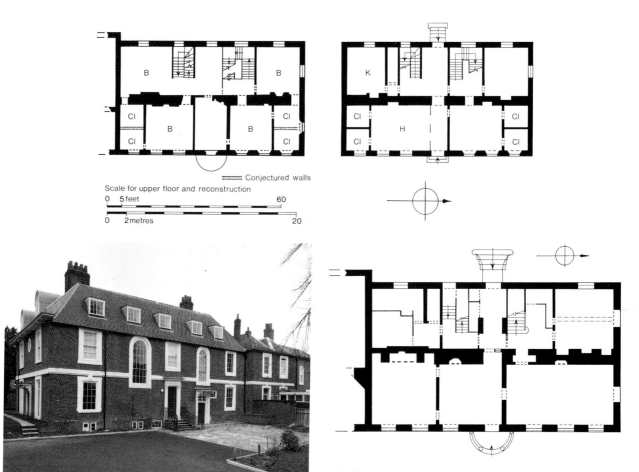

132 *The Grange, Hoddesdon: from the north west*

133 *The Grange, Hoddesdon: ground-floor plan (bottom)*
reconstructed ground and first-floor plans (top)

square entrance-hall, with a staircase-hall of equal size behind it. The middle axis thus created separated two pairs of rooms on each of the two principal floors, and if, as is very likely, there was a second staircase originally, it would have been for servants. Indeed, Childwick Bury has a second stair beside the main staircase but, since the latter is a splendid late 19th-century creation, it does not argue an early date for this arrangement. The axis formed by entrance and staircase-hall was the most important feature these houses had in common. At Childwick Bury the chimney-stacks were banished to the outside walls, leaving the middle axis apparently unheated – a hardly credible conclusion which better evidence might well correct. A different solution, one which proved more acceptable to later builders, was adopted at Westbrook Hay; at the front of the house at least, the chimney-stacks flanked the entrance-hall and so provided a fireplace to heat it, while in the rear hall a third stack backed on to the staircase-hall. For some reason not perfectly clear, a fourth stack, probably serving the kitchen, was placed on the back wall; it was left to a later generation to produce a completely symmetrical arrangement of transversely placed chimney-stacks.

Larger double-pile houses

The two Lomax houses are closer in their proportions to a form of double-pile which has a different ancestry and was built by a superior stratum of gentry. Houses of this kind have a long rectangular plan, usually about twice as long as wide. From a purely architectural standpoint, The Grange, Hoddesdon [**132**], can be said to provide a starting point in Hertfordshire, although, as noted above, in social terms it was utterly different. It represents the adaptation to the double-pile form of the social arrangements implicit at Aston Bury Manor or, on a larger scale, at Rothamsted Manor; the latter comes to mind because the differentiation of the staircases is much like The Grange, one being smaller and simpler than the other, yet not a servants' stair. And the use on both floors of lobbies rather than corridors produces a backward-looking plan that contrasts with a forward-looking external appearance [**133**].

A progenitor having been found, it has to be said that all its supposed descendants have vanished, so that the family tree has to be reconstructed almost entirely from old drawings and estate maps. Yet it may be worth doing because three houses so linked together were among the most important new buildings in the county during the late 17th century. Fortunately, the graphic evidence is good enough to suggest that they formed a comparatively homogeneous group.

The superior status of Broadfield, Cottered, as the house of one of the richer gentlemen of the county, is expressed externally by virtue of the first-floor windows being larger than the ground-floor ones. They must denote an upstairs dining room, a suite of important rooms to go with it and a staircase of appropriate grandeur; some of it, especially the windows, in a rather old-fashioned idiom when compared with the advanced style of Balls Park a few years earlier. The disposition of windows is significant. They do not alternate in size, three-light and four-light, but are arranged symmetrically on each side of the middle axis formed by the porch and the pilasters above it. Two great chimney-stacks in the Buckler drawing also show that there were important rooms at both ends.

Although by the standards of the surviving late 17th-century buildings, Tyttenhanger is large, it is the loss of most of its contemporaries which makes its size appear unusual. Throcking Hall, Cottered, and Hertingfordbury Park and Goldings (both in Hertford) were also nine bays wide, and the first two, having a high basement, cannot have been much smaller than Tyttenhanger. One very important feature of these houses with high basements is that the services, including the kitchen, were transferred there, thereby permitting better views of the park and gardens; but how far such large houses really stood clear of minor buildings is open to doubt, as is shown by Celia Fiennes' comment on Coleshill House.[15] Unfortunately, the basements of such houses are now very difficult to study from their architectural remains. Oxhey Place, Watford Rural, Offley Place [134] and Brookmans, North Mymms, seem to have come somewhere between the really large houses and a house such as Childwick Bury, and were matched in size by the late 17th-century parts of Bushey Hall which were added to an older building.

134 *Offley Place* (Oldfield)

Courtyard houses

It is really very surprising that, with all the inventiveness displayed in late 17th-century house planning, and despite the powerful drive towards the compact, centralised house, a handful of small-courtyard houses, a type that first appeared in Elizabeth's reign, continued to be built or produced by alteration until the beginning of the 18th century. The situation is further complicated because the only completely new house of this kind has been pulled down and the two others were adaptations of existing buildings.

The Hoo, St Paul's Walden, built in 1661, was apparently intended to be approached from the north, the only direction from which its four groups of chimney-stacks had the symmetrical appearance evident in Drapentier's and Buckler's drawings [135]. Unfortunately reconstruction of the original plan, which suggests symmetry, is hampered by the drastic reorganisation which occurred when the entrance was moved successively to the east and west sides, but with this limitation in mind it may be suggested that the surviving great staircase was matched by a second one, and that the whole house was intended to form two sets of chambers on the first floor, and possibly the second floor too. If this is correct, The Hoo was a larger version of such earlier houses as Pishiobury and Balls Park in having an extra storey with good bedchambers, but although formally it perpetuated the same plan, it no doubt resembled its contemporaries in the way it was divided internally.

The very latest courtyard house of all, Beechwood Park, Flamstead [136], completed about 1702, was created by doubling the size of a house with two front wings which had been built only a generation earlier [137]. An 18th-century plan showing a covered way built across the middle of it from front to back demonstrates the obvious inconvenience of a courtyard; why, then, was it adopted in preference to doubling the depth of the old house to make a double-pile? The twin considerations of difficulty and expense lay at the root of the decision. To make a satisfactory double-pile by filling in the space between the wings would have involved putting one or two chimney-stacks in the middle of the new house, and to give the 1670s range anything of a view, or even to light it adequately, would have entailed demolishing the existing chimney-stacks; while to put the new range behind the old would require refronting the old range. By doubling the size of the house around a courtyard, demolitions were avoided and loftier rooms were created where most needed. It avoided a situation in which the floor levels associated with the early 18th-century elevation are considerably higher than those in the range behind it, such as exists at Stanstead Bury, Stanstead Abbots. Probably the same factors perpetuated the courtyard plan of Hitchin Priory when it was rebuilt in 1655.

Palaces

John Evelyn did not apply the word 'palace' to Cassiobury Park lightly, with the intention of paying a compliment or

135 *(above) The Hoo, St Paul's Walden* (Drapentier) **136** *Beechwood Park, Flamstead: north-east and south-east elevations*

harbingers seeking accommodation for Queen Elizabeth's progresses [138]. This range was so out of keeping with the notion of a country house at the time of the second transformation by James Wyatt, that it was not included in the plan that recorded for posterity the splendid house about to disappear [139]. Yet the existence of such a range must surely denote an intention on the part of the owner, however improbable it may seem as late as 1677–80, to entertain a large body of people which could only be the royal Court.

The point appears to be confirmed by the way the Caroline house was planned. To the right of the entrance lay two large rooms, one of them, at over 50 ft (15.2 m) long,

137 *Beechwood Park, Flamstead: perspective drawing; the 1670 elevation (above); the house in 1702 (below)*

138 *Cassiobury Park, Watford: engraving showing the pre-1804 house*

expressing its size relative to other country houses. He was conveying the idea that Cassiobury was different from the other great houses of the county not merely in size but in fundamental matters of planning. Most remarkably, in a house that underwent a costly transformation at the hands of Hugh May, it retained well into the 19th century a lodgings range of a kind that would have been familiar to the

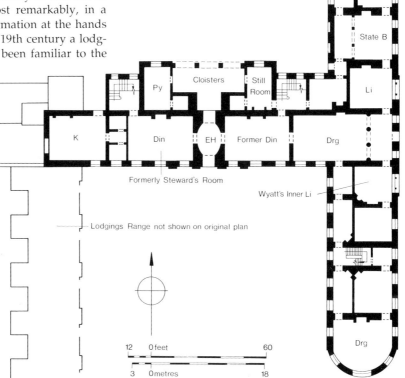

139 *Cassiobury Park, Watford: ground-floor plan of the pre-1804 house*

83

being exceptionally large; with the entrance-hall they formed an enfilade, and from the end of it two arms branched out like the top of the letter T. To one side, facing the garden, lay the State Bedroom, Best Chamber and the principal staircase and, although the names of the rooms are as in 1800, there is no reason to suppose that they, or equivalents, were not late 17th-century names. In the opposite arm of the T were Lord Essex's rooms. Each part had its own staircase, the greater one (now in the Metropolitan Museum, New York) being originally at the extreme end of the State wing, and although a direct comparison with Mackerye End, Wheathampstead, is slightly ridiculous, the complete separation of the principal suite in the smaller house may have been paralleled in the larger one. Unfortunately, how the upstairs rooms were organised is uncertain, yet even in the little we do know the sense of a palace is apparent. This is heightened by the way the two sets of apartments were approached from the enfilade, not by corridors but through a series of passage rooms, each serving also as an ante-room to a particular chamber, for at Cassiobury, as in greater palaces, the importance of great personages was enhanced by a multitude of attendants who awaited their coming and going. Clarendon House, Piccadilly, built 1664–7, suggests a model for this kind of planning; there, three of the four corner pavilions were divided between large rooms facing the courtyard and others only half as wide behind.[16] If Arthur Capel, created Earl of Essex in 1661 for his loyalty to the Crown, did indeed hope to receive Charles II in his own house, there seems to be no record of it, and the King's political and religious leanings finally dashed them; but the period just before 1677, when Essex was still Lord-Lieutenant of Ireland, and the following years, when he was at the Treasury rebuilding Cassiobury, provide a suitable background.

No other house suggests a similar aspiration, but in Tring Park [140] royalty was certainly entertained and, significantly, this house has features in common with Cassiobury while differing markedly from any other house of the class of large double-piles to which it is most closely related. It was built in the 1680s by Christopher Wren for Henry Guy, then Gentleman of the Privy Chamber to Charles II and subsequently Secretary to the Treasury. Though Charles, for whose benefit the house was perhaps built, never visited it, William III did, in 1690; however, it was not to stay with a great train of attendants in the manner of Elizabeth and James I, but only to dine. As with Cassiobury, no documentary evidence exists to show that a royal visit was hoped for, but the house is so unlike its contemporaries as to make it certain that some special purpose was intended and, since its owner was not a great noblenan to whom its stateliness might appear natural, the entertainment of royalty may be a credible explanation. The idea is reinforced by Roger North's remark, prompted by the alteration of the entrance steps, to bring them indoors, whereas they had been intended to be outside: 'Perhaps *courtiers* could not venture to mount so high in wett weather'.[17]

Tring Park has been described by the convenient phrase 'triple-pile'. The problem of lighting the middle range of the

140 *Tring Park* (Oliver)

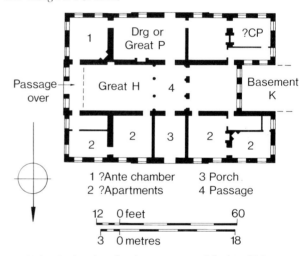

141 *Tring Park: plan showing room use of the late 17th century. The staircase is to the right of 4*

three was overcome comparatively simply because the presumed purpose of the house reduced that part to three compartments, two of them open from the ground floor to the attics and all purely for stateliness [141]. Unlike nearly all other late 17th-century houses, Tring Park was entered by a small internal hall or 'porch' (Roger North's word for it). From here the visitor proceeded into the 'passage', defined by columns to right and left which separated it notionally from the great staircase and great hall respectively. At the opposite end of the passage from the porch lay the 'withdrawing room or Great Parlour, I remember not well which', says North. In fact, the passage was the centralising element of the ground-floor plan through which most movements between the major elements of the plan had to take place, including the ascents from the kitchen and up to the first-floor suites. Commensurate with their pivotal importance, the passage and gallery faced the hall with 'a double order of Columns'.

The only other house anything like this is Cassiobury

Park, and each house helps to explain the other. At Cassiobury in 1800, the internal porch led successively into the dining room and drawing room, and the order of these two rooms may suggest that the hall at Tring was a very grand dining room served by the basement kitchen no more than its own length away. Possibly the dining room at Cassiobury was also a lofty room rising the height of two storeys, and the drawing room too, for that will explain the two free-standing columns and their responds at the east end, supporting a gallery, which, like the one at Tring, served to connect in a very dignified and stately way the two first-floor suites.

Their similarity in this respect emphasises a striking difference between the two houses: Cassiobury was very large and the state rooms formed only a part of it, for, in addition to a sizeable family wing, the chambers at the west end, to the left of the entrance, were no doubt good ones. Not so at Tring. Here the principal staircase, more spacious than anything at Cassiobury, rose up to the gallery from which two more or less identical suites were reached. Although the original dispositions are not quite certain, each side appears to have had in the middle, opening off the gallery, an anteroom from which were reached two apartments comprising a large room with a smaller one beyond it, probably dressing room and bedroom respectively; the importance of the ante-room and dressing room was conveyed externally by the use of sash windows instead of the mullion-and-transom windows used elsewhere. While there were also attics, these were probably only for servants, and the whole impression is of a house laid out for an utterly different purpose from, say, Tyttenhanger. Henry Guy, like all his contemporaries in politics and at Court, wished to establish himself and his descendants in a country estate, yet his career as a Member of Parliament, civil servant and boon companion to Charles II, suggests that life as a country gentleman was not important to him. Taking this and the evidence of his house together, it may not be too far fetched to suggest that Tring Park was built primarily as a place to entertain the Sovereign, and that its builder sacrificed all other considerations to that end.

Again there is a remarkable contrast with Cassiobury Park. The Earl of Essex was the only magnate in the county to rebuild his house in the most up-to-date and sumptuous way while retaining a lodgings range, as if the whole Court might need accommodation. Yet in the matter of progresses, as in so much else, the Restoration restored the old ways with a difference, and certainly the kind of progress made by Elizabeth and the early Stuarts had gone for good. But this can only have become clear gradually. What were once important representational occasions, the King's public dining days, were resumed in 1661 but discontinued in 1663.[18] It would hardly be surprising if some great courtiers expected the progresses of old to begin again. Unfamiliar though the concept of a progress may now appear in a Restoration context, Charles II undertook one in 1663 to the Marquess of Worcester at Badminton, to the Lord Chancellor at Cornbury and to four lesser grandees. Thereafter, from inclination as well as policy, he made only

'sea-progresses' in 1671 and 1675;[19] otherwise, his visits with his retinue to his greater subjects were conducted, like every other aspect of Court life, with less formality than his predecessors had demanded. Nevertheless, the royal arrival made considerable demands on a host's hospitality, as at Norwich in 1671; then Lord Henry Howard, later 6th Duke of Norfolk, showed John Evelyn the Ducal Palace, especially 'the contrivances he had made, for the entertainement of their Majesties & whole Court not long before, & which, though much of it, but temporary appartments fram'd of boards etc. onely, were yet standing'.[20] Occasions like this perhaps prompted Clarendon, referring to the Scottish gentry's hospitality during Charles I's progress in 1633, to remark that 'all cost was employ'd to make their Entertainments Splendid, and their Houses capable of those Entertainments' – a practice, he says, rare till then, 'though it hath since grown into a very inconvenient custom'.[21]

The only progress made of the old kind did not occur in England; it was left to the Duke of Beaufort, as President of the Council of Wales, to perform in viceregal state the last such journey in 1684.[22] But with Charles II's death, even the progress of the Court as a seat of pleasure rather than of government died; no longer did a cleric of stubborn principles like Thomas Ken have to refuse to lodge 'a woman of ill repute' under his roof.[23] The death of the progress is marked by an account of William III's visit to Tring Park in June 1690: 'The 4th, the King sett out on his royal voyage for Ireland early in the morning with a small retinue; he went in a coach and six horses with the earls of Portland and Scarborough with him. His Majestie did Mr Henry Guy the honour to dine with him at Tring . . . and his Majestie lies at Northampton'.[24] Even had the King chosen to stay at Tring Park, the kind of lodgings preserved at Cassiobury would have been unnecessary; it is remarkable that such an anachronism survived so long.

If Cassiobury and Tring Park were built with royalty in mind, Moor Park, Rickmansworth, was built for a man with royal blood in his veins and ambitions to wear the crown himself. The Duke of Monmouth seems to have begun his great new house in 1680, at about the time his supporters' hopes that he might replace the Duke of York in line of succession to the throne provoked a second Exclusion Bill, and it may not be coincidence that Moor Park, like the other two houses, appears to have been distinguished by a vast hall rising through two storeys; for although it cannot be established with certainty that this feature was present in Monmouth's house, it could hardly have been created during the alterations of the 1720s without an almost total rebuilding, which seems not to have happened.

The relation between elevations and plan

That the late 17th century is the period in which English houses became symmetrical is a truism. A little-explained

142 *The residence of Peter de Noüal at Berkhamsted: an engraving of 1805*

144 *Goldings, Hertford* (Oldfield)

point about the process is how the considerable variety of elevational treatments was gradually reduced to a few standard types subsequently used throughout the 18th century. Not that the standardisation of appearance should be overemphasised because some of the predictability of appearance which existing country houses now tend to present is due to transformations made in the 19th or 20th centuries with the aim of producing conformity to an ideal. Markyate Cell and the house of Peter de Noüal at Berkhamsted [142] serve as reminders of how far a manor house or a gentleman's residence might depart from the accepted canons of

design, and a glance at 18th-century pattern books dispels the notion that the men of that age had any instinctive feeling for proportion.

The general direction of change in late 17th-century architectural design can be seen most clearly in the transition from the broken outline presented by the gabled elevations of Rothamsted Manor [143] and Furneux Pelham Hall to the compact and smooth appearance of Goldings, Hertford [144], or The Grange, Hoddesdon, but appears, too, in the change from the bold projection of the two wings at Tyttenhanger to the slight break forward of the pedi-

143 *Rothamsted Manor, Harpenden Rural*

145 *Aston Bury Manor*

mented centrepiece at Tring Park. Change of fashion and the growth of interest in classical architecture are usually thought sufficient explanation, and of course they do go some way to explain why particular forms of gable and window and a host of details alter, especially when considered over a fairly long period; however, they do not account for the use, in houses of comparable size, of wings at one period and a rectangular, double-pile plan at another, still less for the contemporaneous use of the two forms. Some late 17th-century architects, Sir Roger Pratt being one, recommended the double-pile for its cheapness, though this consideration is unlikely to have decided the form of the larger houses. In looking for deeper causes the next step is to classify houses by their appearance.

Symmetry with unequal bays

Symmetrical design is normally associated with the principal elevations of houses. Its beginnings in the late 16th century were primarily a matter of visually balancing the two halves of the front on the axis of the doorway, as at Little Court, Buntingford, and not long afterwards on a much larger scale at Hatfield House. Balls Park achieved a quite

unusual degree of symmetry, extending to three and perhaps even all four elevations, although there is some doubt about the fourth; and with this greater symmetry went a degree of uniformity quite unusual for the period, so that the regular fenestration of the two principal fronts was broken only by a centrepiece, crowned by a pediment. By the 1680s, uniformity of this kind was usual and remained so for most of the 18th century, with the result that houses that do not conform to convention are apt to be undervalued.

Aston Bury Manor illustrates the conflict between the fashionable trend of the time and the practical needs of house design. As the ground plan, except for the staircases, is perfectly traditional, so is the ground-floor front elevation [**145**] in which windows are proportioned according to what goes on behind them. Why, then, was the situation so different upstairs? There, seven completely uniform windows lit rooms of two distinct orders of importance, the larger ones having fireplaces and the smaller ones being unheated closets, so that the two rooms in the middle of the house received no more light than a closet less than half their size. The inescapable answer, that on this floor symmetry prevailed over other considerations, is confirmed by the window depicted by Buckler in the west gable, which can never

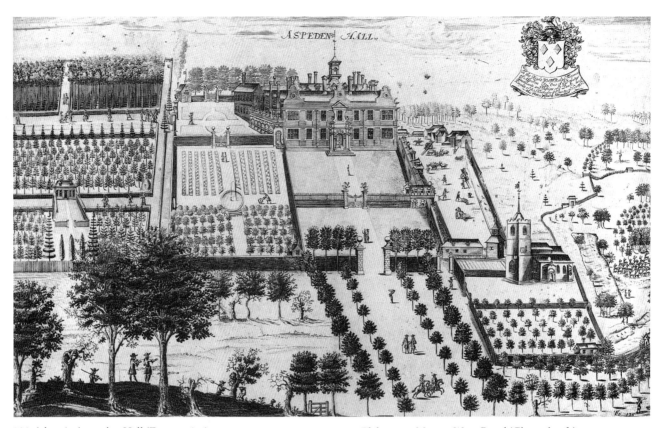

146 *(above) Aspenden Hall* (Drapentier)   **147** *Blakesware Manor, Ware Rural* (Clutterbuck)

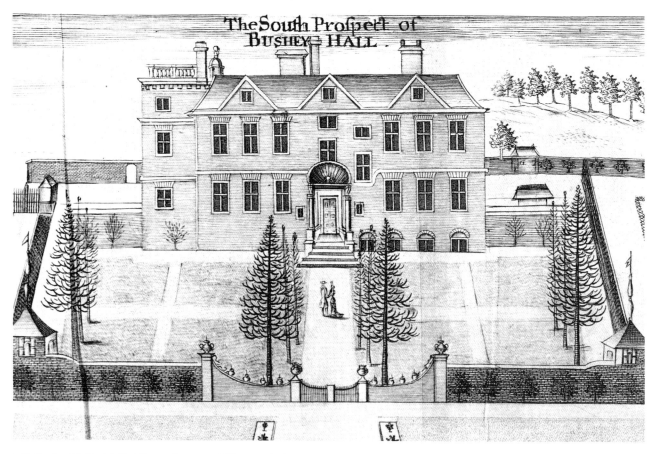

148 *Bushey Hall: detail of the south prospect* (Drapentier)

have been glazed over its full width, if in fact it was ever anything more than a dummy. The gabled attic storey, the end gables with symmetrically placed chimney-stacks and the balanced rear elevation all proclaim a wish for external uniformity which was met everywhere but in the ground-floor front. Although no satisfactory explanation can be offered, that last resort of the architectural historian – change of intention during building – may be legitimate here, with a change of design matching a change in the method of construction.

The frontal symmetry missing at Aston Bury Manor was achieved at Broadfield, Cottered, in a very unusual way that reinforces earlier assumptions about the plan. On each side of the middle axis and on each floor, a large window was flanked by two small ones, and the one end elevation which Buckler drew gives the impression that overall symmetry may have been attained. What the front suggests is an internal division into two parts, for otherwise the form the symmetrical rooms took, given that Balls Park had already set the example of uniformity, would have been whimsical. Force is given to this observation by the appearance of Aspenden Hall following its recasing in brick some time after 1665 [146]. On either side of the frontispiece are the same number of windows as at Broadfield; their relative sizes are the same, but they are disposed differently, with

the large windows at the end, not in the middle. The difference between the two houses must spring from a different relation of the principal rooms to the lesser ones on each side of the entrance. Conjectures of this kind, which on first consideration may seem quite unwarranted, receive some support from Rothamsted Manor, where Sir John Wittewronge's refronting of the house permitted him to achieve a required level of symmetry; and although the mirror-image pairs of Dutch gables on either side of the storeyed part do indeed seem symmetrical, closer inspection shows that the five-light windows on the left-hand side serve to differentiate the more important part of the house from the rest, where the windows have only four lights.

With Broadfield and Rothamsted can be grouped two more enigmatic houses. The first is Blakesware Manor, Ware Rural [147], where a comparatively long elevation was punctuated at regular intervals by the porch and by two unusually prominent bay windows; the second, Bushey Hall [148], had in its post-Restoration part a symmetry comparable to Broadfield in not being composed of uniform members uniformly spaced. Here, the windows themselves are uniform, but have a deliberately irregular spacing – two and one – forming a balanced composition on each side of the door.

All four houses fall early in the period, all are large, all

149 *Newsells Park, Barkway* (Drapentier)

have an element of duality in their appearance. In the only survivor, the plan conforms to the expectations created outside, that is to say it is divided into two parts, one of which is inferior to the other but not very much – not as much as the service end of a medieval house. Aston Bury Manor, where on the ground floor the connection between room function and external appearance is almost as close as in a medieval house, provides a contrast.

Houses with one wing

Bushey Hall and Blakesware have been discussed solely in terms of their late 17th-century elevations, yet they had in common another feature which is remarkable in two country houses of considerable pretension: a large wing flanking the front and breaking its symmetry. It is possible to dismiss Bushey Hall as the unfortunate result of altering an old house, whereas at Blakesware the wing, which may conceivably have been built thirty years after the already large house of 1664, is, to a modern eye, a surprising impairment of the original design. That contemporaries found such an

arrangement aesthetically acceptable is confirmed by a third house, The Bury, Rickmansworth, where, despite difficulties of interpretation, the wing is certainly coeval with the reconstruction of the main house in the middle years of the 17th century. What purpose did such wings serve? A single wing for service purposes is unlikely at the front of the house, especially if it is an addition. In both houses the wings probably provided accommodation comparable to that in the main ranges – rooms for family use and perhaps including one or two specially large and well-appointed ones for display – and so might be seen as another manifestation of the division into two parts which is so marked a feature of both plans and elevations. An observation of Lawrence Stone's is relevant to the argument – the number and size of rooms essential for family life in the gentry class is fairly constant; the corollary is that, beyond a certain size, anything extra has to be accounted for either as family space or stateliness – parade, in the 17th-century term. At The Bury parade is hardly in question; family seems to be the answer – and if so, it must correspond to some kind of kin group, perhaps related elementary families.

90

If, on Hertfordshire evidence, the functions of front wings and their importance relative to the main body of the house remain unclear, the contrast between them and the long back wing at Rothamsted Manor is instructive. That wing is a service wing, incorporating the kitchen, pantry and other rooms, with sizeable chambers upstairs. Although it can be argued that the position of this wing was determined by a pre-existing kitchen range, the fact that a short wing with a loggia was added in the course of rebuilding shows that a change could have been made had it been desired; in other words, the position and known function of these wings imply that front wings were of a higher status.

Symmetry with two front wings

A much commoner kind of elevation is one which has two wings projecting in front of the main range, sometimes far

enough to provide a room, sometimes less. Mackerye End, Wheathampstead, and Little Offley House are of the first kind; Tyttenhanger House, Brent Pelham Hall and probably Newsells Park, Barkway [149], of the second. Of the four houses where the original plan is known, all are divided on the first floor into two suites. Two houses are rebuildings, not new work of the late 17th century, and some details of their planning can reasonably be attributed to that. Not so Tyttenhanger, a new house where the plan arises by deliberate choice.

Why should Sir Henry Blount, celebrated as a traveller and a man who moved among the fashionable and influential, have chosen to build his house like that? Tyttenhanger may be attributable on stylistic evidence to Peter Mills, a member of the 'artisan mannerist' school.[25] This label, devised to distinguish craftsman-architects from court-based architects and carrying purely stylistic connotations, here conceals the fact that whoever was responsible for the house produced a design excellently adapted to what can

150 *Stagenhoe Park, St Paul's Walden* (Drapentier)

151 *Hertingfordbury Park, Hertford* (Drapentier)

now be seen as the demands of the time. The duality of accommodation was matched by just as much external classical detail as the social situation warranted; the first floor was emphasised by alternating segmental and triangular pediments along the whole of the front, as if to stress the equal importance of all the rooms behind, but this treatment carried on round the west side (but not the east) where the principal suite lay. Function, form and ornament made an excellent fit.

When Mackerye End was rebuilt in 1665, a different effect was sought, or perhaps the results were simply less happy. All the emphasis given by gables and larger windows is on the wings where, indeed, on both floors, lay some of the principal rooms – the parlours and the chambers over them; yet what the design failed to achieve, by comparison with Tyttenhanger, was adequate emphasis of

the 'large chamber over the hall' to which the grand staircase led.

Uniformity and symmetry combined

In the same years as some owners were seeking symmetry with unequal bays or front wings, others were achieving an overall uniformity broken only on the middle axis. The beginnings of this treatment go back to the eve of the Civil War, to Balls Park where the courtyard house, though approached through an elaborate frontispiece, had a regular and restrained front elevation lacking the movement favoured at the time and achieved by the use of wings, porches and bay windows. Stagenhoe Park, St Paul's Walden [150], begun about 1650, had, according to the Drapentier engraving of *c*.1700, resemblances of detail to

Balls Park, but a more important likeness is the regular symmetry on either side of a two-storey porch. At the Restoration Sir Jonathan Keate built The Hoo, St Paul's Walden, with a larger and more sober version of the Balls Park elevation, having a very restrained emphasis on the middle axis. Towards the end of the decade the beginning which was made with the rebuilding of Salisbury Hall, Shenley, shows that it was intended to be a stylistically updated version of Stagenhoe Park.

Pediments and their purpose

Knowledge of the pediment as an architectural form in Hertfordshire goes back at least as far as Knebworth House in the early 1560s. There it was a product of Court taste, used to give the courtyard elevations a uniform appearance irrespective of whether the great withdrawing room or a pantry lay behind the windows; elsewhere, until the late 1670s, it was an even less significant obeisance to classical architecture. By then, if Cassiobury Park is correctly interpreted as a palace, the use of the pediment there is entirely in keeping with Roger North's reference to it as 'a piece of state'.[26] Two pediments adorned the house. The smaller one marking the entrance and spanning three bays may have corresponded to a large upstairs chamber, as the balcony to the middle bay suggests, but no first-floor plan exists to establish this. The second and larger pediment on the east front marked externally the enfilade of state rooms, though its width also embraced on the ground floor two rooms which do not appear to have been of any particular significance. Again, the upstairs arrangement is unknown; if the suggestion of a gallery (see p 85) is correct, the relation of pediment to rooms of parade is quite direct.

Appropriately enough, Tring Park is the only other house where the pediment is employed precisely to locate the rooms of state. At the front, giant order pilasters and a pediment framed the entrance and also a room above it distinguished by a large window; at the back, they framed the principal ground-floor room which Roger North called the withdrawing room or great parlour. Not much later than Tring, three houses of less pretension were also dignified by pediments: Goldings, Hertford, Thorley Hall and Hertingfordbury Park [151], all probably complete by the mid 1680s. In all three the connotation of the pediment as conceived by Roger North had been somewhat weakened. The only one to follow the example of Tring in having pediments back and front was Goldings. Since each was five bays wide it is unlikely to have corresponded exactly to internal room arrangements. The use of the pediment established in a general way that the principal rooms were in the centre, and so proclaimed a break with the mid-century social division of a house into two distinct parts. By about 1686, when Brent Pelham Hall was refronted, its two-staircase constricted-middle plan was thought compatible with a central pediment, the aim presumably being to emphasise the common centre of the house. But the general tendency is clear enough: increased use of the pediment corresponds broadly to the growing centralisation of plan.

The implications of late 17th-century planning

During the Commonwealth, a mode of planning is found which has as its principal characteristic a division of the house into two distinct parts, always with some indication of the superiority of one part over the other. Examples of such division continue until the beginning of the 18th century. The question of when it first appears is impossible to answer from Hertfordshire evidence, and may well be difficult in most counties because of the alterations earlier houses have undergone. Pishiobury, Sawbridgeworth, illustrates the problem. Sir Thomas Hewett's inventory of 1662 implies a division of the 'houseful' (all the occupants of a house) not unlike that evident in Rothamsted Manor in the early 1650s and raises the possibility that social arrangements not unlike those of 1662 were found in the 1680s; while what is probably the last fling of such ideas occurs as late as 1702 at Beechwood Park, a house oddly reminiscent of the building enterprise envisaged in Thomas Heywood's play of 1633, *The English Traveller*:

> *Reginald:* 'Tis Supposed
> He hath late found a wife out for his son;
> Now, Sir, to have him near him, and with nearness
> Too without trouble, though beneath one roof,
> Yet parted in two families, he would build,
> And make what's picked a perfect quadrangle,
> Proportioned just with yours . . .[27]

An implausible situation plucked from a Caroline play does not satisfactorily account for a fairly widespread architectural phenomenon. An alternative explanation lies in the entertainment of social superiors or, conceivably, social equals. The plan of Pishiobury might have been designed to enable its builder to entertain in the same way as Robert Cecil intended at Hatfield House, moving out of the best rooms to let his hoped-for royal guest take over.[28] 'Sir Thomas Hewett's own closet' in 1662 was near the back staircase, as if the best rooms arranged about the grand staircase were available for others' use as need arose. An explanation on these lines would fit all the bigger late 17th-century houses; it certainly applies to Cassiobury Park and Tring Park, and such houses as The Hoo, St Paul's Walden, and even one as small as Mackerye End, Wheathampstead, can be interpreted in this way. The problem presented by the architecture is to know who occupied the better rooms when hospitality was offered; how far down did the Hatfield House pattern extend? Or did that pattern exist only in the grandest houses, which were divided into husband's and wife's sides?

Broadfield, Cottered, may be significant here; begun during the first Civil War and left unfinished at its builder's death in 1689, it was renovated by his grandson who, among other things, made 'lodging-chambers on the West Side thereof'. It sounds as if the one aspect of the house the original builder, Arthur Pulter, had not thought worth finishing was guest accommodation. This may have had some-thing to do with the anomalous social position of someone who opted out of the Civil War, because grand hospitality (if that is what the duality of suites implies) continued throughout the Commonwealth, as Rothamsted Manor attests. Whatever the social exchange envisaged, the plan-ning of houses at every level of gentry society enabled a suite of two or more rooms called an apartment to be placed at the disposal of a guest, the number varying according to the size of the house and the importance of the visitor. John Evelyn, denying his presence at a scandalous ceremony at Lord Arlington's Great House at Euston (Suffolk), expresses the notion of separate suites clearly: 'I neither saw, nor heard of any such thing . . . though I had been in her Chamber, & all over that appartment late enough'; and again Evelyn, wishing to get away from the various enter-tainments offered, had 'more often recesse to my prety apartment . . . & had leasure when I would to converse with bookes'.[29] Both uses imply a suite of two or three rooms.

Alternatively, the houses in question may have been occupied by two households. At the superior vernacular level, they certainly were (see p 106); yet to suggest the exis-tence of some kind of dual household is to deny the current orthodoxy that the elementary family was universal in England in the 17th century and indeed earlier. Nevertheless, at Rothamsted Manor, for example, it would have been perfectly possible for two families to have lived their lives quite separately, except for dependence on a common kitchen and services, yet the theory has no docu-mentary support. Aspenden Hall, which was a very large house indeed, was inhabited by two brothers, William and Ralph Freeman, of whom Chauncy says specifically that they held manorial courts in their joint names. Arthur Pulter and his son seem to have occupied Broadfield, Cottered, jointly; and Wyddial Hall was the seat of James Goulston (who was Sheriff in 1684) in the lifetime of his father, who lived until 1686. Such two-generation house-holds may have been common; for example, Henry St John, Viscount Bolingbroke, and his father are said to have lived together in the manor house at Battersea until the latter's death in 1708, even after Henry's marriage in 1700.[30] And in a variation of this pattern, in North Yorkshire, two families,

of brother and sister, lived side by side from 1662 to 1702 in the two buildings forming East Newton Hall.[31]

In a house divided between father and son, the son can be assumed to have occupied the superior part if he were Sheriff, but not necessarily in other circumstances. The sec-ondary suites of rooms could have been inhabited by more distant blood relations. Hatfield House could accommodate the largest family and leave ample room for relatives, dependants and the sons of other leading families, which is just what the room names from the middle of the 17th cen-tury onwards suggest; they include Sir Arthur Capel's chamber and the Duke of Gloucester's chamber. Similarly, at Bedwell Park, Essendon, Thomas Atkins, in his will of 1699, mentions 'my cousin Goodfellowe's chamber'. This was normal practice. Outside the county an instance is pro-vided by John Evelyn who noted in 1649 that he 'had a Lodging, & some books' at his father-in-law's house, Sayes Court.[32] Such provision of chambers is one expression of the sense of family remarked on by Sir John Habakkuk in con-nection with Burley House, Rutland.[33]

Such feelings may have been common and may underlie the building of two houses where one would normally be expected. Temple Dinsley, Preston, is one such case, although the second house was not built until the early 18th century; an earlier instance is Stanstead Bury (see below, p 132). At both, the complete demolition of one of the hous-es in the early 19th century means that only its existence and probable 17th-century date is known. Arrangements of this kind may have been an alternative to a family's having two houses on adjoining estates. No systematic search for evi-dence of this practice has been made, but two further exam-ples, one before and one after the period for which information would be most welcome, are known. Robert Chester's two houses, Royston Priory and Cokenach, have been mentioned earlier (p 63); Sir John Jennings, who bought Cokenach in the early 18th century, also bought the adjoining Newsells Park and built at both. Some of these instances may be explained by Samuel Johnson's remark, made in attempting to dissuade Lady M'Leod from aban-doning her family seat: 'Most of the great families of England have a secondary residence, called a jointure house . . .'.[34]

Chapter 6

Vernacular houses from the Dissolution to the end of the 17th century

The suppression of the monasteries corresponds approximately to the time when vernacular houses ceased to have a hall with an open hearth and were beginning to be two-storeyed throughout. This change was gradual and began with the larger farmhouses, many of which had been built or rebuilt *c.*1500 and to become wholly two-storeyed needed only the insertion of an upper floor and the building of a chimney-stack in the hall. An open-hall house with a storeyed bay at each end had only one less room – a large room over the hall – than a fully storeyed house of three-room plan. To many house owners, this addition to the existing two or three upstairs rooms was probably not important, which would explain why some halls appear to have remained open to the roof until well into the 17th century.

Chimney-stacks in the two-storeyed vernacular houses occupied a characteristic position unlike that seen in some late medieval manorial halls. The difference of practice between social classes rests on a combination of social and structural reasons. The fundamental need was to perpetuate the hierarchical distinction between upper and lower ends of the hall, expressed by the position of the seat and canopy of honour; efficient heating and lighting were subordinate considerations. A fireplace could be placed across the upper end, as at Dartington Hall, Devon,[1] and Hertford Castle. In this case, the seat of honour presumably had to be moved to a side wall, as near its traditional transverse position as possible. There is no trace of the customary canopy and panelled seat, although these must surely have existed. Nor could the fireplace go at the lower end without obstructing the service doorways and removing warmth from the upper end.

In a vernacular house, the smaller family and hall permitted an easy solution, that of placing the chimney-stack with its back to the entrance-passage. This preserved much the same social distance between entrance and seat of honour as before; in both cases, the master's seat was diagonally opposite the entrance, but by the late 16th century it was reached from behind the chimney-stack; access to and from the service room was conducted without ceremony and was evidently not impeded by the change. By the time two back-to-back fireplaces became customary, the fixed bench with the seat of honour at one end had been abandoned in favour of movable furniture. This period may perhaps have first seen what became the traditional placing of the master's seat next to the fireplace, near the jamb farthest from the point of entry to the room.

The brick required to build an external chimney-stack was expensive, as its restriction to the houses of the landowning classes before the late 17th century demonstrates. The alternatives were a smoke-bay[2] – a phenomenon not noted in the course of the present survey except in kitchens – or a timber chimney-stack. To build the latter externally may have presented difficulties in maintaining surfaces subject to heat and cold, dryness and wetness, even allowing for the strength and elasticity of pargetting.[3] A second obstacle to adopting upper-class practice was the manner of lighting halls by opposed windows that appear to have been unglazed, with diamond mullions and shutters which could be closed on one side or the other against the prevailing wind.

Since the building of a lateral chimney-stack precluded opposed windows, it was difficult to light a hall properly and at the same time to exclude draughts except by using glazed windows; the cost of glazing is likely to have restricted its adoption in vernacular houses.

Certain display features of the late medieval house invited development in fully storeyed houses. The jettied first floor was one, the gable surmounting a wing another, and in the second half of the 16th century it seems to have been comparatively rare for the two to have been combined in the same house. There were structural reasons for the decline of the gable: given a building of two storeys throughout, the simplicity of roof construction that was the prime structural advantage of the Wealden over contemporary types could become general. Not until the roof space came to be used for attic rooms did the gabled front become a fashion capable of meeting strictly functional needs.

The continuous-jetty house

Continuous-jetty houses are uncommon in the countryside. A large well-built one, now Nos 30/32 High Street at Puckeridge in Standon (virtually an urban context), has been so altered as to leave only the basic frame; Great Barwick Farm, Standon, has unexplained anomalous features;[4] and to one or two more, full access by the Royal Commission was not allowed.

152 *Old Rose and Crown, Braughing*

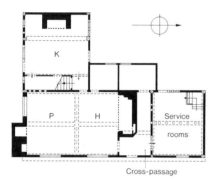

153 *Old Rose and Crown, Braughing: plan*

At vernacular level, the first stage in the break away from the open hall can be seen at the Old Rose and Crown, Braughing [**152**]. Its ground plan [**153**] comprises three cells and an internal chimney-stack backing on to a cross-passage, so the principal differences between it and its predecessors are the flooring over of the hall, the continuous jetty and a chimney, which was probably of timber. The space occupied by hall and chimney-stack together is square, and if the area of the stack between the jambs be taken to correspond approximately to that of a large open hearth, the traditional room proportion was maintained, the passage being additional. The customary pair of service rooms below, and an unheated parlour, are present; and the subsequent building of a kitchen wing establishes that there must have been a detached kitchen when the house was first built. A less well-finished house at much the same stage of development is Chapel Farm, Ardeley. Two houses in Albury parish, Tudor Cottage [**154**] and Kennel Farm, both built in the second half of the 16th century, are other examples of the jetty being developed as the prime feature of architectural interest, and Mingers, Much Hadham, exemplifies the renovation of so many outdated houses to the same effect.

Tudor Cottage is the most interesting. It is in some sense a successor to the three-cell open-hall house, yet analysis of its plan [**155**] reveals differences which imply important social

changes. Although the hall is still in the middle of the house, the cross-passage has been suppressed in favour of a lobby-entrance, a change which brought about a new relation between the single service room and the hall. The second room with a fireplace is quite short (in the axis of the house) and must always have been a kitchen, that being the only heated room to which such proportions seem to have been thought appropriate in the past (a generalisation applicable to most of Hertfordshire but not necessarily so elsewhere).[5] Does this correspond, at this social level, to the abandoning of the detached kitchen and hence the bringing of cooking into the house, or were the functions of the kitchen merely transferred from the hall? If the example of Bramfield Bury, a house at a somewhat superior social level, is relevant, probably the former is true.

What, then, was the function of the unheated inner room, the largest room in the house? It showed no sign of having been partitioned structurally and is too large relative to the other rooms to have been a single service room equivalent to the old buttery and pantry; as much as anything, it resembles in size and the lack of a fireplace the two-storey jettied blocks (such as the one at No. 40 Stocks Road, Aldbury) which are presumed to have stood at the upper end of an open hall. If that analogy be accepted, what we see at Tudor Cottage is not the process of alternate rebuilding, for it was all of one build, but rather a concept of alternate development; the notion of a large unheated parlour, for that is what it must surely be, was the most recent improvement to the

154 *Tudor Cottage, Albury: from the south east*

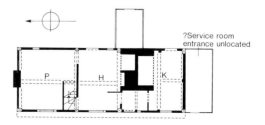

155 *Tudor Cottage, Albury: plan*

96

medieval hall and was taken over unaltered and the remainder of the house improved. At this stage in the design process it was decided to incorporate a kitchen and, if the interpretation of the largest room as a parlour is correct, there must have been a service room adjoining the kitchen where, until recently, an outshut stood. An alternative sometimes put forward in such cases, that the unheated room was subdivided by light partitioning, is impossible to prove or disprove.

When the house was newly built (with a wooden chimney) it probably had no upstairs fireplace, although it is impossible to establish this with certainty. The best-finished first-floor room, that over the supposed parlour, was distinguished by its wall timbers being faced up flush below the wall-plates and tie-beams so that what is called in probate inventories the chamber over the parlour retained the pre-eminence it had in the later open-hall houses. No other partition was detectable upstairs and the structural evidence suggested a single large space within which movement was restricted only by curved braces below the tie-beams, a tapering wooden flue and a staircase, as if the whole were devoted to work or to the storage of implements and produce. This is surprising only in the light of later developments; the very gradual development of every aspect of material culture has been recognised by archaeologists from Montelius and Pitt-Rivers onwards, and it need not be cause for astonishment that house design was improved by a long succession of small steps forward.

Lobby-entrance houses

Although Tudor Cottage, Albury, can perfectly well be described as a three-cell house with a lobby-entrance, to do so omits its most significant architectural feature. Those houses best described under this heading have a general resemblance to it in plan but lack the structural display provided by the jetty, so that to a degree many of them can fairly be described as poor relations, or, since they are of late date, poor descendants. A straightforward house of this kind is Briggens Home Farm, Hunsdon. Originally it must have had a timber chimney which, from the space its brick successor occupies, probably served two fireplaces in rooms of equal size, and there was a smaller service bay. It is an unusual house of its kind in being apparently of one build, although enlarged and altered in the 19th century.

Houses of this plan type fall broadly into three categories. The first consists of those incorporating a minor part of an open-hall house, or those where the succession of building phases implies that an open-hall house once existed. A second category comprises those houses where no trace of a medieval structure exists, nor can any be inferred. The feature common to many houses of this kind is the apparent lack of a service room in the original build. There are usually two ground-floor rooms with fireplaces, and a third, often the largest room, which may or may not have had a fireplace originally but shows no sign of subdivision. Where was the unheated room needed to store food and drink? That question provides the starting point for inquiry and the answer will usually lie in alteration or rebuilding as between the domestic and service parts of the house. The third category is the most difficult of all. It comprises those houses where the concealment or destruction of evidence leaves the investigator certain that there has been a complicated development, but unable to specify what it is; two negative indications, the lack of structural uniformity and the failure to conform to a known type, qualify a house for inclusion.

These three categories embrace a high proportion of all the late 16th and 17th-century houses examined in the course of this survey, the number of new-built, three-room lobby-entrance houses being small. Repeatedly, houses selected for their apparent simplicity and as being representative of known types proved to be multi-period structures. One example will serve for many. A house thought to be a three-cell lobby-entrance house, now converted into two cottages, Gouldburns and May Cottage, stands at Hadham Ford, Little Hadham. Inspection soon produced evidence of an open hall and the search for a simple late 16th or early 17th-century house was frustrated. With hindsight, the lack of height in the first-floor rooms should have been recognised from the outside as indicating a floor inserted in an open hall.

While this kind of complication is not unexpected in south-east England and East Anglia, the inferences have been pushed to greater lengths than usual and have thrown up two conclusions. First, the change from impermanent earthfast construction to fully framed timber building appears to have been a long, drawn-out process. Secondly, houses of one build conforming to a type seem to be comparatively rare. Rather, the notion of types arising mainly through alteration is closer to reality and a larger sample might produce a typology of transformation of one house type into another. This would extend beyond simple alterations such as the flooring-over or rebuilding of an open hall to instances where the function of one or other part of the house is so radically changed that its earlier form is not perpetuated and has to be inferred.

Fragmentary late medieval houses

The house now forming Gouldburns and May Cottage has already been mentioned for the deceptive appearance it presents. Bury Green Farm, Little Hadham, is similar except that less remains of the first phase. It looks like a small, late 17th-century house with a lobby-entrance and two-room plan. Only the survival of one clasped-purlin roof truss, soot-encrusted on one side and clean on the other, makes it certain that there was originally an open hall. Three other pieces of evidence combine to suggest that the bare framework at least survives under the wall plaster: the mixture of smoke-blackened and clean rafters, the proportions evident in the cross-section and the manner of thickening the principal post at its head.

More tenuous evidence can be interpreted in the same way at another small house, Oundle in Bushey. Unlike Bury Green Farm, its appearance has been transformed in a succession of changes from the 18th to the 20th centuries, but in so far as its architectural features are datable, they are of the late 17th century. Perhaps little more than the shell, a framework of principal posts and beams, survives from the late medieval hall, or possibly only the outline of its ground plan is preserved by a later structure which has replaced it piece by piece. The final result did not differ much from Bury Green Farm in that the ground plan comprised two heated rooms, and one of the two principal bedrooms also had a fireplace.

Supposed two-room plan houses

The principal alteration which left both Oundle and Bury Green Farm as they now stand was the replacement of a partially heated main range by one in which both rooms had fireplaces. In the earlier phase a place to store food can be found, but not in the later one, unless some outshut or wing can be shown to be coeval with the heated rooms. There are, in Hertfordshire and elsewhere, houses which appear to lack any kind of provision for food storage.[6] But this is unlikely, for we cannot assume that the permanent structural provision for a pantry that is a hallmark of late medieval buildings, and persisted in the form of a generalised service room

156 *The Cottage, Cromer, Ardeley*

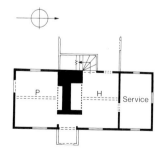

157 *The Cottage, Cromer, Ardeley: plan*

in a house like Briggens Home Farm, Hunsdon, was abandoned in the late 17th century only to reappear in 18th and 19th-century houses.

Many houses of this type have an ostensibly later wing or lean-to which could have been a pantry, and others have evidence that something of the kind existed. Two such houses are in the hamlet of Cromer in Ardeley parish. The Cottage [**156**, **157**], predominantly of the mid 17th century, shows slight traces of earlier work which seems to have incorporated a third room, the predecessor of the present one which has no fireplace. Cromer Hall nearby also lacks an original pantry or service room, and it can reasonably be assumed that the present outshut replaces something coeval with the main structure if it is not itself an original feature disguised by alteration.

Unconfirmed medieval houses

It is apparent that vernacular houses evolved by small steps. The gradualness of change is clearest in the occasional late 16th or 17th-century house which looks as if its peculiarities ought to be explicable in terms of an earlier origin, whilst not presenting any features which can definitely be said to be medieval. Turk's Cottage, in Braughing [**158**, **159**], is a conspicuous example. Its form, a hall range and two gabled cross-wings, is rare but not unknown in the late 16th century. It contains one first-floor post suggestive of a Wealden house but in the timberwork elsewhere are certain inconsistencies, to all of which some form of composition has been applied to make them less obtrusive, with the result that the evidence no longer shows exactly what has happened. As with the fragmentary and allegedly two-room houses, the most that can be said is that the present Turk's Cottage was certainly influenced by and perhaps incorporates parts of a predecessor. This process of change makes the notion of pure plan types untenable for many Hertfordshire houses built before the 18th century.

Longhouse derivatives

The first and most controversial category of change is defined in a doubly negative way; it assumes not only the removal of part of a house but also the removal of a function, ie, a byre. All the kinds of plan here assumed to have their ultimate origin in the longhouse are found in the western fringe of Hertfordshire. Most of them are of medieval origin, even though no vestige of medieval fabric now survives: for example, Old Raisins Farm, Wheathampstead [**160**, **161**], where the process of alternate development clearly implies a medieval predecessor.

A diagnostic feature of a former longhouse is that the superior part, the former hall, is entered from an architecturally inferior part – which is typically of a different build –

158 *Turk's Cottage, Braughing: from the south east. The hipped roof to the left is the oldest feature visible; the chimney-stacks date from the end of the 17th century*

159 *Turk's Cottage, Braughing: plan*

160 *Old Raisins Farm, Wheathampstead*

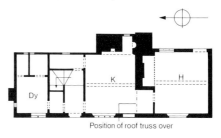

Position of roof truss over

161 *Old Raisins Farm, Wheathampstead: plan*

by a cross-passage behind the chimney-stack. A plan and structure like this, albeit in different materials, would be perfectly at home in South Wales, the Welsh Marches or the West Country and capable of interpretation as a longhouse rebuilt in two stages, beginning with the hall in the mid 17th century. (Recently, the vernacular houses of the North York Moors have also been defined in this way.)[7] The Retreat, Chorleywood, can be viewed similarly; it may have had the byre incompletely separated from the hall, and subsequently rebuilt with two storeys like Old Raisins Farm. Entirely post-medieval houses which can be interpreted as belonging to the same class by the criteria outlined above are Dell Cottages, Chorleywood, and Shootersway Farm, Northchurch. Holly Bush Farm, Nettleden with Potten End, Delmerend Farmhouse, Flamstead, and Delaport Farm, Wheathampstead, should probably be considered as well.

Houses claimed as belonging to this class of longhouse derivatives sometimes, and perhaps frequently, have halls of less than the squarish proportions usually found elsewhere, that is, they are shorter than they are wide; this applies both to altered medieval houses and to later ones, such as Dudswell, Northchurch. This may be an indication that the hall had lost some of its importance relative to the parlour; or it may be because the hall was used for cooking and that the customary proportions for kitchens as, for example, at Tudor Cottage, Albury, were deliberately adopted.[8] Whatever the explanation, this proportion of hall to parlour

is not uncommon in areas such as Dorset, where the occasional longhouse still exists beside many derivative forms.

One of the more unusual variants appears at Town Farm, Aldbury [162]. The earliest part of the house was timber framed and consisted of a hall open to the roof and, at the upper end, a shorter bay of two storeys; at the lower end there is no trace of an entrance-passage or service rooms. In due course a kitchen wing was built at right angles to the hall instead of at the lower end, as if there had been some impediment to its being there. Subsequently, everything at the lower end was demolished and rebuilt in 1736 as what would conventionally be a parlour, then called simply the 'best room'. These facts do not establish the former existence of a byre at the lower end of the hall but are consistent with it; and although the position of the parlour can be explained in other ways, the siting of the kitchen, coupled with the lack of service rooms at the lower end, provides the key to the development of Town Farm.

A final category of plan which has been the subject of considerable discussion and which, according to one view, may be a derivative of the longhouse,[9] is represented by a timber-framed house of two bays at Chorleywood, Nos 4/5 Chorleywood Bottom. This house formerly had a large end chimney-stack and the gable end flanked by the entrance, such as is commonly found in South Wales and Hertfordshire, and it is the placing of the entrance other than in one of the long elevations which is so strange in an age when houses were one of the principal forms of display at any social level. The rebuilding of a longhouse, beginning

99

162 *Town Farm, Aldbury: ground and first-floor plans with room uses as in an inventory of 1736*

with the house part and providing an entrance of appropriate quality from the cross-passage, but thereafter demolishing the byre rather than persisting with the original intention to rebuild, may explain this regional phenomenon better than a short-lived change of fashion. Moor Cottage, Water End, Great Gaddesden, is a further example of a house to which this kind of interpretation can be applied.

Improvements to the medieval house

Parlours

Town Farm, Aldbury, shows one of the commonest ways of improving a medieval house by the addition of a parlour. Over much of England and Wales a customary way of doing this was to add a new block, with parlour on the ground floor, and best chamber above, considerably taller than the hall; this occurs in Hertfordshire as often as in the old county of Monmouthshire where it was first recorded.[10] Such additions vary greatly in size and function.

The smallest parlour blocks had only one room on each floor and, since they were added to small open halls, the staircase encroached on the room space; a stair turret or projection was too grand for such modest buildings. When, in the 17th century, an addition of this kind was made at Green Street Cottage, Little Hadham, the contrast between the heights of the hall and parlour had a greater impact than it would have had in later years when tall buildings became commonplace, whilst inside, the application of brightly coloured patterns to every surface, whether of wood or plaster, was just as impressive in a different way. Green Street Cottage is unusual in preserving so much evidence of wall

painting; in most other houses the remains are fragmentary, but, thanks to the devoted labours of Dr Clive Rouse[11] in following up every trace in Hertfordshire, it is clear that vernacular buildings of the late 16th and early 17th centuries were decorated in vivid colours and bold patterns to an extent not previously realised. Although parlours seem often to have been singled out for such treatment, it should be remembered that almost every room of even a comparatively modest house like Manor House, Great Wymondley, was painted, and there is no reason to suppose that it was unique.

In the same parish and at a somewhat earlier date, probably the late 16th century, Ashmeads, Little Hadham, was improved by the addition of a jettied parlour. The way the addition was made, and the subsequent alteration of the hall range, are as interesting for the continuity they reveal as for the considerable improvement in living standards which they imply. The new block was entered by a modestly ornamental doorway placed diagonally opposite the entrance in the traditional way [**163**]. This doorway led, possibly through a lobby, to the staircase leading to the chamber over the parlour, then the only important upstairs room, as well as to the parlour itself, which had usurped some of the most important functions of the hall to become the major living room in the house.

163 *Ashmeads, Little Hadham: doorway to parlour*

164 *Hollands Close and 2 Ford Hill, Little Hadham*

Near Ashmeads is a similar enlargement at the house now called Hollands Close and No. 2 Ford Hill [**164**], which also began as a little timber-framed hall and had a tall brick parlour block of two storeys with attics added in the middle of the 17th century. By then the opposite doorways, or cross-passage, which entailed traversing the hall to reach the parlour, had become obsolete and were replaced by the lobby-entrance: the functions of the parlour had become indistinguishable from those conventionally ascribed to the hall. Whatever may have been the arrangement at Ashmeads, the parlour here had a small room, perhaps a closet rather than a service room, partitioned off, and an irregularity in the ceiling plaster suggests there was a lobby at the stair foot. Upstairs was a good bedchamber, probably with a closet opening off it, and an attic chamber. Since no access to the old house was possible at these higher levels, the parlour block entailed a division of the household as complete as in any open-hall house. Perhaps, too, in the late 17th century the romanticised farmhouse kitchen familiar from Victorian descriptions had its beginnings: the room where family and servants ate together and from which the family then retired.

A more developed separation of polite and working parts of the farmhouse occurred when a parlour wing was built at Moat Farmhouse, Much Hadham. Again, it was added to an open-hall house, but here are two sizeable rooms on each floor, not one plus a service room or closet. They indicate recognition of the social changes that were taking place, and instead of a confusion of functions there is the clear acceptance that hall and parlour, or eating parlour and best parlour, whatever they were called, were quite distinct from the kitchen and the farmhands' accommodation. The principal link with the older style of planning is the way of entering the house, with the front door still opening into the hall range, which by this time was a definitely inferior part of the house. Piecemeal rebuilding thus created a social paradox that was not to be endured for long.

In Westfield farmhouse, Little Hadham, the process reached its logical conclusion. The 'parlour' achieved full recognition as the principal living room, the remainder of

101

the wing becoming an entrance and staircase hall, with the kitchen, part of the old house, and its attendant offices being relegated to the status of a back wing.

By the middle of the 17th century the three-cell house, even with two full storeys and two heated ground-floor rooms, was inadequate for the better farmhouses. Developments in the second half of the 17th century did not lead to the emergence of an easily recognisable dominant type and mostly the story is of improvements achieved in a variety of ways.

The kitchen incorporated in the house

It is not always easy to recognise a room built as a kitchen. When a hall fireplace is wide and deep, equipped with low benches or shelves in one or both jambs, and has one or two 'keeping-holes' (a northern term for cupboards without doors) at the back, it may well have been used for cooking. Such a fireplace usually has brick jambs of the middle or late 17th century, though the wooden lintel spanning the opening may be older. Were the earlier timber fireplaces like the one in Town Farm, Standon, used for cooking? No evidence of associated shelves was observed, and perhaps the use of herring-bone pattern brickwork to form the fireback discouraged the building of cupboards. Food preparation may indeed have been carried on in a detached kitchen. In a house with three ground-floor fireplaces we may presume that one serves a kitchen, and if it is of later date than those in hall and parlour, it probably replaces a detached kitchen. At the Old Rose and Crown, Braughing, the kitchen wing added to the original three-cell plan still had a bay open from ground to roof in which cooking was done, as did a building as grand as the Bishop's Palace, Much Hadham, at about the same period. In these early examples a wing replaced the detached kitchen with comparatively little structural change. Progress was rapid, and by 1616 the compiler of a glebe terrier could refer to an 'old building called a kitchen although it hath no fireplace'.

By the middle of the 17th century, a farmhouse of any size that did not incorporate a kitchen would have looked old-fashioned. At just that period Hammond's Farm, Pirton [165], was transformed by rebuilding everything below the upper end of the hall to produce what was in effect a new house with an unconventional plan [166]. The intention in putting the kitchen at the rear of the new cross-wing and keeping the parlour at the front was perhaps to use either hall or parlour for dining, as occasion demanded; one of the many instances where the function of these two rooms is confused.

Hammond's Farm was unusual in undergoing such a dramatic transformation of plan and material. Such changes generally took place over a longer period, as at Causeway House, Braughing [167], which was built with three ground-floor rooms; the room at the south end was probably the kitchen, as it certainly was later. The weathering of the roof

165 *Hammond's Farm, Pirton*

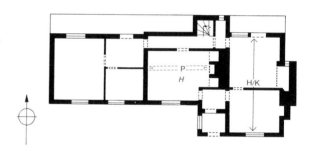

166 *Hammond's Farm, Pirton: plan*

gable establishes that the present service bay is a later addition, yet the argument used in connection with alleged two-room houses, that a service room of some kind must have been needed, applies here; either it was partitioned within a not particularly large kitchen or the present structure can be inferred to have replaced an earlier and lower one, which was presumably the relic of a late medieval house. From a functional standpoint, the most important of several alterations which took place c.1650–80 were the rebuilding of the chimney-stack in brick to incorporate what is definitely a kitchen fireplace, and replacement of the service bay.

Kitchens of the 16th and 17th centuries that were purpose-built rather than conversions are generally recognisable by their customary proportions; they are comparatively short rooms, that is to say, less than square, for example, at Tudor Cottage, Albury, where the fireplace occupies most of one cross-wall. During the 18th century, when it became common to build lateral chimney-stacks within the shell of quite small farmhouses, this proportion was maintained, sometimes for the principal rooms, sometimes for a specialised kitchen. The former case appears to imply a combined function as living room and kitchen.

Rook's Nest Farm, Walkern [168], is instructive in this

167 *Causeway House, Braughing*

168 *Rook's Nest Farm, Walkern: from the south east*

169 *Rook's Nest Farm, Walkern: plan*

respect. It was a rather superior farmhouse, resembling a gentry house in its sharp division between family rooms and service rooms. The division was expressed as fully in appearance as in plan by giving the family living quarters slightly greater height and an altogether more impressive symmetrical appearance than the service wing [**169**]. The domestic rooms comprise, on each side of an internal stack, hall and parlour with chambers and attics over, the plan being given a roughly cruciform appearance by a two-storey porch at the front which is balanced by a stair turret at the back. Quite clearly, cooking was never done in this hall, yet the wing in which the kitchen stack stands is of a different build and may be as much as thirty years later if a date cut into the brickwork is to be believed. Its predecessor must have been a survival from an earlier house. When the service range was built it incorporated a pantry between hall and kitchen, and there was a further room, unheated and of unknown purpose, beyond.

Around the time the improver of Rook's Nest Farm was emulating gentry standards, the owner or tenant of Hyde Farm, Abbots Langley [**170**], was departing from them, and the two houses afford an interesting contrast. At Hyde Farm, the 16th-century hall was turned into a parlour, and the addition to make an L-shaped house took the form of a new hall with a kitchen behind it [**171**]. What had hitherto been a distinguishing mark of a gentry hall, the lateral chimney-stack, here became a rather oversized example of a feature which was becoming common in the better vernacular

buildings, an external chimney-stack serving a parlour. Neither of these houses, though they provided much the same number and kinds of room, really conforms to any late 17th-century type.

Although Rook's Nest Farm and Hyde Farm could be classified formally as L-plan houses, it would be unwise to create a type where such houses vary widely in everything but overall shape; that most of them are of two periods of construction is a less significant objection, because a type may emerge through alteration. The diversity of the L-plan incorporating a kitchen wing is shown by Lower Farm, North Mymms, which was built as a three-room lobby-entrance house in the early 17th century. Alteration has made it impossible to know if either of the two original

103

where the dairy or milk house, cheese room, smoking room and storage for firewood were. Before the end of the 17th century a whole range was added parallel to the main part of Lower Farm containing ample provision of unheated rooms, to none of which can a specific use be assigned.

Lower Farm was obviously prosperous. Great Hormead Dane, Hormead, a continuous-jetty house of the 16th century, did not fare as well in the 17th. There, too, an L-plan was adopted, but it entailed conversion of one of the small service rooms, possibly both, into a kitchen and the addition of one or two ancillary rooms beyond its chimney-stack.

Elongated lobby-entrance plans

A number of comparatively large vernacular houses, all of the second half of the 17th century, lack wings or outshuts and achieved their size by simple increase of length; instead of three cells there were four. Where the extra rooms were provided in a wing the staircase could be so placed as to give access to at least some rooms in the main range as well as those in the wing, so that a measure of the centralisation towards which house planning was moving could be achieved: a tendency that, at manorial or landowning level, was already producing the double-pile house or T-plan, and cruciform houses like Hammond's Farm, Pirton. Evidently there were several acceptable ways of enlarging the old three-cell plans and now that the houses have, without exception, been so much altered that the original use of minor rooms is irrecoverable, the factors determining the choice of one type or another are difficult to understand.

Some lobby-entrance houses were simply made more or less symmetrical, with two cells on each side of the central chimney-stack. At Hall Farm, Broadfield, Cottered [**172, 173**], seats in the jambs of one of the fireplaces show that this was the hall, a point confirmed by the main staircase at the opposite end, for the stair was usually closely related to the hall. A small room opposite the stair foot was a service room of some kind, probably a pantry, and beyond was another large room with a small fireplace characteristic of a parlour of c.1700. In that case, what was the function of the room on the far side of the main stack, the one which might equally well be called the parlour? A curious feature of this room is the positioning of the bearer to one side, as if to allow for a passage through to the unheated room at the north end of the house, which perhaps served some farm purpose such as a dairy. Yet if there were such a passage, there is a disproportion between fireplace size and room size in the two parlours so considerable as to raise doubts about the functions assigned to the two middle rooms. Possibly the 'hall' was primarily a kitchen, and the smaller room served as what the gentry would have called a dining parlour, although, too, it may well have served the more general purposes of a living room, likewise taken over from the hall; an unsatisfactory explanation in so far as it makes the position of the main staircase anomalous.

170 *Hyde Farm, Abbots Langley*

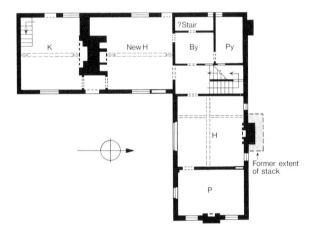

171 *Hyde Farm, Abbots Langley: plan*

ground-floor fireplaces was used for cooking, so that adding a kitchen wing in the latter part of the century could as well represent the transfer of an existing function as the incorporation of a new one, and only on general grounds is the latter view more likely. It would be interesting to know the social standing of the man who built this wing; like his fellow at Rook's Nest Farm, though in a very different way, he was giving a farmhouse some of the attributes of a small gentry house, in this case the separate dining room and the hall with something of the air of an entrance-hall. What the house lacked was the centralised access to all family rooms which was provided by a cruciform plan and attainable in great measure with a T-plan.

It is rarely possible to reconstruct how long wings such as the one at Lower Farm were used in their entirety, because any evidence of purpose has long been swept away; indeed, the supposed brewhouse which stood next to the kitchen at Lower Farm had become a ruin and was demolished recently. With the general suburbanisation of Hertfordshire and the demolition or drastic conversion of all rooms and most buildings connected with farming, it can only be conjectured

172 *Hall Farm, Broadfield, Cottered*

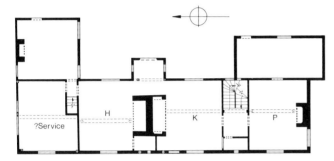

173 *Hall Farm, Broadfield, Cottered: plan*

174 *Gaytons, Much Hadham*

175 *Gaytons, Much Hadham: staircase of the late 17th century*

Hall Farm illustrates the difficulties of accommodating these elongated houses to the conventional interpretation of those with three cells and a lobby-entrance. The historian's difficulty is that, in the late 17th century, room uses were changing without any corresponding change of nomenclature. In a society still largely governed by custom and tradition, there was no pressing need to devise appropriate names for rooms which were changing their use. A problem of exactly this kind exists in farmhouses in South Wales at the present day;[12] the removal of cooking from the room which began as the hall and was later the kitchen has made of it a kind of parlour. Therefore, to distinguish it from the original and now little-used parlour, a term is taken over from suburbia and the latter is called, quite inappropriately in an isolated straight range of rooms, the 'front room'. Such problems of nomenclature exist everywhere where old farmhouses are altered to meet contemporary needs.

The vogue for a symmetrical front encouraged the growth of elongated houses. Whether this consideration weighed with the builder of Hall Farm is hard to say; it certainly did at Gaytons, Much Hadham [174]. Here, some of the advantages of the lobby-entrance plan were still prized at a comparatively late date, notably the economical use of space and the high degree of centralisation that the conjunction of entrance, chimney-stack and staircase permitted, all combined behind a perfectly symmetrical front. In this house, the plan type was adapted to separate the service rooms from the rest: kitchen, pantry and another small room to one side of the entrance, hall and parlour to the other. What is lacking by comparison with small double-pile plans is independent access to the parlour from entrance and staircase.

Gaytons is a bigger and better house than Hall Farm; it has a grander staircase [175], sizeable attic rooms and the remains of superior internal fittings and decorative design that were wholly successful as an architectural composition.

Only its position in a village street, making a proper appreciation of the long front more difficult than if it were in the open countryside, disguises a certain awkwardness arising from the clash between a five-bay elevation, four rooms and three gables. If the windows had originally been larger, this would certainly have modified the present strong impression of symmetry, yet the illusion of weight coming over openings created by the roof valleys is aesthetically uncomfortable and must always have been present whatever the size of the original windows.

The smaller and less ambitious Causeway House, Braughing, where the fourth bay which might have produced a unified elongated plan was never integrated with the rest of the house, overcame this difficulty; the three bays of the timber frame match the three dormer gables. What is so interesting about vernacular development in the second half of the 17th century is the variety of ways in which a new architectural consciousness manifested itself at the same time as the need for an increase in the number and variety of rooms. In Hertfordshire the effort to solve both problems, culminating in the symmetrical brick front of five bays, took longer and was more difficult than in some areas with a different vernacular tradition, such as the Cotswolds.

Several of the considerations governing house plans at this period can be observed at Mackerye End Farm, Wheathampstead [176] (now The Manor House). It is higher and wider than most houses of its kind and may be of two builds. Its plan combines the standard unit of the period – two rooms and lobby-entrance – to which was added the service rooms appropriate to a rather superior farmhouse, that is, a kitchen, a staircase and two small unheated rooms, one of which was a pantry. It is the combination of those two fundamental ways of meeting contemporary domestic needs which reveals a unity of purpose belied by the variety of appearance of the houses in which they occur. Mackerye End Farm has much more in common with Rook's Nest Farm, Walkern, than the very different shape of their plans would suggest, and its service half is much like the wing added to Lower Farm, North Mymms, which is so different in other respects; and although the staircases at Mackerye End Farm and Hall Farm, Broadfield, differ in form they stand in the same relation to the hall.

177 *Leggatt's Farm, Kings Walden*

178 *Bridge End and The Whare, Little Hadham: from the west. This may be an example of the unit system*

The unit system

Anyone visiting a farm today expects to find one house, the farmhouse. It was not always so. A 17th-century observer of the Hertfordshire landscape would have seen in a number of farmyards two houses standing close together which nowadays, with few exceptions, have been united. The two houses were not necessarily equal in size but their form and detail show that they were equal in status. This phenomenon of joint occupation was first recognised in Wales and named the 'unit system'[13] from the existence in one place of two or more units of domestic building, not all of which were necessarily independent houses. Although the basis of the system is primarily the extended family, the only relevant documentary study makes it clear that persons other than relatives could participate.[14]

Hertfordshire can show one perfectly clear example at Leggatt's Farm, Kings Walden [177], where two houses, each with hall range and cross-wing were built on parallel alignments and almost touching corner to corner. They are joined on the ground floor by a little connecting block, a feature observed in several Welsh examples which establishes Leggatt's Farm as an instance of the unit system. Another, about which some doubts may be felt because of its position in a village, is provided by the houses called Bridge End and The Whare in Little Hadham [178]. They stand close to one

176 *Mackerye End Farm, Wheathampstead*

another in a way unlike farmhouses on adjoining plots in a village street, as if to suggest that they may once have been connected with the same farm. Houses as nearly equal in size and appearance as these are rare.

Certain features differentiate such houses from the elongated ones described earlier (see p 104). Those forming a straight range of buildings are generally larger than the four-cell lobby-entrance farmhouses. Those of L-shaped plan or consisting of two ranges at an angle to one another have an overall length which is both striking and inconvenient. Where two front doors exist, dual occupation is clear enough; where one is blocked, some other explanation may be possible, such as a change from open hall to entrance-hall.

When can the unit system first be detected in the architectural record? It is impossible to point with certainty to a late medieval example, although several incorporate one open-hall house. The explanation may be that replacement of joint by single occupation, as happened almost everywhere, necessitated changes additional to those dictated by fashion or the new requirements of domestic or farm life and so destroyed more evidence than usual. Even so, a few instances of two houses in one yard may be late medieval, for example, those at Little Hadham. Others are the Dower House, Westmill, and Piccott's End Farm, Hemel Hempstead, in both of which two open halls are inferred. In each case two houses have been incorporated into one and their date, rather than the existence of the unit system, is the matter at issue here.

The question of origins is difficult to discuss from architectural evidence alone because of the phenomenon of alternate development, for if that can explain a house of two parts, neither complete in itself, it may be applicable to two small houses forming part of one establishment. This is the more relevant if the two adjoining houses were not always totally independent domestic units.

Holt Farm, St Stephen, embodies two houses, possibly late medieval; they are joined corner to corner, not at right angles but skewed. The way the houses are related physically to one another and to the approach road is likely to have reflected quite closely the integral status of the two households, although architectural evidence alone cannot define this more closely. Holt Farm expresses a degree of dominance in one of the partners in the joint farming enterprise which did not exist at The Dower House, Westmill, where equality, or something approaching it, must be assumed. Complete equality was rare. Only when the two houses were identical and stood in an identical relation to the farm approach was this possible, as is the case with the semi-detached farmhouses at Arnford, Long Preston, Yorkshire,[15] where late 17th-century stone details and identical elevations and plans make the social equality clear.

The closest example to this in Hertfordshire is provided by New Hall, Ware Rural [179], where the external equality and symmetry of the two units is not matched by symmetry of plan because the division into two parts was accomplished by enlarging a medieval open-hall house. It is not the general appearance of New Hall that gives away its duality of plan, for the central two-storeyed porch [180] and

179 *New Hall, Ware Rural*

180 *New Hall, Ware Rural: detail of porch*

the gabled wings can be matched in normal farmhouses, and its length of 75 ft (23 m), though considerable, is surpassed by some of the elongated lobby-entrance houses with which it might at first sight be confused. What is so unusual is the pair of identical doors sheltered by the porch, one opening into the cross-passage of the old hall-house and the other into the lobby-entrance of the added second unit; this is the sole piece of evidence unequivocally linking New Hall to the unit system.[16]

The point is confirmed in different ways by Cross Farm, Harpenden [181], and Green Tye Farmhouse, Much Hadham. Cross Farm has, for a farmhouse only one room in depth, the quite remarkable length of 95 ft (29 m) which provides five large rooms [182]. It lacks the symmetry of New Hall, nor can even a rough equality of rooms be claimed when the fireplaces in the two ends of the house are so different, one set for polite use, the other for working purposes. Nonetheless, there were two doorways side by side, only

181 *Cross Farm, Harpenden*

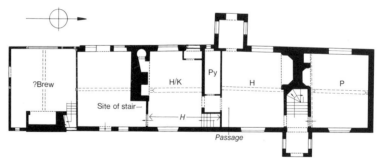

182 *Cross Farm, Harpenden: plan*

one of them masked by a storeyed 17th-century porch. It is impossible to see the jambs of the blocked doorway clearly enough to say whether it is contemporary with its neighbour in the porch, so the possibility that the present front door replaces an older one has to be borne in mind. Without denying that this may be the case, it is hard to think of reasons for moving the front door a mere 9 ft (3 m) sideways; if the door were to be moved at all, the plan suggests that half that distance would have been more satisfactory. Green Tye also has two doors side by side, which hints at the existence of a unit system.

The unit system in operation

Walnut Tree Farm, Pirton [**183**], provides a model of how the unit system developed and worked, although it must be

stressed that this is not the only possible way. The present house was built in the late Middle Ages as a timber-framed building of which only a two-storeyed cross-wing survives (phase 1) [**184**]. Coeval with it was a hall, assumed from its low proportions to have been open to the roof, although very little evidence remains, and it is also assumed that there was, as usual, a service bay. In the late 17th century a handsome new house of brick was added at the west end (phase 2), much like the front part of Rook's Nest Farm, Walkern. With its two storeys and attics, up-to-date lobby-entrance plan and two-storey porch, it must have overshadowed the old house, and at this stage the unit system can definitely be said to have come into being. Perhaps within a year or two, the contrast was diminished by a partial rebuilding of the older part (phase 3), which may have been intended from the first. The way the new brickwork is bonded into the old suggests two building campaigns to carry out a single intention, with toothing left for the continuation. In the newer

183 *Walnut Tree Farm, Pirton*

part, a second porch, identical in detail with the first but very slightly narrower, was built in front of the old cross-passage. The passage itself was blocked by a wide fireplace to create a lobby-entrance. After another comparatively short interval, both parts were enlarged to double depth and provided with more rooms and good staircases.

Clearly, the evidence raises problems of interpretation. So little remains of the first phase that it has to be interpreted conventionally. With the second phase begins the problem of the relation between the two parts. In terms of a normal lobby-entrance plan, the ground-floor rooms are a new hall and a well-lit parlour at the freestanding end of the new build, so that the original service room continued to serve that purpose in relation to the new hall, and possibly the hall was used for cooking. Yet it is hard to see why the cross-wing at the lower end of the old house should have remained had an independent household not been using it, for otherwise the kind of piecemeal replacement envisaged at Great Barwick Farm, Standon, and many other houses would surely have occurred rather than enlargement. In this third phase, the building of a second porch, almost equal to the first, establishes the existence of two households to some degree independent of each other. What is absolutely clear is the careful distinction between the two in status and function. The new east house had a smaller parlour, its principal fireplace differs from any in the west house in being intended for cooking, and even the porch is fractionally smaller than its counterpart in a way which recalls the marginal differences between the two staircases at Aston Bury Manor.

What do the differences imply? Having only one kitchen-type fireplace is crucial, by implying that food was cooked in the inferior house for the occupants of both, so that in this respect Walnut Tree Farm operated as a single unit. Nevertheless, the separation into two parts was sufficiently complete to warrant two porches and two good staircases, so that some fairly sharp distinction must have been drawn between the two households comprising the houseful. The greater degree of separation on the first floor is apparent

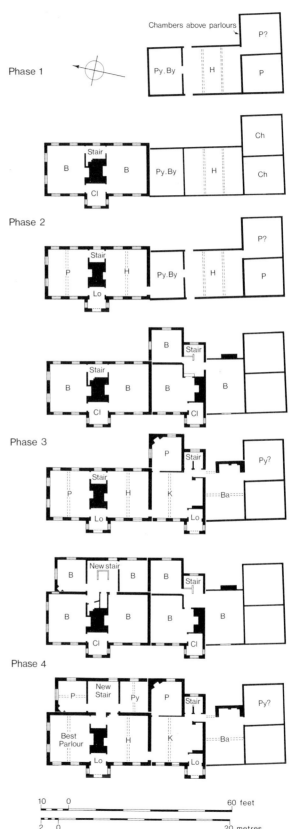

184 *Walnut Tree Farm, Pirton: development plans*

from the inconveniences that attended the unification of the house. What had first been built as the superior unit retained its superiority in the form of a better staircase and improved bedchambers. The little room over the porch provided a closet for one of the two principal rooms, and one of the two rooms flanking the staircase was perhaps a dressing room for the other important bedchamber. In the east house the arrangements were simpler; the principal bedchamber over the kitchen had a closet over the porch; there was a smaller but quite good bedchamber at the rear; and a third and definitely inferior chamber over the old hall. Evidently, both households were of very similar size.

Walnut Tree Farm strengthens the interpretation of New Hall and Cross Farm. All look like houses in which two households living under the same roof were sufficiently independent to require separate entrances, while living a communal life to the extent that the division of the ground plan into a purely domestic and a domestic working end could be maintained. That conclusion must follow from the existence of only one kitchen and, if accepted, it assists the interpretation of other unit-system plans, none of which conforms to normal types.

Wakeley, Westmill [185], was built as two houses. The north house has a large kitchen with a fireplace designed for cooking, the other has nothing remotely like it. Tenuous plan evidence suggests that a link exisited between the two houses from the first and permitted one kitchen to serve both. How this hypothetical communal cooking arrangement worked is even more conjectural, but bearing in mind the existence of detached kitchens not so many years earlier, we may suppose that food was carried from the kitchen through a passage to the principal room of the north house. An arrangement something like this may explain Wickham Hall, Bishop's Stortford [186], which now has an extraordinarily elongated L-shaped plan with the north arm over 60 ft (18 m) and the east arm about 70 ft (21.5 m) long; the north arm alone is as big as an elongated lobby-entrance house like Gaytons, Much Hadham. The complicated development of both ranges may imply dual occupation antedating the predominantly late 17th-century character of the house by a hundred years or more, yet it is in the latter period that some separation of functions is discernible; for while at that period there was no possible cooking hearth in the east range, there was one in the north range, plus what looks like an original corridor connecting the supposed kitchen to the superior house; all this is reminiscent of the interdependence found at Walnut Tree Farm. At both places food was prepared in the one room that was obviously a kitchen and perhaps eaten by the two households separately.

Gentry houses and the unit system

Although a unit system can be argued for a few more houses, the more important have been analysed. One striking conclusion is the general similarity of plan in functional terms, between Walnut Tree Farm and the gentry house, Aston Bury Manor. Naturally, the latter, being of one build,

185 *Wakeley, Westmill*

186 *Wickham Hall, Bishop's Stortford*

has a tidier plan, yet the element of duality represented by its two staircases is paralleled at Walnut Tree Farm, where it is proclaimed to the outside world by two entrances. Mackerye End, Wheathampstead, is not very different from Aston Bury Manor, and little about Rothamsted Manor except its size would have been unfamiliar to those who lived at Walnut Tree Farm, or Wickham Hall, Bishop's Stortford, another divided manor house. It looks as though the houseful was divided for some purposes but not others, and that the division, whatever the architectural form it took, did not usually preclude the maintenance of a common kitchen, even where two separate houses existed. In the light of this finding it is regrettable that Leggatt's Farm, Kings Walden, could not be examined fully because there, if anywhere in Hertfordshire, two households may have lived side by side, each largely independent of the other. As for the other unit-system houses, it is difficult to believe that the two households were unrelated; but despite this it has been stated that 'there slept together under each roof in 1600 only the nuclear family, with the addition of servants when necessary'.[17] This cannot be wholly true of Hertfordshire, as Walnut Tree Farm and New Hall prove. The situation can best be explained by postulating the existence of kin groups within which varying degrees of separation existed, such as parents and children plus grandparents, or brothers or cousins, each with a family. Whatever the composition of the group, its expression in bricks and mortar implies an expectation of long continuance.

It appears that actual separation of households was stronger among farmers, most of whom were no doubt copyholders, than among gentry. If as many as one third of the jointly occupied farms at Yetminster, Dorset, were held by unrelated sets of people,[18] structural divisions would be needed. Walnut Tree Farm would not meet that case unless simply locking a door was regarded as sufficient, but Leggatt's Farm or Bridge End and The Whare, both in Little Hadham, would. The externally less marked physical separation among the gentry may be connected with the sense of a house as the seat of a landed dynasty, providing for more than the nuclear family.

The stylistic qualities of 17th-century vernacular houses

By the end of the 16th century the continuous-jettied front had fallen completely out of favour in farmhouses and the flush-walled house of two storeys that took its place has not survived, or never existed in sufficient numbers in Hertfordshire for its architectural qualities to be easily discussed. Popefield Farm, Hatfield, suggests that a timber and plaster equivalent of the gabled Cotswold style was favoured for some small houses in the 17th century. A few of the larger three-cell Elizabethan or Jacobean houses seem, like many a gentry house, to have incorporated two-storey bay windows to striking effect, one to each cell and surmounted by a dormer gable (in the original sense of an unwindowed gable). At Egerton House, Berkhamsted, which was pulled down in the 1930s and must have been one of the most striking examples, each bay was capped by a pediment, whereas at the generally similar house, now Nos 59/61 High Street, Barkway, the bays terminate under jettied gables.

Because many houses had been built before about 1530, much of the effort put into Elizabethan and Jacobean farmhouse building was devoted to the addition of parlour blocks, often of two storeys and attics, at the end of an old open hall. Whether these additions were of squarish plan or were longer cross-wings, they were invariably roofed at right angles to the older building, unlike the 'in-series' additions of an earlier period, so that the high gabled roof, conveying size and modernity, towered over the hall. Two of the many examples have already been mentioned, Ashmeads and Hollands Close, standing within sight of one another at Hadham Cross in Little Hadham parish. The sought-after effect is reinforced at Hollands Close by its being on rising ground at the upper end of the quite low range adjoining.

Not until after the Civil War did a distinctive vernacular aesthetic come into being, and although some of its elements are also common to gentry houses of the period, they are used in somewhat different ways. Two elements in particular stand out, the continuous gabled elevation and the decorative chimney-stack, and both are as much functional as ornamental. More floor space and headroom were gained by building three or four such gables on the wall-plate than could have been had with dormer windows set in the slopes of the roof. This in itself produced the impression of a much taller house than was the case when the roof space was unused or where there were only the two gables of cross-wings.

Brick chimney-stacks with carved shafts and concave-sided octagonal caps, perhaps ornamented with curious spiky projections, sometimes replaced wooden stacks which presumably had a quite simple rectangular top rising only a short distance above the roof. Sir John Wittewronge built chimneys like this at Rothamsted Manor in 1651, whereas the richer and widely travelled Sir Thomas Pope Blount had plainer panelled stacks only a few years later at Tyttenhanger. But at vernacular level, ornamental chimney-shafts were used differently, often combined with a lobby-entrance so as to gain maximum effect from being on the same vertical axis as the front doorway.

The popularity of ornamental brick chimney-stacks is not wholly explained by the apeing of gentry fashion, for its timing coincides with a general increase in the use of brick for building. Whether the rapid spread of this fashion coincided with the replacement of a wooden stack or with the complete replacement of an open hall, it was the concomitant of a marked improvement in housing which included upstairs fireplaces. This kind of pride accounts for a name such as Six Tunnels Farm, Great Gaddesden, 'tunnel' being an old word for shaft or flue.

The first such room to be heated in vernacular houses was generally the chamber over the hall and, as with the change in style of chimney-shafts, the emulation of gentry fashion was an important factor. Another was the wish to allot more specific functions to rooms, and to avoid having looms, beds, cheeses and other things all together in the parlour. A brick stack could be adapted to serve a further fireplace with comparative ease, so that even though the cost of brick compared to other materials must have been falling, it may still have been cheaper to build one stack serving three fireplaces than the two or three separate stacks that ground-floor living would have required; and if display was a consideration, money was more effectively spent if the shafts were grouped together.

To serve the upstairs bedrooms, and particularly the great chamber over the hall, a good staircase was required. This was the other feature of architectural display for those farmers who could afford it. In earlier vernacular houses any upstairs bedrooms had been in wings or additions, as was the case with the late 16th-century houses which had tall parlour blocks added to them; a few large houses of that period were built with cross-wings, yet neither type of dwelling seems to have included a staircase of any pretensions. It is as if the late 17th century saw a change in the dignity and importance of upstairs rooms, even though, in some cases, the use to which they were then put had begun earlier.

111

Chapter 7

Eighteenth-century country houses and seats

During the 18th century the houses of the landed classes increased in size. At this social level a new house was likely to be larger than its counterpart of fifty or a hundred years earlier and an old house was likely to be extended when it was renovated. Obvious exceptions are the great Elizabethan and Jacobean houses, especially those of courtyard plan; their various fates, described below (pp 127–32), did not include enlargement. Overall, house plans became simpler, with fewer but larger rooms. Nevertheless, they are more difficult to categorise than their late 17th-century predecessors, because so many are the result of adapting older buildings. Yet more complications were introduced by what appears to have been a new attitude on the part of owners towards their houses. Changes in manners combined with the desire for a display of status and the pleasure of building for its own sake led some owners into endless tinkering with their houses. As Sterling, the hero of *The Clandestine Marriage*, says: 'The chief pleasure of a country house is to make improvements, my lord. I spare no expense, not I. This is quite another sort of place from when I first took it . . .'.[1]

On the limited evidence provided by a single county a typology of houses is impossible. Classification has to be in more general terms than for any preceding period and can be attempted in three ways. One is to distinguish how the principal rooms of a house were related to one another by identifying features or elements fundamental to them, and so group disparate houses together. A second is to analyse actual room usage and classify characteristic groupings of rooms – this is especially difficult because so little information is to be had. The third, the one most commonly used in writing architectural history, is to begin with types of elevation and relate them to certain broad categories of plan, but since this method of classification has been extensively treated elsewhere, it will be ignored here.

Finally, developments in the gentry part of the house will be dealt with separately from those in the servants' part, for although planning of the service quarters necessarily responded to the family's needs it did not do so in a uniform way at any given time. More than one response was possible depending on several factors, which included the form of the house, its relation to the gardens, stables and home farm, and the ability or willingness of the owner to alter one or more of these.

Below the nobility several levels of gentry can be discerned, and for those at the lower end of the scale who needed only the minimum of rooms there were few architectural problems. For them the simple double-pile, five or perhaps seven bays wide, remained appropriate for a long time with comparatively little change. By the reign of George II it was difficult to distinguish the houses of the minor gentry from those of prosperous and socially ambitious farmers; perhaps at this social level it always had been so. The point is made in a description of the establishment maintained in 1740 by the poet Crabbe's uncle, Mr Tovill, who was one of the 'first-rate yeomen of that period – the Yeoman that already began to be styled by courtesy an Esquire'. The house, its moat, dovecot and fishponds 'were such as might have suited a gentleman's seat of some consequence'; the difference between what sounds like an old manor house and a gentry house lay in the kind of life lived within it and the presence of the farmyard at the back.[2]

Members of the gentry class were absolved by their private means from Mr Tovill's necessity to work. Their foremost concerns were to devise ways of passing the time both for themselves and for visitors, whilst those who became Sheriff would certainly have needed somewhere to deal with correspondence, to meet those who came on business, and to host receptions. Meetings may not always have demanded a special room – a parlour or any suitably furnished room could be pressed into service and official papers may simply have been kept with title deeds and family papers. All gentry who were Justices of the Peace had need of some facilities of this kind, however modest. Although few can ever have conducted business as grandly as Charles II's great Chancellor, Clarendon, whom Pepys once found 'busy in trials of law in his great room' or 'Room of Causes' with its 'lawyers lobby'[3], many at some time carried out the duties of a magistrate and must have made provision for doing so in their own houses in ways not now easy to recognise.

The kinds of plan favoured at the turn of the 17th century were developed to meet these social and official needs in several ways. One was the abandonment of whatever social custom dictated the provision of two staircases, and the accompanying division of the upstairs rooms, in favour of centralisation as the key to planning the gentry rooms. Another was the development of passages, servant staircases and basements as a means of increasing the privacy of those waited upon in a household containing many servants.

Simple double-pile houses

At the beginning of the 18th century the contract plans for Cole Green Park, Hertingfordbury, show some of the new developments in use [187]. The plan is divided by two transverse walls into three nearly equal compartments. In the middle is the hall, open to the broad, imposing staircase at the back; to the left are two large, square, intercommunicating rooms, the dining room and drawing room; and to the right are two inferior rooms, linked via a lobby at the foot of the servants' staircase, which encroaches on both. The wide fireplace in the back room establishes it as the kitchen, and the front room, by its proximity to both kitchen and back stair, must have been the common parlour, with closets for servants' dressing rooms. In the number of rooms it provided, although not in their size, Cole Green Park represents just about the minimum gentry requirement and is not an innovative house; that quality was provided by a structural feature, the tripartite division of the plan by brick-built cross-walls as thick as the outer shell. The middle part of a house like this was marked by a projection, usually of three bays, at back or front or both which defined

the space between the two cross-walls on which are placed chimney-stacks. Depending on the size of the house, these are sometimes the principal stacks, sometimes the only ones, but either way they reveal the broad outlines of the plan. Popes, Hatfield, Much Hadham Hall and probably Briggens, Hunsdon, were among a considerable number of houses like this.

Double-pile houses of a simpler kind and unquestionably of gentry status were built at the beginning of the 18th century. One such is the Golden Parsonage, Great Gaddesden [188], now much reorganised internally, where greater importance attached to the largest room which was still a hall in the older sense. Hence, the Golden Parsonage reflects

188 *Golden Parsonage, Great Gaddesden: front elevation*

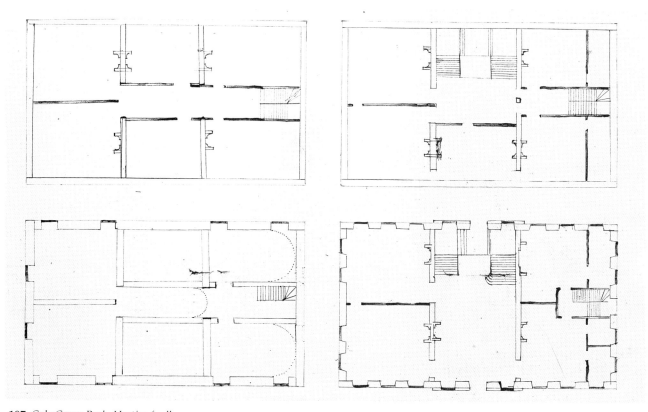

187 *Cole Green Park, Hertingfordbury*

the survival of a mode of social life which may have been bound up with the existence of a larger household, for the handsome pilastered brick house was joined to an older, probably timber-framed, building where the servants lived and worked. That much can be guessed from the paucity of the ground-floor rooms in the red brick part and is confirmed by old maps which show that the present service range replaces something older. The impression left by the Hertfordshire evidence in general, and the Golden Parsonage in particular, is that in all but a very few cases that part of the house where the gentry lived was viewed as an architecturally separate entity to which the necessary ancillary buildings were virtually irrelevant; this is borne out by most house plans published in the 18th century as well as by Oldfield's and Buckler's choice of viewpoint to hide whatever conflicted with the architectural ideal intended by the owner.

The Golden Parsonage is one of several houses in Hertfordshire which are small relative to their owners' status. Temple Dinsley, Preston, is another, and it suggests an alternative explanation; for there two houses stood close together for about a hundred years until one of them was pulled down in the 1820s. Today, only documentary evidence establishes the existence of the larger house of the two, and internal knowledge of the existing one gives a misleading picture of the whole 'house' and its social importance. Where similar contrasts exist, the possibility that a second house has vanished completely ought to be considered.

and suppressing the minor rooms and its social function was changed by creating an enfilade extending through five front rooms.

The rebuilding of Cokenach, Barkway, in the 1720s produced a house with resemblances to Cole Green Park in overall size and general appearance, but there the similarity ends, for the incorporation of two wings flanking the rear courtyard at Cokenach necessitated the provision of two staircases rather than one and resulted in an imperfect version of formal planning – if, indeed, that is what was sought. Where the original staircases stood and how important they were cannot be confirmed.

Where a series of grand rooms and an enfilade was not needed, an alternative way of enlarging the double-pile was to remove the staircase from the entrance axis and put it to one side, as had been done long before at Tring Park. At Brickendon Bury, built in the early years of the 18th century, this idea was adapted to a more modest house. The plan was something between a double and a triple-pile. The hall and the grand room behind it, no doubt the saloon, each had natural light, although not very much can have reached the middle of the house; and, on the other side of the hall in the space corresponding to the main staircase, there was probably a secondary stair, which may have received some natural light. This arrangement, despite the difficulty of using all the space in the middle to advantage, produced a comparatively large and remarkably compact house.

The double-pile enlarged

A straightforward way of gaining further accommodation was to enlarge the simple double-pile. Cole Green Park as originally planned had four rooms grouped around the entrance-hall and staircase, then, as enlarged a few years later, eight [189]. Its size was increased by adding wings

Triple-pile houses

A landowner superior in rank and fortune to the local gentry needed something bigger than a simple double-pile. If his social status were sufficiently high, he might develop the triple-pile form first exhibited at Tring Park. The only possible rival to Tring in this respect, as well as in sheer size, was Tewin House [190], built 1716–18. This was an

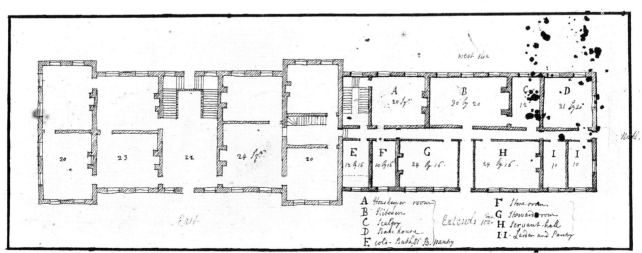

189 *Cole Green Park, Hertingfordbury*

190 *Tewin House: detail from Arthur Devis's painting of Colonel and Mrs J Sabine (private collection)*

apparently square house of nine bays, sufficiently large and splendid for George I to have visited, but its demolition in the late 18th century makes conjecture about its plan hazardous.

More modest than this, but a good-sized house by any standards except those of the great landowners, is Langleybury, Abbots Langley [191]. The principal planning problem was how to light the centre of the building, since

the huge room rising through two storeys at Tring Park was not needed and the equivalent space was divided into two floors. By bringing the staircase as far as possible towards the centre of the building, the problem could be alleviated, as the centre received borrowed light from the staircase window [192]. To have brought it in more and so created two short wings would have solved the problem altogether, but only at the cost of creating another, that of providing easy access from the staircase to all the principal bedrooms without using corridors or lobbies. This planning difficulty may be one reason why the triple-pile was so rarely adopted; the only other possible example in Hertfordshire is Albury Hall, where it may be datable to the 1740s.

191 *Langleybury, Abbots Langley: front elevation with kitchen block, formerly detached, to the left*

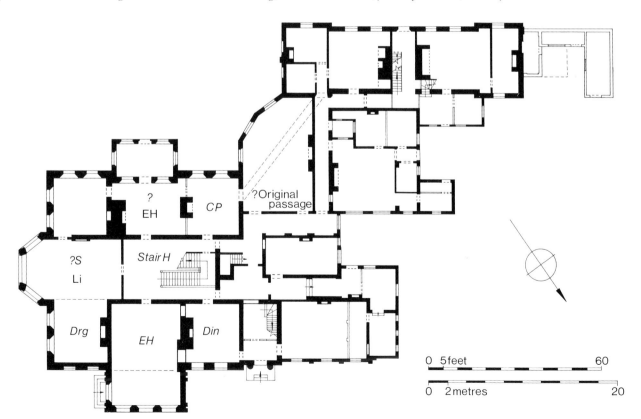

192 *Langleybury, Abbots Langley: plan*

The compact house

The villa

From the 18th century to the present day it has been usual to distinguish between a country house and a villa. As used before the 18th century, the word 'villa' seems often to have denoted no more than a small house, a usage which persisted into the early 19th century, for example, in an engraving of a small three-bay house devoid of architectural pretensions captioned 'Mr Ginger's villa at Hemel Hempstead' [193]. Even then, usage was inconsistent. Cecil Lodge, Abbots Langley [194], a house only three bays wide with two wings of one-room plan projecting at the corners, is just the kind of house one might expect to be called a villa, yet the caption to Oldfield's drawing calls it, quite correctly, a seat; for no less a personage than the 7th Earl of Salisbury lived there before his accession to the title. On the other hand, Bengeo Hall, a larger house illustrated in the same collection,[4] passes as a villa. The word appears never to have conveyed much specific architectural significance beyond compactness,[5] as opposed to the size and sometimes sprawling appearance of a country house, and of elegance in contrast to weight and grandeur.

193 *'Mr Ginger's villa at Hemel Hempstead' (by permission of the British Library)*

194 *Cecil Lodge, Abbots Langley* (Oldfield)

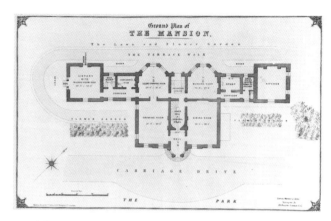

195 *Colney Park mansion, London Colney: plan of the late 19th-century house*

Compactness as a defining quality of the villa manifested itself most noticeably in a small entrance-hall instead of a hall large enough to be a reception room. In this respect, the villa is a phenomenon of the second half of the 18th century. At Colney Park, London Colney [195], the hall was where servants assisted the gentlefolk to take off their outdoor clothes and was not big enough for anything else; Moor Place, Much Hadham, Ashlyns Hall, Berkhamsted, and Marden Hill, Tewin, all had this feature in common, although in appearance they differed much. The increasing efficiency of top-lighting made it possible to remove the main staircase from an outside wall and put it centrally within the house, surrounded by rooms and approached from two or three of them; while the fashion for circular spaces coupled with structural improvements in the support of stairs permitted a greater use of winders with yet further economy of space. Compression of hall and staircase did not go hand in hand. In both respects Colney Park (of *c.*1775) can be regarded as a villa, yet Moor Place, built 1777–9, combined a small hall with a spacious staircase; and Wormley Bury, Hoddesdon, retained the old style of hall with both principal and back stairs packed tightly in the middle, surrounded by rooms great and small.

In the second half of the 18th century, compactness became a virtue sought in every kind of house to some degree, whether villa or not. It became easier to achieve when the division of the interior into a series of more or less equal spaces by means of longitudinal and transverse walls was abandoned. Gorhambury makes an interesting contrast to Cole Green Park or Langleybury in this respect [196]. It had two differently planned staircases, the better one circular, the inferior one straight, but neither against an outer wall; a satisfactory suite of four large rooms carefully differentiated in size to suit their function was contrived by a freer disposition of cross-walls than the old system permitted. The change from square rooms at Langleybury to oblong ones at Gorhambury must have been dictated by fashion, but may have been made easier by improvements in lighting, with thinner glazing bars and smaller sash boxes, and in heating, with more efficient grates.

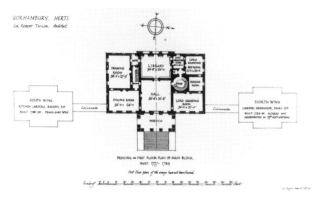

196 *Gorhambury, St Michael: first-floor plan (after J C Rogers)*

The unified country house

The middle block of Wrotham Park, Potters Bar, has been called 'palpably a villa',[*] a tribute to its elegance, which ignores the conflicting aims observable in its plan and elevation [**197**]. A recurrent feature of architectural design is the attempt to give a house an attractive appearance from as many viewpoints as possible and only the most grandiose, like Moor Park, succeeded in subordinating all the service quarters to this ambition. Some service functions were difficult to accommodate. The kitchen, for example, had to be of more than the usual room height to disperse heat and fumes; that was as true of Wrotham Park in 1734 as of Hatfield House in 1612. This, and the desire to exclude the smells of cooking from the house, were two of the factors causing the basement kitchen to fall into disfavour and to be transferred to somewhere more distant from the public rooms. At Moor Park, Rickmansworth, and in a less grandiose way at Langleybury, the kitchen was in a detached building linked to the house only by a corridor. This solution was modified at Wrotham Park by adopting the Palladian formula of a main block connected to flanking pavilions by corridors which themselves fronted rooms, and it was easy to sink the floor of one of the pavilions well below ground level to provide a kitchen. The house may

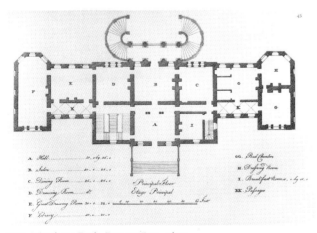

197 *Wrotham Park, Potters Bar: plan*

have been sited with that in mind and, where the fall of the ground permitted, the pavilion solution might equally have been adopted in improving an old house such as Newsells Park, Barkway. Whatever Wrotham Park may owe to the villa concept in appearance, compactness was not one of its virtues; the two staircases, both very grand, confirm that it has as much in common with the spacious, spread-out country house of the early 18th century as with the villa ideal.

Perhaps large houses of this kind, in which the principal part has a villa-like appearance, are not solely the result of influences from villa designs, but rather of convergent development, two quite different strains being bred with a similar end product in mind. Several factors are involved: the separation of services from the gentry household; the desire to unify the house and all its appurtenances, except, usually, the stables, and the need to relate the principal rooms to one another in a coherent sequence. These aims, realised at Bayfordbury [**198**, **199**], were facilitated by the use of top-lighting for staircases, a development fundamental to the superior compactness of late 18th-century plans both large and small.

In Hertfordshire the earliest manifestation of these ideas is at Moor Park, Rickmansworth, where all kinds of outbuildings were assembled in one huge symmetrical composition and every activity not directly related to the family and guests was relegated behind curving colonnades at the front and plainer symmetrical elevations at the back. The ideal of the country house presentable on every side was thus achieved at enormous expense and so was the ideal of separating the gentlefolk from all that might remind them of the labours on which their comfort depended; only essential food and fuel supplies were kept in the house proper. Top-lighting of the two staircases ensured that the plan could be compact, relative to the great size of the principal rooms. This plan must result from the recasting of the earlier large house, the Duke of Monmouth's in the 1720s, but although it possesses some of the virtues that were to be characteristic of villas, it is remote from them in size and purpose. Nor does Wrotham Park really embody the villa idea in its plan, so the type cannot be said to appear in the county until Bayfordbury was begun in 1759, if then.

Bayfordbury presents some intractable problems stemming from an enlargement of the house in 1809–12, making it difficult to reconstruct what it was like as first built, but a key may be provided by the thick walls within the seven-bay shell of the main block, which are likely broadly to represent the earlier disposition of rooms. A squarish space adjoining the present staircase can be interpreted as the well of a predecessor more like the one at Wrotham Park and lit by a window in the outside wall. If this were so, Bayfordbury's resemblance, in its original state, to a villa depends little on the comparative smallness of the entrance-hall; perhaps the verdict in this case should be 'not proven', although the architect aimed to produce something different in kind from the enlarged Cole Green Park or Cokenach.

The compactness of Bayfordbury owes much to the relegation of the subsidiary functions of the house to pavilions

198 *Bayfordbury: entrance front*

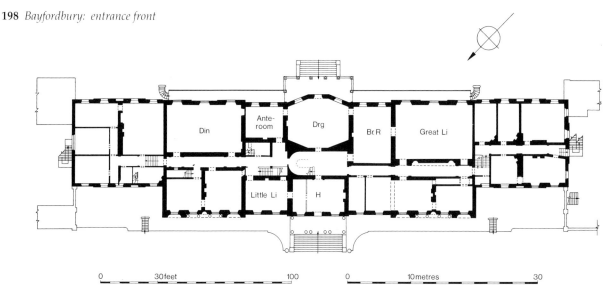

199 *Bayfordbury: plan*

rather than to a service wing. It is this development, combined with the use of top-lit staircases, which increased the proportion of room to circulation space and finally gave the country house the likeness to a villa. Two such houses were begun in Hertfordshire in 1777. At Woodhall Park, Watton-at-Stone, both great and back staircases were together in the middle of the house and around this top-lit central space were grouped all the public rooms. Gorhambury, St Michael, a larger house, retained the older fashion of a large, square entrance-hall with a library (in place of a saloon) behind it, and this, in conjunction with a private suite of rooms for the owner, negated the compactness achieved by locating the staircases in the body of the house.

Compactness was not solely the prerogative of those who built new houses. Undated plans, perhaps of c.1754–69 [**200**], suggest two ways of transforming Beechwood Park, Flamstead, into a compact house. Both involved demolition

of the older half of the house. In one, the wings were retained and the space between them filled up with two rooms; in the other, the walls of the wings facing inwards to the courtyard were demolished and the whole of the rear half of the house, behind the longitudinally placed staircases, was replanned.[7] Hall, dining room and drawing room were the same in both proposals; in the remaining part of the ground floor the questions at issue were how to fit in a library, breakfast room and an apartment comprising bedroom and dressing room. Both plans assumed top-lighting for the staircases. The entrance-hall was to be large but smaller than the library, which corresponded in position, as nearly as an altered house would allow, to the saloon at Bayfordbury, and no doubt it had a similar social function. Only for the more radically altered ground-floor plan does the corresponding first-floor plan exist; it provides at the front for a large ante-room above the entrance-hall between

118

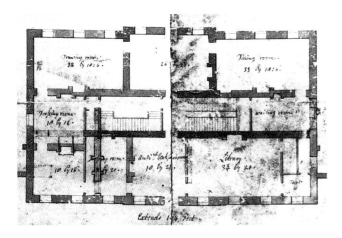

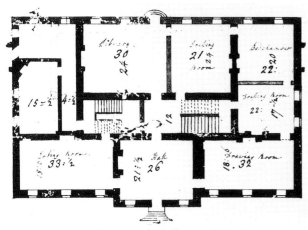

200 *Beechwood Park, Flamstead: plan proposals; ground floor (c.1761) (top); ground floor (c.1754–69) (bottom)*

two large bedrooms, each with a dressing room, and to the rear three smaller bedrooms with dressing rooms. This was a design for entertainment on a noble scale.

How the house was used

The ground or principal floor

Beechwood Park and its analogues illustrate the difficulty of producing a formal typology of late 18th-century country houses, when the relation between the public rooms is elusive and changeable. This difficulty may be resolved in a larger sample where more comparisons can be drawn. In some instances we are helped by the survival of late 18th-century plans; especially valuable are those at Newsells Park, Barkway, which show how every room of a large house was used.

A starting point for the discussion of room use is provided by the observation that the minimum requirement of

a country house in the 18th and 19th centuries was an entrance-hall and four good-sized reception rooms; 'the establishment of this minimum size effectively excludes the 18th and 19th-century villas . . . which were designed for private domestic use rather than for public display and entertainment'.[8] The essential rooms were hall, dining or eating room, drawing room and library and one other. A very grand house like Wrotham Park, Potters Bar, had three other rooms – a saloon, a second or great drawing room, and a breakfast room – and other houses might have one or more of these in addition to the basic four. All these were public or reception rooms in the sense that their use was not confined to family members', but most large houses also had a suite of three private rooms on the principal floor. Wrotham Park had two bedchambers and a dressing room whereas elsewhere, for example at Beechwood Park, Gorhambury and Brocket Hall, Hatfield, one bedchamber might be flanked by two dressing rooms.

From the scanty evidence available, a preferred relationship between the principal rooms is discernible, most clearly in the smaller houses. The most basic conjunction is that of hall and dining (or eating) room and usually where this arrangement is found the dining room lies to the left of the hall on entering; this is the case at Beechwood Park, Brocket Hall, Gorhambury and Wormley Bury, but the arrangement varies in relation to the position of the kitchen. It is in direct descent from the earlier relationship of hall to dining parlour (or great or long parlour) that became common in Elizabeth's reign and persisted throughout the 18th century at Knebworth House and Newsells Park. A second and apparently less constant relationship existed between hall and drawing room (on the right-hand side of the hall), completing a suite of three principal public rooms: dining room, hall and drawing room. Beechwood Park and Brocket Hall were like this, and probably Wormley Bury too, but at Gorhambury, where all the rooms to one side of the central axis were private, the approach to the drawing room was either from the dining room, keeping close to the original sense of 'withdrawing room', or through the library: a different kind of suite with a grander and more logical sequence of rooms.

A library was to be found in any house with pretensions to gentry status but its position relative to the hall varied very much. This was because the function of the room itself was changing throughout the century, from a place where books were stored and read with serious purpose to one which was in effect another drawing room, where the wider range of books by then available might as often be read for entertainment as for information.[9] The contrast between old and new attitudes is revealed in proposals for rebuilding Rothamsted Manor in the 1770s; they show the house as it then existed with a comparatively small study where, no doubt, books were kept along with the owner's private and official papers, and the remodelled house with a bow-windowed library more than twice its size [**201**].

The social purpose of the new room is made clear by its relation to the dining room, intercommunicating with it and replacing the withdrawing room which was immediately

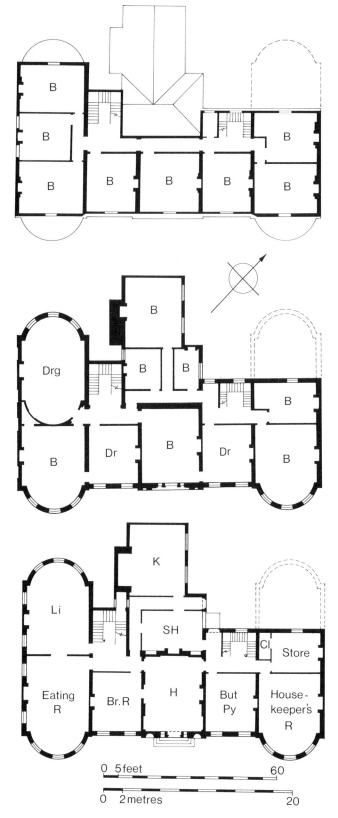

201 *Rothamsted Manor, Harpenden Rural: plans showing proposed alterations, c.1770*

above; functionally, the two must have been more or less interchangeable. For Beechwood Park something similar was proposed. The new library was to face the garden and in one proposal the door into it terminated a vista across the house from the front door, whereas the Great Room it was intended to replace occupied an altogether larger wing, standing a little apart, and similarly at Newsells Park and Wrotham Park. These houses demonstrate successive stages in the evolution from book room to large library with good lighting and pleasant view, then to library as drawing room, and culminating in the last quarter of the century at Watton Woodhall, where the library is near the billiard room and was served by the same dressing room.

In some large houses, the hall declined in importance when its function was usurped by the saloon. Although the hall at Wrotham Park and Watton Woodhall is still much more than the vestibule it was later to become, at Wrotham Park, particularly, it was effectively a large antechamber to the suite of fine rooms that faced the garden, with their vista from dining room to library. Brocket Hall is the only house where the saloon, being twice the size and height of the hall, completely overshadows it and indeed every other room. No doubt this saloon was intended for very grand balls, although it is difficult to know how much the room arrangements here, which differ considerably from anything found in a new-built house, arise from its piecemeal rebuilding.

It is not only the saloon that was different at Brocket Hall. A common dining parlour, perhaps equivalent to a breakfast room, was not so closely related to the hall or the dining room or both, as was the case at Watton Woodhall, Wrotham Park and Rothamsted Manor. Since a breakfast room was also a morning sitting room,[10] its location near both the library, which was a more important room performing a comparable function, and the billiard room was perfectly appropriate; it put the informal leisure rooms on one side of the house and the rooms of state and display on the other. It was a quite different division from that at Gorhambury but equally a functional one. One other ground-floor room deserving mention is the waiting room, where servants waited to be called; they would have been inconveniently far away in the basement, and perhaps the system of bells for calling them was not yet sufficiently perfected for that to be feasible. At Watton Woodhall it was placed between breakfast room and library and next to the back stairs; at Beechwood Park it was to be between dining room and library in the proposed mid-century rebuilding; and at Hatfield House Arthur Young reports its existence without making clear where it was.[11]

The upper floors

Less information is to be had about upstairs rooms because first-floor plans are less often published than ground plans. The likelihood is that the practice of putting reception rooms upstairs was in decline, so that by the second half of the 18th century the old system of two staircases serving two principal groups of rooms had disappeared entirely. This must correspond to some fundamental change, whether of entertaining or of household composition. Late 17th-century plans convey the impression that they were intended for the reception of some socially superior person, rather like a scaled-down version of the relation between royal and private apartments at Hatfield House. Later houses provided a series of apartments, each comprising a bedroom and dressing room, which were all approached from the principal staircase, as if for the less formal reception of equals.

An aspect of the country house so far little explored here is its role as the seat of a family, almost of a dynasty, to which quite distant relatives would feel an attachment, which they would periodically visit, and where unmarried members of the family might take up permanent residence. Briggens, Hunsdon, appears to be an example of this. Cussans lists the monumental inscriptions to Robert Chester, the builder of the house, who died in 1732 in his 57th year, and his sister, Mrs Jane Chester, also of Briggens, who died four years later, also in her 57th year.[12] Presumably Jane had only a bedroom of her own, not necessarily one of the grander ones with a dressing room, and lived as a member of the household; no doubt she had at least one personal servant. The distinction between relatives of her status, whether living in the house permanently or visiting, and the kind of people for whom the principal apartments were intended, was no doubt sharply defined.

What took the place of the two suites of rooms, one grand and one less so, was a series of apartments each comprising a bedchamber with a dressing room, and a number of less important bedchambers without one. Pairs of closets seem only to have remained where they could not easily be removed. Had the courtyard plan of Beechwood Park been abandoned and the house turned, as Matthew Brettingham, the architect, intended, into a rectangular block, the two principal bedchambers would have been reached through a large ante-room, and whereas one of them could also be approached via a dressing room from the staircase, the other could not. These must have been the two principal bedchambers, with either a sitting room or the ante-room which Roger North recommended[13] between them, and were possibly for the owner and an important guest. The proposed scheme entailed demolishing the older rear part of the courtyard house and was not adopted; instead, the front part, built in 1701, was altered to provide three principal bedchambers and dressing rooms in the same space by omitting the ante-room behind. Flanking the courtyard were the two lesser chambers, each with a correspondingly smaller dressing room; and in the range closing the courtyard was another, not particularly large, room, perhaps corresponding to the ante-room at the front, from which the principal bedchambers could easily be reached.

In a grand house like Brocket Hall the chamber (or first) floor had at one corner an apartment consisting of a bedroom and two dressing rooms; it was directly above an identical ground-floor apartment. The remainder of the floor was occupied by five apartments, each comprising bedroom and dressing room. There was also a 'bedchamber with light closet', an expedient adopted when space did not permit a bedroom of reasonable size to have its own dressing room: the bed was placed against one of the short walls of the room between two light screens which partitioned off two closets, the one on the outer wall being well lit by a large window and the other one dark. The same device was proposed at Beechwood Park but for different reasons; the more important of the two principal apartments was provided with both a drawing room and a 'light closet' (probably a powder closet), with the dark space serving as a lobby between bedroom and drawing room. Broken lines on the plan indicate that light closets were also considered within a dressing room at the south-west corner, but if this were implemented it would have made the dressing room itself rather dark, which may be why the proposal is shown tentatively. At Wrotham Park the larger of the two ground-floor bedrooms had light closets; perhaps it was a mark of status to have them as well as a dressing room, even if the latter were shared.

Types of plan

Arrangements for service accommodation

A difficult problem in respect of 18th-century houses is to know how service accommodation evolved: plans and estate maps do not always help to clarify the situation. Brickendon Bury is a typical example. By 1793 it had a service block, hardly smaller than the house itself, to the right of the front elevation, yet around 1790 none of this existed and the services were in a long, narrow back wing [202]. So carefully done were the alterations that the change cannot be deduced from the existing building.

The difficulties the gentry had in deciding where to locate the essential services of cooking, brewing and laundering arose from their changing perceptions of houses and their setting. However large the house, the stables and pos-

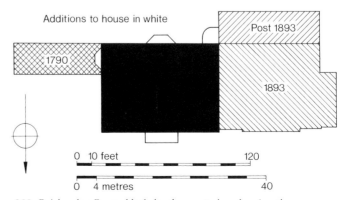

202 *Brickendon Bury: block development plan showing the changing locations of service rooms*

sibly the laundry and brewhouse too, had to be sited away from it, so that, unless such buildings were completely concealed from the house, one of the elevations looked out upon them. When houses were inward-looking, courtyards, cloisters, long galleries and enclosed formal gardens provided privacy and quiet while serving to mask unsightly ancillary buildings; but by the start of the 18th century, house owners had come to demand more of their surroundings and, wherever possible, wanted uninterrupted views from all sides.

Drapentier's engravings show how readily household needs could be adapted to architectural formality, provided the house was intended to impress only when seen from the front or the garden. But the wish for total harmony between house and garden, integrating the house with the landscaped park, became harder to achieve as the numbers and types of household staff multiplied, leading to a greater separation of gentry and servants, with the consequent difficulty of achieving a full architectural integration of the staff accommodation.

In the 1660s and 1670s one closet of the pair opening off the principal bedchambers in houses like Aston Bury Manor would be for a personal servant to sleep in. At Bonningtons, Stanstead Abbots, other servants slept in the almost detached block, large in relation to the house, which housed the kitchen and all service rooms except the cellar. Making the service block inferior in appearance, disposing it as inconspicuously as possible, and hiding it with trees was one way of dealing with it. As a continuator of Defoe's *Tour* remarked of Broxbourne Bury: 'There are also new offices erected at a little Distance from the House, in a Quadrangle. They are placed behind a large Plantation of Trees, so that they do not appear until you are near upon them, yet a convenient Distance from the Mansion house'.[14]

Alternatively, the service functions could be treated as a proud appendage to the house. This was how the problem was solved at Langleybury in the 1720s, where the stable and service ranges, each with a quite imposing front, were arranged on opposite sides of a small courtyard and were joined to the house by a covered passage [203]. Probably there were other houses in Hertfordshire where the service range was treated as monumentally, but all have since disappeared.

For a grander house than Langleybury, a version of this treatment was to unify the whole composition by means of colonnades, as was first done at Castle Howard (North Yorkshire) by Sir John Vanbrugh at the beginning of the century; nearer to hand, Cliveden (Bucks) had been treated in this way by Thomas Archer about 1705.[15] This solution first appeared locally in Benjamin Styles' palatial rebuilding of Moor Park, Rickmansworth, where two enormous quadrant colonnades, concealing extensive service rooms on one side and stables on the other, produced an effect of unity and monumentality unsurpassed in the county. Only the colonnades and not the service buildings themselves were actually joined to the house, probably because the servants and services in direct contact with the gentry household had their quarters in the basement that underlay the whole

203 *Langleybury, Abbots Langley: kitchen and stable blocks* (Buckler)

of the huge house. Not for another thirty years was anything like this solution adopted elsewhere. Instead, a long, straight elevation was preferred in which the bulk of the house was enhanced by single-storey ranges connecting it to two-storey outbuildings. Wrotham Park presaged the popularity of such elevations in Hertfordshire, but its exceptional length was due to the fact that the house behind this noble front was itself unusually large. Even then, no space was found for the kitchen, which, with the stables, was completely excluded from the architectural composition of main block and wings terminating in pavilions. Soon after Wrotham Park was finished, this idea of a long, straight elevation with two pavilions was taken up at Bayfordbury, with terminal blocks in which were located, on one side, the kitchen and on the other the brewhouse and wash-house. The stables were left out of the formal plan and elevation. To incorporate the necessary yard, and at the same time to preserve a long unbroken garden front, would have entailed wings as extensive as those at Moor Park.

Anyone building or rebuilding a house in the last quarter of the 18th century could choose either curved or straight colonnades according to preference. At Gaddesden Place, Great Gaddesden, they curved back from the entrance front to embrace part of the garden; at Balls Park they curved forward, and at Watton Woodhall a hybrid front in two planes broke forward slightly by means of short, curved walls. These big houses were designed to impress; for buildings of a more modest scale, the pattern of Bayfordbury was preferred, whether for the new house at Colney Park, London Colney, or for additions at Beechwood Park, Flamstead, and Boxmoor Place, Hemel Hempstead [204].

T-plan and end-entry houses

The plans of new-built 18th-century houses give the impression of being rectangular in outline and varying in size rather than shape: the result of the double-pile principle. It

204 *'Mr Mead's seat on Box-Moor'* (Oldfield)

excludes from consideration service wings and linked pavilions. Among the exceptions to this uniformity are three houses of T-plan, all of them imperfectly known because two have now lost nearly all their original internal features and the third has long been demolished, yet the break with customary modes of planning that they represent is still of some interest.

The Grove, Sarratt [**205**], is the better preserved of the two survivors. The explanation suggested (see Inventory), which rests on the concept of alternate rebuilding and the analogy of Cassiobury Park, presupposes the existence of an older house of which virtually nothing is known. From the first phase of rebuilding in 1754–61, a house of T-plan emerges [**206**], having as its most significant characteristic two elevations of equal importance: one was the principal or entrance front, the other facing the garden, and in an age which showed as much concern for gardens and parks as for the house they surrounded, that was probably the intention of the design. If an older service wing survived at that

205 *The Grove, Sarratt: front elevation*

time, the consequent limitation of the view in one direction provides an additional reason for building an imposing garden front. Ware Park, Ware Rural, seems to have been broadly like The Grove, in so far as any conclusions can safely be drawn from the very slender evidence.[16] Its most striking feature was the front to the park, sited on a slope to enhance the impression of height, and at the rear of this range was another at right angles to it which must have contained the entrance-hall.

The third house of this little group is The Bury, St Paul's Walden [**207**]. To a house which had been built (or rebuilt) *c.*1730 was added in 1767, perhaps by James Paine, a range at right angles to it, producing a T-plan. This addition incorporated an innovation which marks a more radical break with the past than may at first appear: an off-centre entrance. For the whole of the long period so far covered by this survey, rural houses of every degree had been entered on one of the long sides. In the grand Elizabethan courtyard houses, once the visitor was inside the courtyard, the hall range which constituted the essential house was always so entered. One of Roger North's 'general rules' was 'To have the *entrata* in the middle, because this position serves the whole better than if it be at one end, which must steal much room for entrys. And it is also uniforme without'.[17] At The Bury, St Paul's Walden, the front doorway led into an entrance-hall between two rooms and from the hall into the older house beyond.

The new asymmetrical elevation was imitated *c.*1780 at The Grove, Sarratt, by the architect Sir Robert Taylor. The original front was extended and a wing, shorter than the existing one and providing a new main entrance, was added to form an imperfect H-plan, so that henceforth a house of ten bays plus wings was entered at the end. Whatever the internal circulation was like, and there must have been some problems, the real merit and principal aim of the design was to provide three good elevations with views over the grounds.

Later end-entry houses lacking the bar of the T served to heighten the contrast with normal practice. Kings Walden Bury had been converted to an end-entry house by the time Buckler drew it in 1832 [**208**]; it resembled The Grove in preserving an earlier entrance front, its later entrance was embellished with a Gothic porch, and in the early 1950s it disappeared unrecorded. No more is known about the end-entry phase of Tring Park, where a new owner in the late 1780s created an entrance into the two-storey saloon. The house is now finished from top to bottom with woodwork and plasterwork in the style of Wren, and so thorough was the restoration undertaken by the Rothschilds *c.*1872 that evidence for the late 18th-century work has been obliterated. At Fanhams Hall, Ware Rural, no more than the shell of the early 18th-century house is embedded in a huge neo-Tudor house of 1900; all trace of the extraordinary-looking end elevation depicted by Oldfield and of the plan that went with it has disappeared. The end-entry type evidently was coming into considerable favour towards the end of the 18th century. Tewin Water was built then, in the older fashion with a long front elevation, but not long after-

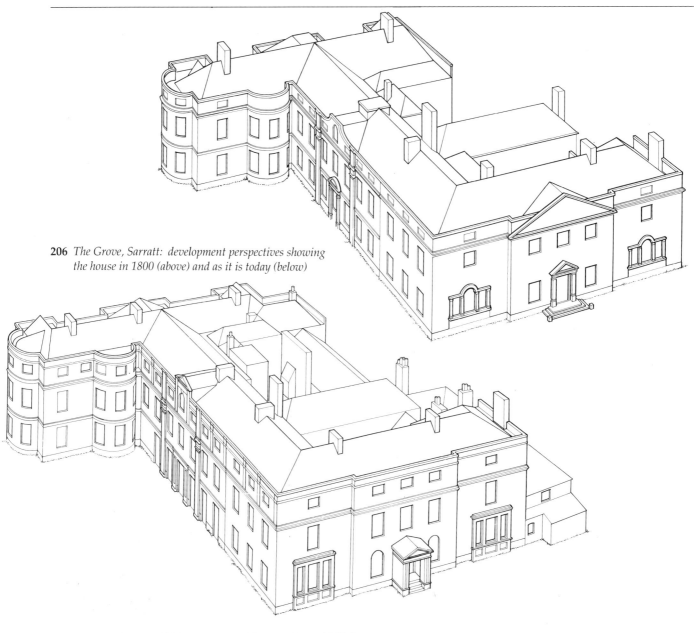

206 *The Grove, Sarratt: development perspectives showing the house in 1800 (above) and as it is today (below)*

207 *The Bury, St Paul's Walden*

208 *Kings Walden Bury* (Buckler)

209 *Tring Park* (Buckler)

wards it was changed in the course of enlargement to have an end-entrance. Unfortunately, hardly any internal details of the rebuilding survived the remodelling by Sir Alfred Beit some hundred years later.

Architectural historians seem not to have discussed the end-entrance plan and, if the fate of such houses in Hertfordshire is typical, little evidence remains. The type persisted into the 19th century but, perhaps because it has not been recognised as a type, examples are hard to find. Stapleton Park (North Yorkshire), now demolished, was perhaps modified to have an end-entrance in about 1820. Another example, also razed, is Tillmouth Park (Northumberland), built in the late 18th century.[18] This plan form may have been favoured because it solved the problem of where to put the service quarters. If they were at the opposite end to the entrance, two long elevations were left clear to face the gardens, or any other pleasing prospect, so enabling more rooms to enjoy an uninterrupted view than could be attained by any alternative arrangement. The evidence is such that this notion is difficult to test, and in any case it cannot apply to all the houses mentioned. Not at The Grove, Sarratt, for example, where the kitchen and other services lay behind one of the long elevations. (Although in a house which presented two important elevations to the

gardens, and had a good entrance front as well, this hardly mattered.) The Bury, St Paul's Walden, with its T-plan, can never have presented quite such an impressive appearance seen from the gardens, and the location of the service rooms is not known, any more than at Kings Walden Bury. The most solid evidence in favour of the idea comes from Tring Park, where removal of the entrance *c.*1786 from its original position left two dignified elevations on opposite sides of the house [**209**]. In plans of this kind, internal circulation depended on corridors flanked by rooms, the corridors often being rather dark as a result. Hunsdon House, rebuilt with an end entry in the early 1800s, may have been modified in the 1860s in order to alleviate the problem, and the top-lighting needed in some parts of the service quarters of The Grove, Sarratt, illustrates the difficulties.

An old house altered: Newsells Park

Most 18th-century building activity took the form of enlarging or partly or wholly rebuilding an existing house. Just that seems to have happened at Newsells Park, Barkway, which is one of only two houses for which the function of every room is known. Rothamsted Manor is the other.

Although Newsells Park was pulled down in the present century, it can be shown with reasonable certainty to have been of 17th-century origin and to have retained into the early 19th century the sharp division between service quarters on one side of the hall and family rooms on the other side and in the rear wing [210, 211]. Features specific to the 18th century are few, principally the large library with what seems to be a later drawing room behind it and, to give the front the general appearance of symmetry, a servants' hall was added on the opposite side with two dressing rooms opening off it. Either the Blue Parlour or the Tapestry Room served as a drawing room to the uncommonly large dining room, itself a grand addition of the late 17th century.

Upstairs, the first floor accorded well with late 18th-century requirements, with very little wasted space. A principal bedroom and its dressing room occupied the whole middle range at the front and there were four more good bedrooms, each with a dressing room, and a fifth with only a closet opening off it (the plan suggests that originally there might have been a pair). The most obvious disadvantage is that some of the passages must have been rather dark. On the second floor, four bedrooms, not counting the nursery and Master Peachey's room adjoining, must have been good enough for the family or guests because they bore names; and it was here that the billiard room was located, well away from the public rooms and conveniently lit by a skylight. Newsells Park was tall enough to have garrets over the attics containing three bedrooms (and four beds) for servants. The only servants to sleep elsewhere were the housekeeper, who had a large ground-floor room, the valet, who had a small bedroom next to the hall, and the menservants, who had separate accommodation over the stables.

We do not know what changes Newsells Park underwent later, but from a comparison of the plan of Rothamsted Manor as existing with the proposals of 1770, the general direction of change in these older manor houses may be suggested. Mostly, the rooms were too small and in the wrong relation to one another, so that the only effective way of bringing such houses up to contemporary standards was by drastic reorganisation of the internal space. This was accompanied by the removal of small external projections to give an up-to-date exterior appearance. Fashion is generally regarded as the most deadly enemy of old houses, and that is true provided fashion is taken to mean not only the current taste in architecture and decoration, but also the contemporary mode of life, for undoubtedly the demands of comfort and convenience posed the greater threat.

210 *Newsells Park, Barkway: 1805 plans of the house and outbuildings; ground floor (below); first floor (opposite below); second floor (opposite above)*

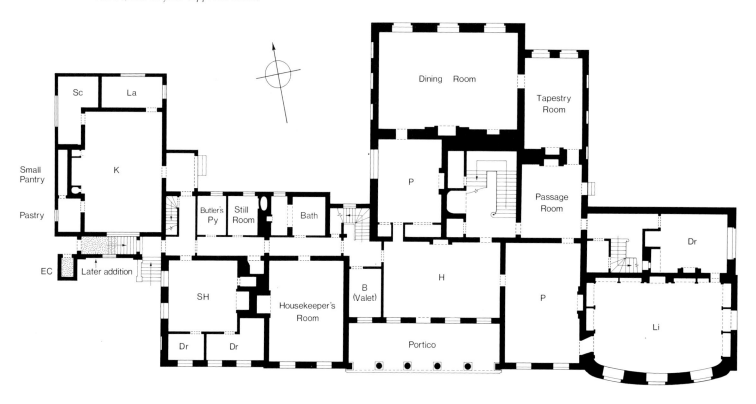

To adapt or destroy?

The question of what to do with the very large houses built before the Civil War troubled the generation which took them on after the Restoration. Arthur Capel rebuilt the greater part of Cassiobury Park and pulled down most of his ancestral house, Hadham Hall, Little Hadham, whereas the 3rd Earl of Salisbury, who adopted Quickswood, Clothall, as his principal residence, seems to have left Hatfield House untouched, carrying out essential maintenance only. A generation later, at the beginning of the 18th century, Knebworth House was completely rewindowed externally and the hall restyled. At Broxbourne Bury, not many years later, the outbuildings were tidied up by erecting new offices around a quadrangle; the owner intended to follow this up with work on the house,[19] an interesting order of priorities. Aspenden Hall seems to have grown continually. It retained its orthodox H-plan, with the medieval hall range, partly updated by refronting, still occupying the traditional position between two wings, until the 18th century. What was originally the solar wing, already greatly enlarged and altered, was then refaced to provide a new principal or entrance front, fourteen bays wide. The date this was done is not known but the change may be the first of its kind in the county except for Cassiobury, which embodies a very different idea of social life.

North Mymms Park followed suit sometime in the late 18th century. Restored in the Elizabethan style in 1893, North Mymms Park now shows little trace of its historical development. Only a late 18th-century drawing reveals that

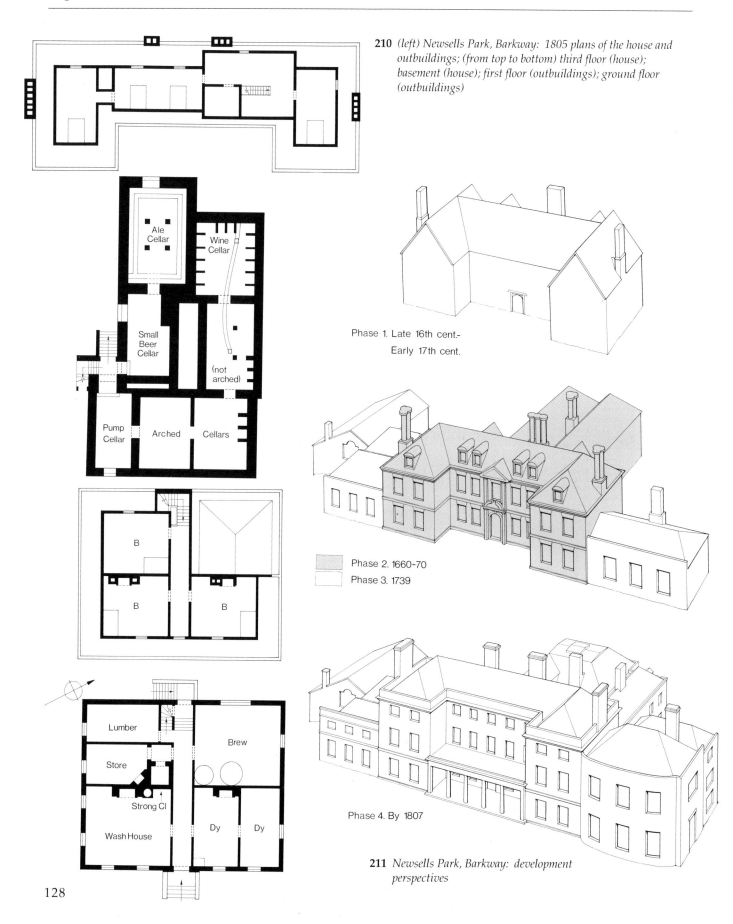

210 (left) Newsells Park, Barkway: 1805 plans of the house and outbuildings; (from top to bottom) third floor (house); basement (house); first floor (outbuildings); ground floor (outbuildings)

Ale Cellar

Wine Cellar

Small Beer Cellar

(not arched)

Pump Cellar

Arched

Cellars

B

B

B

Lumber

Brew

Store

Strong Cl

Dy

Dy

Wash House

Phase 1. Late 16th cent.- Early 17th cent.

Phase 2. 1660-70
Phase 3. 1739

Phase 4. By 1807

211 Newsells Park, Barkway: development perspectives

212 *North Mymms Park: watercolour by T Baskerfield (Meynell Collection)*

the west wing was refaced in the mid 18th century to become a symmetrical entrance front [212]; the original (and present) front underwent little alteration except for new sash windows in the Elizabethan hall. Probably very few of the late 16th-century fittings survived this renovation, which affected principally those parts of the house likely to have had the best fireplaces, doorcases and panelling, that is, the parlour wing and the hall.

Even the informed visitor could hardly guess what has befallen North Mymms Park without knowledge of the 18th-century drawing. Nor is anyone likely to be aware, when looking at Hatfield House, of what occasioned the comprehensive restoration, extending to virtually the whole of the interior apart from a few very important features. It was undertaken to remove all evidence of the changes made by the 7th Earl of Salisbury in the early 1780s, following his decision to demolish Quickswood and renovate the family's principal seat at Hatfield. To make the house suitable for full occupation, after a hundred years of merely keeping it weatherproof, he transformed the east wing (the old royal apartments) into as close a likeness to a house of his own day as the shell permitted, and the wash drawings of his architect's proposals show room after room all in late 18th-century style except for the outer walls, which were left unaltered. In essence, Hatfield House had been brought up to date in the same way as Aspenden Hall or North Mymms Park, in that much money was spent on the family wing while retaining the hall range and service wing because it would have cost too much to replace them. The extraordinary feature of Aspenden Hall is that a house lacking the historic associations of Hatfield should have retained the old hall through a long sequence of alterations.

By these means three large old houses acquired a new lease of life. All had from their beginnings relegated the kitchen and other services to a convenient distance from the family quarters; the continued separation of the two by the hall effectively prevented cooking smells from being a nuisance, whatever inconveniences of communication it may have entailed. At Hatfield House, both the original and the new entrance fronts faced avenues and parkland, and

the refurbished rooms faced the garden; Aspenden Hall and North Mymms Park were no doubt similar. All three houses had the advantages which Repton in his Red Book ascribed to Tewin Water: 'its vicinity to the capital . . . gives it all the Convenience of a Villa, while the size and stile of the house, together with the extent and character of the place, make it an adequate residence'.[20]

The virtues of compactness so widely recognised in the late 18th century brought about a crisis for the huge unwieldy survivals from the age of Elizabeth I and James I. Aspenden Hall survived because its courtyards had earlier been opened up, but even in that reduced form it proved to have no long posterity. Other houses fared worse. Standon Lordship, swept away in 1826 except for its gatehouse, is an instructive example of the difficulty of adapting an old house in changed circumstances. Drapentier's engraving, made presumably in the 1690s, shows a coach-and-six wheeling up to a quite recently opened or rebuilt doorway on the east side of the house. The original gateway had lost its importance and the courtyard its function as an approach. The status of the rooms in that range had changed, no doubt for the worse, and the cost of partial demolition and the building of new accommodation would have been very considerable.

Soon after the turn of the century, Knebworth House had evidently become intolerable and various proposals were made to remodel it. A major problem was the inconvenience of getting from the gatehouse to the house entrance on the opposite side of the courtyard [213], so the first idea was to connect the two by a covered way [214] (an idea once proposed, and perhaps executed, at Beechwood Park) and at the same time to demolish the parlour range and retain the service wing. This was not very promising. Since the approach from gatehouse to hall would still have been long and inconvenient, the idea of the covered way was abandoned and without it the old service range, no longer screened from the approaching visitor, had to go too. The hall range alone remained to form the core of the new house, a long rectangle that presented the old problem of where to put the servants and the messier parts of their

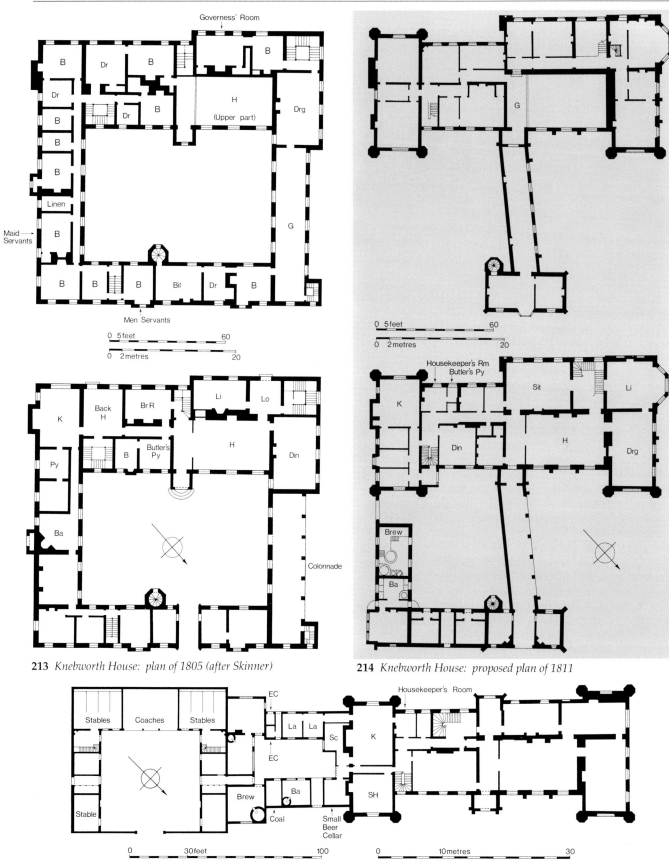

213 *Knebworth House: plan of 1805 (after Skinner)*

214 *Knebworth House: proposed plan of 1811*

215 *Knebworth House: plan of house as rebuilt in 1811*

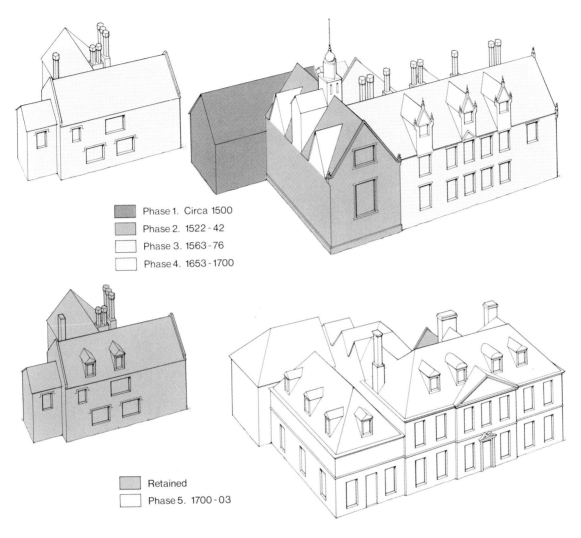

Phase 1. Circa 1500
Phase 2. 1522 - 42
Phase 3. 1563 - 76
Phase 4. 1653 - 1700

Retained
Phase 5. 1700 - 03

217 *Stanstead Bury, Stanstead Abbots: development perspectives*

Retained
Phase 6. 1800 - 33

216 *Knebworth House: perspective drawing from the west of the proposed 1811 rebuilding*

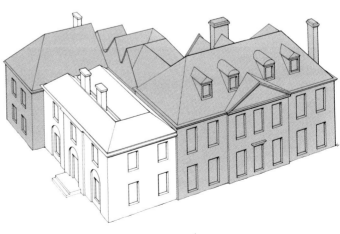

217 *Stanstead Bury, Stanstead Abbots: development perspectives*

work. The idea of an end-entrance was never considered; instead, a service court was sited as far from the front doorway as possible without encumbering the long front and rear elevations and tastefully executed in the Tudor style to match the house [215, 216]. In that way, and by keeping the entrance near one end of a large building, most of the aims of the end-entry plan were achieved with minimal disruption.

Compactness could be achieved in a variety of ways. At Stanstead Bury [217], it was easy to demolish the less important of the two houses that still existed at the end of the 18th century and to create a new entrance front at right angles to the former one: almost a smaller version of The Grange, Sarratt, with the service rooms in the angle between the two arms of the resulting L-plan.

Some houses were so huge and rambling as to defy contraction. The monstrous sprawl of Nyn Park, Northaw, had become a white elephant which could only be pulled down; the job was done so thoroughly that even its site is unknown. Just as unwieldy and inappropriate to contemporary needs were Ashridge House, Little Gaddesden, where only a medieval undercroft survived to form part of James Wyatt's new house, and Hunsdon House, where the cellars are the most obvious remains of what was in some respects the most remarkable house the county ever possessed. It is difficult after nearly two hundred years of alterations to country houses to appreciate just how odd many of them were by the canons of Georgian, and more particularly neo-Georgian, taste. Smaller houses than these could be

trimmed into a more desirable shape, as happened at Markyate Cell which, by the end of the 18th century, must have been a fantastically inconvenient house. Unusually, it is possible to infer something of what the interior was like and how this extraordinary house functioned, and the complexity of the entrance arrangements have been conjecturally restored (see Inventory) to illustrate why some owners found it preferable to demolish rather than to alter.

Houses for the minor and aspiring gentry

While new forms of the country house were developing, the lower gentry and those who aspired to join them continued to build the simple double-pile house. It was also the accepted form for minor houses built by grandees who owned much larger ones, for example, the Duke of Cumberland's hunting lodge at Redbourn, Cumberland House [218]. Such houses vary in size rather than in elevation and it is sometimes difficult to decide which were really gentry houses and which not. Size is one consideration, so is the first-floor plan. It would be possible, by studying the owners' means and way of life, to decide this question more satisfactorily, yet this might still leave uncertain a person's real, rather than assumed, status. Consequently, it may be worth looking for architectural criteria to assist in forming judgements of this kind.

218 *Cumberland House, Redbourn: garden elevation from the south east*

219 *Julians, Rushden*

At the top end of the scale, a seven-bay house like Julians, Rushden [**219**], is unquestionably a minor country house and has been so since the mid 18th century; Fanhams Hall, Ware Rural, and Westmill Bury have to be included on grounds of size, but what about Bayley Hall, Hertford [**220**], and Clare Hall Manor, Potters Bar? A significant difference between these and larger houses may be the abandonment at all except Bayley Hall of the entrance-hall as a room and the substitution of a passage leading to the staircase-hall at the rear, rather like a town house. This mode of planning eliminated the hall as a room as effectively as did the compact planning of country houses some forty years later and need not invalidate their claims to be gentry houses. Three essential rooms – dining room, drawing room and a third which could be library, morning room or breakfast room – are present in all, and in Julians and Westmill Bury a fourth room can accommodate another of these functions.

More significant are the upstairs arrangements. Julians, the one undoubted country house, has four bedrooms, three with dressing rooms; Bayley Hall and Clare Hall Manor have three, two with dressing rooms. It is perhaps the exis-tence of at least two apartments, one of which was available for guests, which established gentry pretensions in the smallest houses aspiring to the name.

220 *Bayley Hall, Hertford: from the north west*

133

That was not the case with all double-pile houses. A modest example at Potters Bar, Salisbury House, has four bedrooms, of which only the principal one has a dressing room; it occupies the space above the entrance-hall; a smaller, later house in Potters Bar, Wyllyots Manor, is similar. Naturally, there is some correlation between these houses in size, number of rooms and number of apartments but it is not particularly close; Newhouse Farm, Ware Rural, bears comparison with Clare Hall Manor in size if the narrow service range of the latter is excluded, but one is a small house aspiring to gentry status whereas the other is a good farmhouse. During the 18th century, the five-bay double-pile house became usual on every farm where a completely new house was required and this type was used for small rural retreats such as Goddards, Widford. By then this kind of elevation had lost its social cachet.

Rectories and vicarages

One manifestation of the rising status of the clergy during the 18th century was the building of rectories and vicarages that were much like the houses of others on the fringe of the gentry. Oldfield's drawings show that a considerable number of clerical residences were rebuilt in the course of the 18th century but only the former parsonage at Bishop's Stortford is at all remarkable. Now called Church Manor

House [221], it was refaced and transformed into a kind of end-entrance plan; the end bays of the three-bay front project boldly forward in a manner reminiscent of Cecil Lodge, Abbots Langley, or Little Cassiobury, Watford; the entrance is in one of the end bays, causing the entrance-hall to be set to one side of the house, as if the constrictions of a town site had operated. From an architectural standpoint, 19th and 20th-century alterations caused most clerical houses to lose whatever interest they originally had, The Vicarage at Abbots Langley, of c.1700, being fairly typical in this respect.

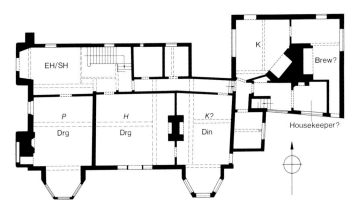

221 *Church Manor House, Bishop's Stortford: plan*

Chapter 8

Medieval towns and town buildings

How different were houses in towns from those in the countryside? Were farmhouses of the type common in the locality gradually adapted to town conditions or were specifically urban house types borrowed from elsewhere? These questions are not easy to answer from the medieval towns of Hertfordshire because little pre-15th-century evidence has come to light. A related problem concerns corporate and other special-purpose buildings, not all of them easily distinguishable from houses; how common are they and where are they located?

Although most towns in this county were small even by English standards this does not mean that the characteristic conditions of urban life did not exist in the Middle Ages, as studies of equally small places elsewhere have shown.[1] Since town building anywhere was governed by the shape, size and accessibility of ground plots it will be necessary first to consider how many places can be regarded as towns and to know where restricted urban conditions applied.

A working definition of a town which will be followed here has been provided by Susan Reynolds. It is a settlement with two principal attributes: the first is that a significant proportion of its population lives by a variety of non-agricultural occupations, notably trade and industry; the second is that it is a social unit distinct from the surrounding countryside, partly because of the difference of occupations and partly because of the greater size and density of its population.[2] This definition embraces three of the twelve criteria according to which urban archaeologists accept town status,[3] namely a relatively large and dense population, a diversified economic base and social differentiation. Some of the other criteria obtained at various periods in several towns. Hertford was the only one to have had defences and a mint; four places had legal autonomy at various times and in different forms; and Hertford and St Albans were judicial centres.

One other criterion, the existence of a complex religious organisation, though more open to interpretation, is applicable to several towns. Hertford, Hitchin and Ware clearly qualify under this head; so do St Albans and Royston which had other religious establishments besides the monastic houses at whose gates they were founded. Berkhamsted and Stevenage, hardly larger than Royston, each possessed a hospital, yet the most surprising case is Standon, now a very rural place, which had three small religious houses. At

Kings Langley, by contrast, the Dominican friary is a piece of royal munificence largely irrelevant to the tiny town.

For Hertfordshire towns to meet this definition fully it would be necessary to establish the occupations formerly carried on in any given place; that, in the present context, is impossible, but the existence of a market is evidence that functions additional to those of an agricultural village were intended, whether or not urban growth actually took place. Within the present county boundary several places are known to have been deliberately founded as towns, or are recorded as having burgesses, or were granted the right to hold a market, and all can be regarded properly as towns or potential towns. Nearly all are known to have had a market or a fair [222] although one place, Harpenden, had a fair but no market and clearly never was a town. Wheathampstead, which once had a market-place, either never grew to be a town or ceased to be one comparatively early. Rickmansworth, on the other hand, of which Leland said definitely that it 'is no market town',[4] was presumably a place of some importance by the early 16th century; the concentration in and around it of men of substance in the late 15th century suggests the existence of a nascent town before the charter of 1542. Hemel Hempstead, which also lacked the formal qualifications of a town before 1539, receives the merest mention from Leland.[5]

Early market-places: their shapes and related streets

Recent work on late Saxon towns has shown that market-places have changed their size and shape to a greater extent than used to be believed,[6] and that a large market-place in a town of pre-Conquest origin may itself be a post-Conquest addition.[7] For Hertfordshire few results of archaeological investigation in towns are yet available and instead the conclusions reached by William Page in his studies of topography are broadly followed here.[8]

St Albans possesses the oldest datable market-place in the county [223, 224]. The abbey was founded c.793 but it was not until c.969, as part of the revival of religious life in

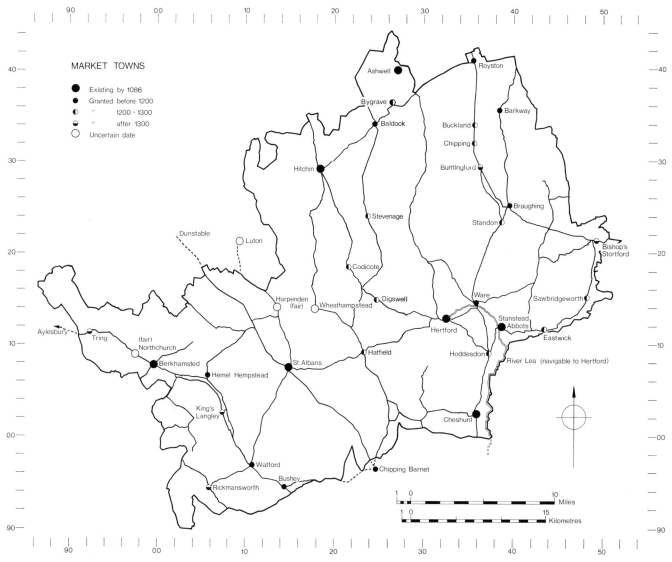

222 *Map depicting market towns in Hertfordshire*

the age of Dunstan, that the monastic community was reformed and a new settlement founded.[9] Its essential element was a market-place forming an elongated triangle based on the abbey precinct and continuing as a wide street to St Peter's church where it narrowed to become the road to the north west. It was larger than later market-places because it was intended to serve the whole of Cashio hundred. The new settlement was built around this large open space, on which were centred the trade and services which caused the place to prosper. It lacked a feature of many later towns: the back lanes providing access to the rear of the long narrow plots of land fronting a triangular market-place.[10] A second trading place was the open space called Romeland[11] where fairs were held; its original boundaries to the south and east are marked by the abbey gateway and what is now George Street, but those to the north and west are ill defined.

Hertford, with 146 burgesses, was easily the largest town in the county in 1086. Formed by two burhs built successively in 912 and 913 to defend the north and south sides of the River Lea, it had two market-places [225]. The one in the earlier burh was approximately triangular and is now represented by Old Cross; it was small by comparison with the similarly shaped one at St Albans. Less is known about its counterpart in the south burh, where the present small market-place appears to be a remnant of something larger.[12]

Another and much smaller borough, Ashwell [226], appears in Domesday Book without mention of any date of foundation. The market-place lay to the south of the church; two lost street names, Old Chipping and Market Hill, establish its existence and late 17th-century references to gardens formerly part of the market-place[13] indicate its late medieval size. The origins of Hitchin [227] are equally obscure and this is the more remarkable because, according to Page, it had a roughly triangular market-place as large as the one at Ashwell or St Albans although now so much built on as to disguise its original form completely. Neither Hitchin nor Ashwell had streets of any importance outside the bounds of the original market-place; in both places the market is likely to have served the hundred, Hitchin and Odsey respectively.

Rectangular market-places are rare in Hertfordshire, the town of Sawbridgeworth having perhaps the only one. Most markets were accommodated in either a small elongated triangular space or a widening of the main street, both types being common throughout England. In roadside settlements a widened street is usual, as at Barkway. Sometimes the widening tapered at one end and had a rectilinear termination at the other, as at Berkhamsted [228], but

224 *Market Place, St Albans: from the north*

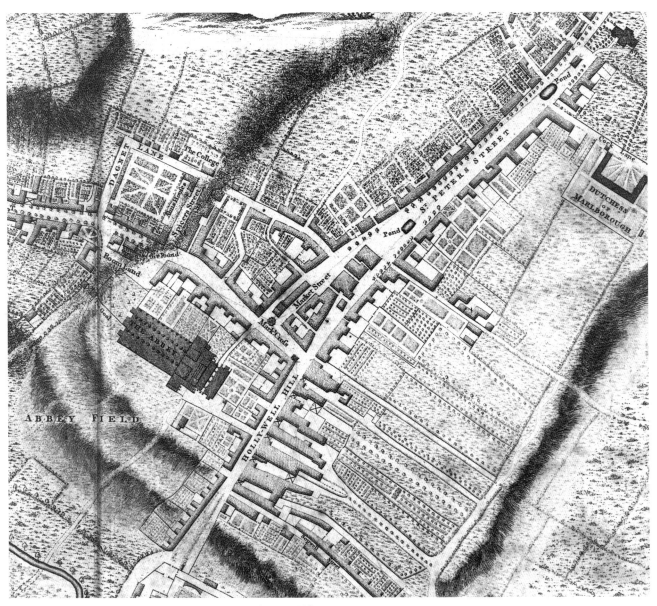

223 *St Albans: detail of town plan by Dury and Andrews, 1766*

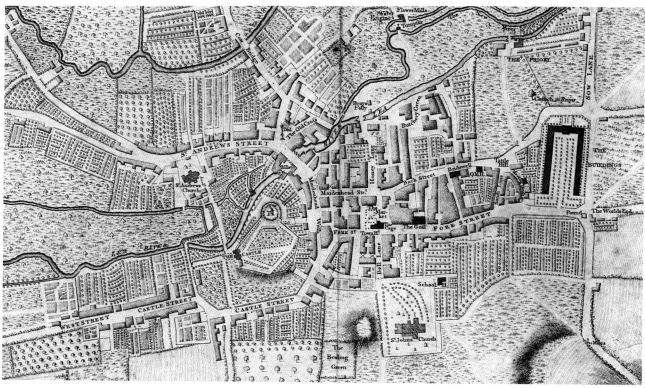

225 *Hertford: detail of town plan by Dury and Andrews, 1766*

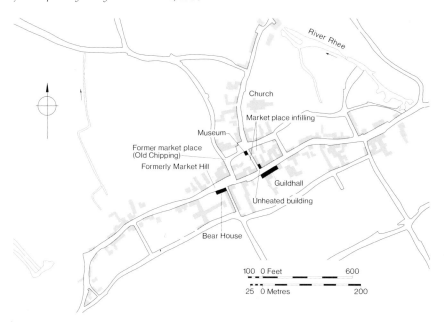

226 *Ashwell: town plan*

in some of the less well-preserved towns, for example, Standon, the precise shape is difficult to establish. When widened streets were used, a through road was diverted wherever possible to ensure that traders had no alternative but to enter the market and pay tolls on the appropriate day; and there was an attempt to ensure that only one place

was suitable for the erection of stalls and the sale of goods. A diversion of this kind may have taken place at Kings Langley [**229**], where, if the street called *Newechepeynge* in 1416 is correctly identified with the present High Street, there is the appearance of small-scale town planning incorporating two back lanes.

138

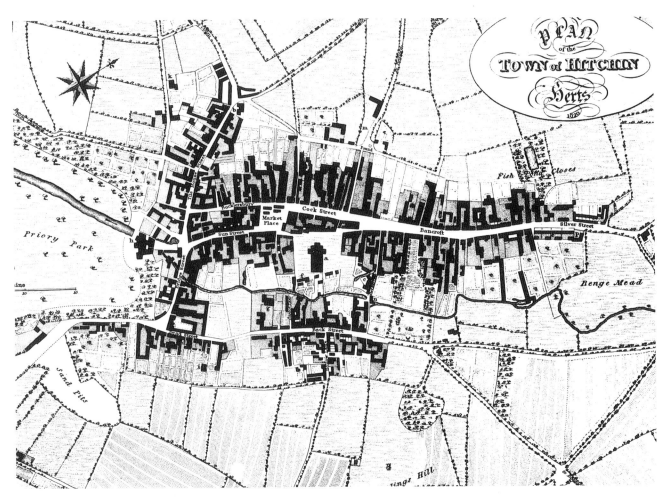

227 *Hitchin: town plan*

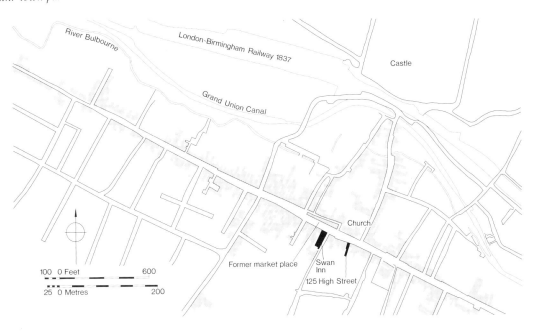

228 *Berkhamsted: town plan*

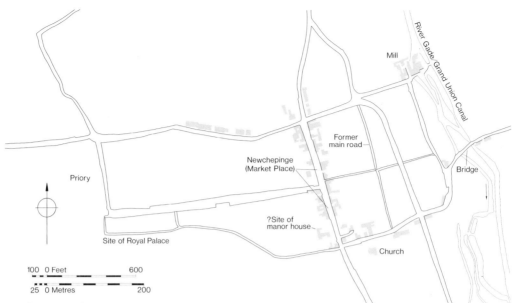

229 *Kings Langley: town plan*

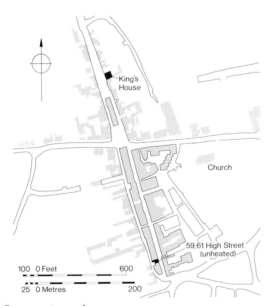

230 *Royston: town plan*

Some towns definitely had more than one market-place. The presence of two at Hertford is explained by the town's origin as two defensive bridgeheads. Two market-places at Royston [**230, 231**], one in Hertfordshire, the other in Cambridgeshire, were created by widening Ermine Street on both sides of the Icknield Way which formed the county boundary; Baldock also has two adjacent market-places [**232**], a large funnel-shaped one forming the High Street and a smaller one at right angles to it forming White Horse Street; but the most unusual case is Ware [**233, 234**], with two market-places in series, the eastern one definitely triangular and perhaps the western one too, set apex to apex. Since such double provision is evidently common, the

explanation may lie either in the sale of different kinds of goods or produce or (less probably) in the use of one of them for fairs as well as markets; for even where the market-place was as large as it was at St Albans, the fairs were held in another place.

The relation of major buildings to market-places

In any town, two major buildings, church and manor house, are not necessarily closely related to the market-place but their siting is potentially significant. In some towns such as Kimbolton (formerly Huntingdonshire, now Cambridge-shire) the church stands at one end of the market-place and the castle, the seat of lordship, at the other.[14] In the towns of Hertfordshire the location of the church is generally obvious, while that of the castle is often hard to find. In Hertford, neither was located with reference to a market-place. At St Albans, where religious and secular authority were in the same hands, the situation was fittingly reflected in the domination of the market-place by the abbey tower and at Royston the situation was similar.

Elsewhere, the close relation of market-place to parish church, and particularly to the churchyard, is significant, for markets were commonly held in churchyards in the 12th century. Historically, the creation of a separate market-place in an ancient town marks the time when trading had grown to the point of needing special facilities and, in a small settlement newly endowed with market rights, the intention of creating a town. Hemel Hempstead [**235**], one of ten towns where the churchyard stands in close proximity to the market-place and a latecomer among Hertfordshire

231 *Royston: view south down Kneesworth Street. On the left (with tall chimneys) is King James's 'Palace'*

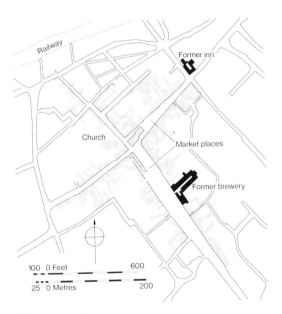

232 *Baldock: town plan*

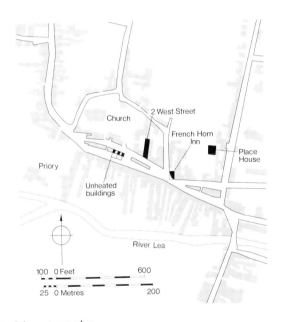

233 *Ware: town plan*

towns, chartered only in 1539, illustrates the latter case. Its late foundation preserved details which have been lost in the older towns. During a legal dispute in 1677, a witness related 'that the ground that is now the market-place was in fields that were plowed there, not being above two or three houses there standing in or near the said place . . . called Churchend, and that when the town had a market granted

then the Market Street was taken out of the fields and built upon'.[15] Some similar process must have occurred in other places where the churchyard flanks the market, such as Watford, Bushey and Tring. The new street at Hemel Hempstead is wider than its approach roads, like the market-places at Barkway and elsewhere, and to the west runs beside the churchyard, from which it was screened by

141

234 *Ware: view east along the High Street. To the left, the market hall; to the right (in background), the French Horn Inn*

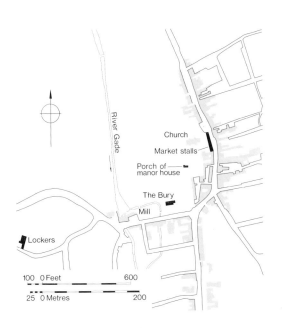

River Gade

Church

Market stalls

Porch of manor house

The Bury

Mill

Lockers

100 0 Feet   600

25 0 Metres   200

235 *Hemel Hempstead: town plan*

the market hall and stalls. The uncertainty felt by the vicar and churchwardens as to what was churchyard and what was market-place is apparent from a mention in the terrier of 'Twelve sheddes used for staules for Butchers, but whether any of these particulars be churchyard land or not wee doe not knowe'.[16]

At Wheathampstead, a similar conjunction suggests that the High Street adjoining the church was the site of the former market-place, whose shadowy existence is otherwise attested only by references in court rolls, and it may not be coincidence that even today, in that one place, continuously built-up frontages on both sides of the street give a faintly urban air lacking in many another village. Generally it is a mark of the successful market town that a screen of shops or market buildings has grown up to separate market-place from churchyard, as at Watford and Hitchin and perhaps once at Tring. In other towns the parish church stood at one end of the market-place: Berkhamsted, Hatfield, Sawbridge-worth, Standon and Ware, and Chipping Barnet which is no longer in the county. In all these places the creation of a market-place may have entailed the separation of commercial from social functions, with the churchyard retaining its importance as a meeting-place on Sundays and festivals.

The building, usually in the 15th century, of church houses or marriage-feast houses, reflects the continuing use for social purposes of both church and churchyard.

Finally, there is a small group of towns in which the market became established away from the original focus of settlement around the church. This occurred at Buntingford (in the ancient parish of Layston), Codicote and Stevenage; and Barkway differs only in so far as the church is quite near the new market, though not related to it by design.

Few Hertfordshire market towns have manor houses. Where a castle existed, jurisdiction can be presumed to have been exercised from it. At Berkhamsted and Bishop's Stortford the castle lay well away from the town and the church dominates the market-place. In some places, a manor house stands near the church, much as it would in a rural parish; Hemel Hempstead and Watford are like this; while at Berkhamsted, where a manor house is hardly to be expected, an unusually large house with an open hall, No. 125, lies on the opposite side of the High Street south of the church. The most interesting town in this connection is Ware, the one place in Hertfordshire which demonstrates as forcibly as Kimbolton the presence of the ecclesiastical and secular authorities. Here, the parish church and the manor house adjoin the broad ends of their respective market-places; both were probably always screened off from the street by a row of shops. Ware is the only town with a manor house (Place House) old enough to be relevant to the medieval plan. In some other places the situation is confused by a much later building known as the manor house, with nothing to substantiate the claim. At Buntingford, a large early 19th-century house stands in an appropriate position, occupying much of the west side of the market-place, and on general grounds the replacement of several market tenements by so big a residence at that late date seems unlikely.

Plot sizes

No work has yet been done to determine the original layout of Hertfordshire towns, and consequently the schematic town plans [226, 228–230, 232, 233 and 235] are based on inferences from Ordnance Survey maps of the later 19th century.

The size and shape of the plots of ground fronting the market-place and main streets obviously were determinants of architectural form. Triangular market-places like that of St Albans might in theory have provided a regular pattern of holdings, yet some interruption is always present. Ware illustrates the point. On the south side, the tenements all run down to the river and the regular pattern is distorted only where the road curves round to the river crossing – a bridge since the reign of King John and formerly a ford. On the north side, since the market-place is sited clear of the church, the manor house provides the only break in a regular layout. It would be of interest to know why the manor

house was placed as if to permit a screen of small buildings between it and the street. This seems to have been usual in other towns where large houses lay at the rear of a court-yard; Shrewsbury affords some striking examples and it may represent a widespread European development.[17] In Ware, from the first, a variety of plot sizes was envisaged and some tenements had very little land; such plots must have been either for the poorest of those inhabitants able to pay rent or were lock-up premises.

Buildings without fireplaces

Lock-up premises are barely mentioned in the literature on medieval town architecture, no doubt because they are assumed to have been too humble to have survived, yet quite large buildings of this kind existed and played an important role in town development. A number are still extant and three were recorded in sufficient detail to establish that none originally had a chimney-stack. In St Albans, 2 Market Place [236] is of three storeys and two bays and was probably built in the early 15th century. Two ground-floor partitions, known only from mortises, suggest that the front room was a shop with a passage from the front to the staircase, permitting the movement of goods to the upper floors. The second partition stood parallel to the first and only 6 ft (1.8 m) away, and a gap suggests that there was a doorway or hatch in it. The space between the partitions is rather narrow for a shop, though not impossibly so, and the remaining space perhaps allowed a narrow entrance from

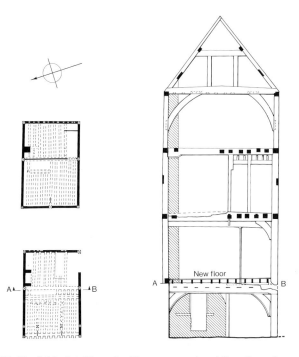

236 *No. 2 Market Place, St Albans: ground and first-floor plans and cross-section*

237 *No. 94 High Street, Ware (extreme right of photograph): the framing was applied during 'restoration' in 1981*

the street to the doorway or hatch; if the latter, the middle part may have been no more than a counter, in its old sense of a place of payment. That leaves open the question of how the rear half of the ground floor was used, and it was perhaps there that the making or preparation of whatever was sold went on. Strangely, there is no trace of a partition separating this part from the rest, whereas both the first and second floors clearly formed two rooms. Possibly the need for some natural light from the front of the building was greater than it was upstairs; certainly any difference of function was not sharp enough to require physical separation.

Another building of this kind was revealed in Ware when 94 High Street was renovated [**237**]. It is altogether smaller, being on a narrower plot and only two storeys high, and has the complication that on the ground floor one of the long walls appears to have been partly open, as if the trading premises once included an adjoining space which could be closed off at will. The third example, 15 Bucklersbury, Hitchin, resembles the Ware building in size. Again, the ground floor was not divided into rooms, the structural division into two bays being emphasised only by a double chamfer running along the binding-beam and down its supporting posts. The only partition was a short one at the back, screening off the original staircase.

All three buildings may have been shops but this can only be suggested by analogy with a building at Ashwell, now the museum, which has the distinctive wide openings of a shop. Each of these was closed by a large shutter, the 'flappet of wood' of the early 17th century, which, when lowered to a horizontal position, could serve as a counter for the display of goods.[18] In other respects, notably the undivided ground floor, this building resembles those at St Albans, Ware and Hitchin.

No other unheated building presents clear evidence of its internal arrangement and the situation is further obscured by the removal of chimney-stacks in order to gain space on valuable town centre sites, yet despite these doubts several

likely examples can be listed. The most prominent and surprising example is the Black Lion public house at Bishop's Stortford [**238**], a building on a corner site which is jettied both at the front towards Bridge Street and on the side facing Devoils Lane; it stands at the foot of the hill leading to the market-place and clearly was intended to make an impression on all who approached the town from that direction. This corner block is richly ornamented by local standards, having two jettied gables on its main elevation as well as the moulded first-floor jetty with a carved corner-post. Pendants below the ends of the tie-beams carry a depressed four-centred arch across the gables – this in addition to the more commonplace close-studding and bay windows with plaster coves below the sills; yet, so far as can now be seen, no provision was made for a chimney-stack, either here or in the adjoining building in Devoils Lane which may have been connected with it.

Also comparable to the Black Lion is 26 Baldock Street, Ware (now the Old Bull's Head). It has a perfectly clean crown-post roof and no trace of an old fireplace or stack, or even the defaced jambs of stone or brick that often remain when a lintel has gone. On the opposite side of the street, No. 45 is representative of several small two-bay jettied houses in various towns. They are rendered outside and bare of old features inside, uninformative about either their date or function but having in common the absence of a large old chimney-stack or a space from which one might have been removed; and they occur surprisingly frequently: No. 21 North Street, Bishop's Stortford, is one, 6 George Street, St Albans, another, which resembles the service bay of an urban Wealden but can hardly be so because the fall of the street precludes a hall at either end.

All these problematic buildings are of two storeys except 23 Market Place, Hitchin, which is a tall and surprisingly narrow (9 ft/2.74 m wide) building. All resemble a cross-wing placed transversely to an open hall set at the side or rear; yet, although it is possible that some halls have disappeared, it is hard to believe that this can often have happened when so many fragmentary ones remain. Nor is the notion of alternate development (p 96) easy to sustain, for in

238 *The Black Lion, Bishop's Stortford: from the north east*

that case some evidence of a substantial post-medieval building might be expected to survive. The removal of wooden chimney-stacks, so frequently postulated in these pages, may account for some apparently unheated houses of this type, but only if it can be shown that such stacks were built against outside walls.[19]

The notion of braziers standing on wooden upper floors is sometimes put forward to permit buildings without chimney-stacks to be interpreted as houses but until such time as the discovery of brazier fragments, tiled places for braziers to stand on, or of references to braziers in probate or other inventories, it can be discounted.[20] Moreover, there is the question of fuel. Charcoal was the only source of heat which did not give off smoke, although fumes remained a problem. In 1621, a witness in a court case remarked of the plaintiff, one of the Six Clerks of Chancery, that the 'usuall fyer which he useth in his lodging and dyning romes in the Country is the same manner of fuell which he soe used in his chamber here, namely charcoale & small coale upon them'.[21] Further reference to stirring the ashes together makes it clear that this fire was made in an ordinary hearth discharging into a chimney, not in any kind of brazier. For these reasons, and bearing in mind that charcoal was relatively expensive, houses without fireplaces or open hearths are referred to here as being unheated.

Unheated jettied buildings exist in towns outside Hertfordshire but have rarely been described as such, partly because the situation is often obscured by the addition of a chimney-stack and perhaps partly because it is hard to envisage a function for such buildings of quality in the English climate. The problem exists in Salisbury.[22]

239 *Nos 59/61 High Street, Royston*

Specially sited buildings in market-places

In Royston High Street, which is on the line of Ermine Street and runs downhill to the centre of the town, there is a two-storeyed timber-framed structure, No. 61, which is of the 15th century and was perhaps once part of a larger building [**239**]. At the north end, facing down the Hertfordshire market-place, this building is jettied, as it is on the east side, with a dragon-beam and carved corner-post. Again, the lack of heating suggests it was not built as a house. It must have been erected for trade or business purposes, but with the evident intention of visually dominating the market-place from its position at the upper and narrower end of it.

It is not the only one of its kind. At the west end of the market-place in Berkhamsted, where the wider market area narrows to the main road, stands a building jettied on two sides, the end jetty facing the church at the other end of the market-place. That is what appearances suggest was intended, although here, as in Royston, only the adjoining building which now masks the end jetty is definitely of a later date, and it may imply that the other buildings are also

subsequent infilling. In the later Middle Ages they formed 'le Shopperowe'.[23] At St Albans, jettying gave prominence to No. 12 George Street, which appears to have had two elevations so treated; one towards the narrow street leading to the parish church of St Andrew,[24] the other, now concealed by the adjoining building, towards Romeland.[25] Its appearance can be appreciated in a Buckler drawing of Hemel Hempstead, showing 60 High Street with one jetty at the gable end facing the street and another on the long wall facing part of the market-place [**240**]. Not that architectural display was confined to the ends of market-places. At Ware a late medieval building somewhere on the site of Nos 65–73 High Street proved, before it was pulled down in 1898, to have unglazed windows with cinque-foiled ogee heads and trefoiled spandrels which, until Middle Row was built, looked up and down the market-place.

Perhaps the exact site chosen for these early timber-framed buildings mattered less than their novelty and their greater height above their neighbours. Although no systematic attempt has been made to discover how the market-places at Royston and Berkhamsted were gradually built over, the jettied buildings clearly imply that the major part was either still filled with movable stalls or that any permanent stalls were of so little architectural consequence that a conventional timber-framed structure stood out among them. Confirmation that movable stalls still existed at a

240 *High Street, Hemel Hempstead* (Buckler): *the building to the left of the spire is now No. 60*

much later date comes from the legal proceedings concerning Hemel Hempstead already mentioned (p 141).

The significance attached to the mode of support of structures in the market-place was expressed in the question: 'Do you know the Market house, Court house and Shambles did stand on pattens or wheels'? Here 'patten' is presumably used to mean a bottom plate or sill, to distinguish between immobile and mobile structures; but the answers are confusing. According to one witness, 'some of the shambles and stalls . . . about thirteene yeares agoe were fixed to the soyle . . . by a brick ground penn and that the same are since digged up and sett upon wheels'; a second said that the Shambles 'are moveably stood on pattens until lately set on wheels'. 'Moveable' is either a mistake or is used in the sense of a movable screen in a medieval hall, as something which could be moved if enough labour were available, because a third deponent spoke of having brought 'about fifty years since . . . timber and gravell to fasten the said Shambles . . . to the ground'.[26] These terms, whatever their precise significance, reveal a situation in which stalls could become permanent structures or be converted back to mobility in response to the policy adopted by the owner of the market rights. This situation contrasts with that at St

Albans, where a change in the terminology of conveyances, from stall in the 13th century to shop in the 14th, has been taken to correspond to the change from impermanent to permanent buildings.[27]

The advantage gained by investing in a building of striking appearance and situation may well not have outlived the builder. At Royston the situation was altered, perhaps less than fifty years later, by the construction on the adjoining plot of a building (No. 59 High Street) which completely masked the end jetty. The newcomer was inferior in so far as it was of only one and a half storeys, not two, but concern for appearances was not neglected and two jetties were provided; only this time the likelihood that the adjacent plot would one day be built on was recognised and both jetties were on the long walls. Even if, as was argued earlier, the jetty was primarily a mode of architectural display (see p 35), other motives may yet underlie its adoption in particular circumstances; for example, it provided some shelter for unglazed shop windows. The earlier of the two Royston buildings, No. 61 High Street, presumably had the shop windows on two sides, like many jettied town buildings on corner sites. If that is so, it implies that there was no stall immediately adjoining to the north, and that when No. 59

146

was built it restricted access to its neighbour. But there is a curious contrast between them. No. 61 was built to front what is now High Street, as if that part of the market-place was perceived to be better for trade. Here, as in other places, encroachment tended to favour one side of the market-place rather than the other. Thus at St Albans the older buildings in Market Street appear to have been better than those in Chequer Street, and in Ware the contrast between the south side of High Street and the generally poorer quality of the buildings in East and West Streets would have been perceptible in the late 15th century.

Official buildings

Few civic buildings have survived in Hertfordshire from the Middle Ages, and the ease with which they were swept away indicates their relative unimportance. Compared with their counterparts in continental towns, English civic buildings are usually small and architecturally disappointing, although the Clock Tower in St Albans market-place, erected between 1403 and 1412, is a great rarity and an exception to the rule [241].

St Albans has a second official building which is fre-quently claimed to be medieval, the former town hall, now 25 Market Place. The only evidence of its purpose is provided by the mouldings on first-floor posts which are returned along arch-braces and tie-beams; they indicate an important room or hall of at least four bays. It was, however, built in the late 16th century and differs only in size and detail from other guildhalls and halls of fraternities. The ground floor was occupied partly by the borough gaol and the rest was given over to some fairly humble use such as the stabling which existed there prior to 1738.

Guildhalls were among the largest and best-finished secular buildings. From an architectural standpoint, the best of them, the building known as The Brotherhood, Hitchin, displayed a remarkable amount of finely moulded timber. Although no evidence of internal subdivision remains on the ground floor, an old photograph appears to show a partition, so it may have been partly enclosed and partly an open structure of posts carrying the upper floor. Upstairs was one large room open to the roof, enriched to provide suitable state for the meetings of the Guild of Our Lady and with mouldings that date the hall to soon after 1475, when the Guild was founded. A year later the Brotherhood or Guild of St John the Baptist was founded at Ashwell, and its members likewise proceeded to build a hall [242]. It, too, was jettied at the front but the plainer timberwork no doubt reflects

241 *The Clock Tower, St Albans: looking north*

242 *Hall of the Guild of St John the Baptist, Ashwell*

the comparative prosperity of the respective guilds and towns. The Ashwell guildhall had a more domestic-looking plan than its grander fellow; each floor was divided into a large and small room, the smaller one upstairs divided by an axial partition into what look like buttery and pantry. These differences of plan suggest some difference of function as compared with guildhalls in larger towns, a purely architectural impression being that the Ashwell building was more parochial, fulfilling purposes like those of a marriage-feast house or a church house like the one at Barley, and with little concern for a splendid setting for the civic power which only the truly urban guilds had. Little is known about other town guilds, and even less about their halls.[28]

Between guildhalls and church houses there were structural resemblances and a functional overlap. Church houses appear hardly to have existed in towns, although No. 43 St Andrew's Street, Hertford, on the edge of St Andrew's churchyard, has been suggested as one. Usually they are found in the larger villages or decayed towns such as Braughing, where the church house was described in a late edition of Defoe's *Tour* in terms which make the difference between it and a guildhall clearer: 'Near the churchyard is an old House . . . which was given with all Sorts of Furniture for Weddings. They brought hither their Provisions, and had a large Kitchen, with a Cauldron, large Spits, and Dripping-pan; a large Room for merriment; a lodging-room with a Bride-bed and good Linen . . .'.[29] Bride-chamber excepted, a guildhall needed the same kind of facilities for feasts, and the absence of a kitchen in guildhalls at Ashwell and elsewhere may be because prepared food could easily be obtained from the many cooks and bakers usual in medieval towns. Defoe's continuator was, of course, referring to a church house as it existed some two centuries later than the guildhalls mentioned above, and the mere difference of date may have brought about the building of a kitchen. A puzzling example of this building type is

Bury Farm, Wheathampstead [243], which was not a farmhouse and has all the appearance of a guildhall or church house, originally without any chimney-stack or fireplace. The existence of such a building in a very rural setting shows that the architectural type represented by the guild or market hall could be adapted to somewhat different purposes.

Open-hall houses

Medieval houses are not infrequently reported from English towns and this usually means no more than that the roof of an open hall has been discovered. The kind of information that might show how the house was used is usually lacking because the ground-floor rooms have been gutted or totally refurbished, and consequently the understanding of such houses is at a lower level than that of farmhouses where, for example, the upper or parlour end is usually distinguishable from the service end. King's Lynn is a rare exception to this, but in Hertfordshire the best that can be done is to single out known town types.

One characteristic kind of urban building appears on the eastern side of the county, namely the small or 'single-ended' version of the Wealden house with subsidiary rooms at only one end of the hall. It occurs in pairs at Hertford – 19/21 St Andrew's Street and 20/22 West Street – and at Hitchin where, until recently, the bold plaster cove to the eaves of the hall, which is a diagnostic feature of any kind of Wealden, could be seen at Nos 31 and 33 Bancroft. Urban Wealdens are best known in pairs or longer ranges and commonly in small towns or in the less intensively developed parts of larger ones, for example, Coventry, but at least two Hertfordshire examples, 3 St Andrew's Street, Hertford, and 8 High Street, Bishop's Stortford, stand alone. Neither shows much in the way of mortises or partitions to indicate how the ground floor of the two-storeyed bay was

243 *Bury Farm, Wheathampstead*

148

244 *No. 137 Fishpool Street, St Albans: from the north east*

used, whether as an ordinary service room or, in part or in whole, as a shop, and so far as present knowledge goes these little hall houses may have been purely domestic.

That the single-ended Wealden is fundamentally an urban house type is proved by its distribution, yet the existence of one in Much Hadham is relevant to the question of what is or is not a town. Morris Cottage is now single-ended; whether it was once double-ended is difficult to establish; even if it was, that may not provide a final answer to the question, for Yew Tree Farm in the same village is structurally, though not visually, a single-ended Wealden, and a shop at that, added to an earlier cross-wing. These examples illustrate the difficulty of distinguishing between urban and rural house types. Just as a village like Much Hadham was large enough to provide employment for some craftsmen, so might houses in all but the market-place or the few fully built-up streets of Hertfordshire towns have been connected with some kind of farming activity. No town in this county has produced evidence comparable, for an arable area, to that of Pickering (North Yorkshire)[30] where nearly all the old houses had an attached byre; but the agricultural component of Barkway, for example, must have been large.

The lack of any clear difference between town and country houses is shown just as clearly by the distribution within the county of double-ended Wealdens. A small one at St Albans, 137 Fishpool Street [244], is disguised by an 18th-century brick front, and another (Brecknock, 52 High Street) at Puckeridge (Standon) is in what was never formally a town but probably had a denser and more urban pattern of development than the lower end of Fishpool Street. Barkway, with urban potential by virtue of its market, has a small double-ended Wealden near the south end of the village and away from what seems to have been the site of the market, and in Stevenage another such house stands in a minor road away from whatever pressure on space was felt in a small market town. Nevertheless, the broad distinction that single-ended Wealden houses are

urban and double-ended ones rural may be valid, despite some exceptions.

Townsmen for whom a Wealden house was too expensive could have a simpler kind of two-bay house, with flush walls instead of a jetty in the storeyed bay. For instance, 20 Baldock Street, Ware, had exactly the same ground plan and one upstairs room as a single-ended Wealden and differed only in having a simpler structure. Being less complex, it was cheaper to build and may be a fairly common type, but since it lacks both the external distinctiveness of a Wealden, even one which has had the hall floored over, it is a type which a selective survey can discover only by chance. St Albans can show several more or less fragmentary late medieval houses which had open halls. One such is 33 St Michael's Street, a house with two bays open from ground to roof and a third with an upper floor. It provided much the same accommodation as a single-ended Wealden except for its somewhat larger hall, yet it lacked the architectural pretensions given by a jettied front. A point of interest is that this house, the one at Ware and the Wealdens all have a hall of greater height than would be provided by the normal hall and cross-wing house such as Walnut Tree Farm, Clothall. Probably structural simplicity was the aim, with a consequent reduction in craftsmen's skill and wages more than outweighing any slight increase in the amount of timber. If this were so, 33 St Michael's Street may represent the lowest social levels of townsmen – small craftsmen, perhaps – who could afford to build in a lasting form of construction.

In towns as in the countryside one of the most common types of house was the one with an open hall and one cross-wing, with the wing not usually longer than the width of the hall; and in both town and country it is commonly only the wing which survives to establish the existence of such a house because the hall range was too low to be worth converting into two storeys and complete rebuilding was simpler. In St Albans, 18 Lower Dagnall Street and, in Baldock, 3/5 Sun Street are like this with 5 Parliament Square, Hertford, one of many possible examples not investigated.

Small jettied buildings with chimney-stacks

Kneesworth Street, Royston, is the site of a residence established for James I and his entourage when hunting in the neighbourhood. It is sometimes called a palace and sometimes a hunting lodge, although the existing buildings and documentary evidence show that it was no more than a collection of disparate buildings varying in age and materials which can never have looked anything like what is normally meant by those terms. One building, now No. 11 [245], had three roof bays and a very short fourth bay at the north end but, although it was formally larger than anything described in the preceding section, it was not really very different in size. In the short bay at the north end, two

haps the term is better reserved for a building of three or more bays incorporating a chimney-stack. Thus defined, continuous-jetty houses are rare in towns. Indeed the only example recorded during the survey, now Nos 53 and 55 Sopwell Lane, St Albans, has a crown-post roof which is presumably late medieval, and no evidence of a chimney-stack earlier than the present one; yet, despite this negative evidence, there must surely have been a chimney-stack, for the building was in all likelihood a small house.

Inns

The large inn, conspicuous in a narrow street by its wide carriage entrance to a courtyard more or less surrounded by buildings, forms one of the most distinctive kinds of urban development. Many of them still possess the one architectural feature by which they can infallibly be recognised, the first-floor galleries needed to provide access to any considerable number of rooms, but so far the only comparatively complete purpose-built inn to come to light in Hertfordshire is a late 16th-century building.

Two types of medieval inn plan have been distinguished.[1] The *Courtyard* type has its principal buildings arranged around a courtyard behind the street front, and the *Block* or *Gatehouse* type has the main part on the street front, with a gateway in the middle, beside and above which the principal rooms are located; but Pantin, who made this distinction, warned against exaggerating the contrast between the two and stressed that some medieval inns may have been indistinguishable from large dwelling houses.

Such Hertfordshire inns as have been examined do not refine this classification. Only two can be dated prior to the Reformation on architectural grounds and the remainder do not display any of the indubitable characteristics of an inn;

245 *No. 11 Kneesworth Street, Royston: from the north west*

beams placed lengthwise, hollow-chamfered on their outer edges and plain on the inner or facing edges, are here interpreted as having supported a wooden chimney (wooden because on general grounds a brick stack is unlikely to have disappeared completely to be replaced by the existing late 18th or early 19th-century stack). Evidence of this kind tends to remain only where the building has declined sufficiently gradually for few destructive alterations to have taken place, yet not fast enough for it to have fallen into ruin.

Storeyed and jettied late medieval buildings that can be shown to have had fireplaces are hard to find. A possible one is a range at the corner of Palmers Lane and Bridge Street (Nos 2/4) in Bishop's Stortford, a little way up the hill from the Black Lion. Its date is open to argument. In favour of its being late medieval is the dragon-beam, the supporting post of which is now removed or hidden by brickwork; against is its two-and-a-half storey structure, a distinctly late 16th-century feature showing no unequivocal sign that it results from heightening. At the back of the middle shop of the three into which the building is now divided is a large and possibly original fireplace.

Buildings of this kind merge into the type, ill-defined in town contexts, of continuous-jetty houses. Two jettied bays are formally enough to qualify a house for this type but per-

246 *The Antelope (originally the Tabard Inn), St Albans* (Buckler)

they could have been altered to serve the purpose. The oldest is the one of which a small part remains incorporated in 18/20 George Street, St Albans [246]. On the first floor can be seen a gallery extending along the rear of the street range and continuing down a wing that formerly returned along Spicer Street. It was once part of the courtyard which was drawn by Buckler and appears in a painting by Varley of the abbey from Spicer Street, but the existing building is difficult to identify with anything depicted by the artists. The George Street range is probably of the late 14th century, a date which is likely also for the traceried openings of the gallery in Buckler's drawing. Another medieval inn may be the former White Swan Inn in Fore Street (Nos 28/30), Hertford [247, 248]; it is separated only by Church Street from the Salisbury Arms. Part of a long range extending down Church Street and forming one side of the courtyard has scraps of evidence to suggest a gallery once existed,

although here, as in a number of other inns in the county, division of what was once a very large building into several occupations makes it difficult to be sure.

The only positive means of identifying an inn other than the presence of galleries is the provision of separate staircases serving groups of rooms, and the later 16th-century Old Bull at Harpenden is the only certain example of this. A medieval inn with this mode of access to rooms may have been the Salisbury Arms (formerly The Bell), Hertford, where successive alterations have long removed the relevant evidence; even the 15th-century date of the oldest parts of this building can now be known only from documentary evidence.

No other medieval buildings so far found in Hertfordshire can be claimed with certainty to have been built as inns, yet a few others which were inns at a later period incorporate medieval work and may well have been purpose-built. One at St Albans, formerly The Christopher and now 3/5 French Row, is known to have had a doorhead with traceried spandrels rather like the window-heads of 18/20 George Street, and is of much the same date but, in so far as the structural development of the building can now be worked out, the gallery, which was undoubtedly present in the 17th century, is an addition. The same is true of The Swan at Berkhamsted, where the front range has an early-looking roof with passing-braces which are likely to be of the 14th century [249]. Here, as at The Christopher and

247 *Nos 28/30 Fore Street, Hertford (formerly the White Swan Inn): from the north west*

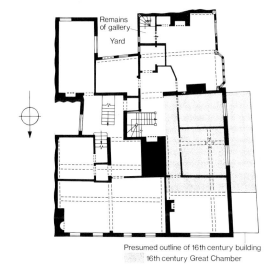

Remains of gallery
Yard

Presumed outline of 16th century building
16th century Great Chamber

248 *Nos 28/30 Fore Street, Hertford: plan*

249 *The Swan, Berkhamsted: roof, combining king-strut, collar-purlin and passing-braces; probably 14th century*

18/20 George Street, there is now no sign of any form of heating. While this is not surprising, if the ranges in question contained lodging rooms upstairs and perhaps downstairs too, any medieval inn must have had a fairly large hall – whether open to the roof or incorporating an upper floor – which had to be heated. At The George, Hitchin, are the remains of just such a large open hall, but nothing in the building confirms that it was built as an inn. Nor was it only in the larger towns of Hertfordshire that inns of this domestic type were found. In Stanstead Abbots, an ancient but not very successful town, the Red Lion perhaps originally incorporated a covered entrance, as, too, did the inn of the same name in the village of Much Hadham.

A photograph taken in 1894 preserves evidence of a different kind. It shows a short two-storey range with an open first-floor gallery then standing in the yard of the George Inn at Watford [250]. This building may once have been linked to the street range, like the galleried wing of The Four Swans at Cheshunt, although it is conceivable that medieval inns had detached lodging ranges, much as later inns appear to have had adjoining, but not intercommunicating, blocks of rooms towards the rear of the yard; a jettied building in the yard of the Red Lion at Stevenage may have been comparable.[32] Its interest lies in showing a structure simpler in its details and finish than the usual conception of a galleried inn, and no doubt more common, and for

250 *The George Inn, Watford: this photograph, taken in 1894, shows a detached building in the inn yard*

that reason it is included here although its date cannot be known with any precision and it could equally well be Elizabethan.

251 *The George Hotel, Bishop's Stortford*

Finally, as Pantin recognised, some medieval inns may have been indistinguishable from large dwelling houses. The George, Hitchin, and The Swan, Berkhamsted, are instances of this (see [289]). So, too, is the quite different kind of structure disguised by the 19th-century appearance of the George Hotel, Bishop's Stortford [251]. There the main range of the complex, the part facing North Street, is a jettied building originally of two storeys which, in both the form of plan [252] and its overall size, has much in common with Redcoats, Wymondley, which was certainly not an inn. The George and Redcoats have exactly the same number and disposition of rooms, but in the main range the George has a rear wing which may well be original; only the near-miraculous survival of a short length of moulded lintel establishes that the hall (c.1500–50) was here, in this way differentiating the two buildings.

Perhaps no medieval house type found in Hertfordshire is either exclusively urban or exclusively rural. The emphasis is on the word 'house' because ranges of shops, especially those at corners, never appear in even a large village; but if it is correct that the upper storeys were not living accommodation, the statement can stand. The limitation of this study to Hertfordshire excludes certain rare forms of open-hall house found in the greater towns, such as the timber-framed house which has a first-floor hall with an open hearth.

Even then, some ambiguity attaches to the words 'urban' and 'rural' in the Middle Ages, when a small town could be smaller than a large village and the density of building hardly differed. What appears to have been a shop built for some trade in need of ventilation forms part of Bear House, Ashwell [253], a place which even at the height of its prosperity in the 15th century can never have been predominantly urban in character; this trading function apart, the

253 *Bear House, Ashwell: from the north east*

12　0 feet　48
3　0 metres　15
Scale for detail

moulded lintel

252 *The George Hotel, Bishop's Stortford: plan*

house might stand in the open countryside. On the other hand, Much Hadham has no claim to urban status, yet it contains urban-style, single-ended Wealden houses and may well have at least one house of the characteristic urban type (hall-and-one-cross-wing) in which the wing faces the street and the hall runs off behind it.

The house known until recent years as the Old Post Office, Offley, is an example of this type but no evidence of its having originally been a shop was noticed. Again it is a question of what is the rule and what is the exception and, whatever argument there may be about the status of Much Hadham, it can hardly be doubted that the single-ended Wealden is found overwhelmingly in town contexts and, if all the variants of size are taken into account, the cross-wing-on-the-street type too. The contrast in this respect between King's Lynn and the Hertfordshire towns makes this quite clear. Conversely, the presence in St Albans of a double-ended Wealden does not significantly diminish the rural character of the type, any more than the bizarre occurrence of a semi-detached pair of cruck houses in Lichfield (Staffs) weakens the rural associations of cruck houses generally.[33]

It is observable, though, that the examples just quoted do not stand on an equal footing. The two variant forms of Wealden do not imply any significant difference of plan and certainly not of structure between town and country, and the third, the hall with a cross-wing facing the street, also scarcely differs in plan or structure in any important way. Much depends on what is thought to be significant and important. Undoubtedly one effect of transposing the one-cross-wing type into a street, whether of town or village – Offley as well as Much Hadham – is to put the jetty on the long front wall, whereas in the country it is at the gable end facing the approach.

If these comparatively slight differences are taken into account, there is still one kind of open-hall town house that has yet to be found in either the countryside or a village, and that is the one represented by 20 Baldock Street, Ware, with one open bay and one storeyed bay of equal height, the whole with flush walls. The open hall as a mode of building demands space compared with the storeyed houses that were developing in the major towns, and it can be regarded as more characteristic of a rural than of an urban environment. As it is at Ware, structurally simple and with a compressed plan, it has achieved an exclusively urban form. The single-ended Wealdens run it close, being found in towns or large villages. Compactness is the essence of both types; at a comparable social level its rural equivalent probably had a single-storey service bay, like Green Street Cottage, Little Hadham, in its original form.

The other distinctive urban type, and apparently a rather rare one in Hertfordshire, is the two-storey jettied house with an end chimney-stack, like 9 Kneesworth Street, Royston. If this house has been interpreted correctly, many like it could have lost a timber chimney, and it would not be surprising on general grounds if a few jettied two-bay houses eventually turned out to have or to have had rear chimney-stacks.

Chapter 9

The growth of the residential town

Hertfordshire towns were founded as trading centres and thrived or failed as such during the Middle Ages. Their social composition was comparatively simple, comprising tradesmen, craftsmen and merchants of various degrees of wealth, and their relatives, dependants and workpeople – that is, their families in the older sense of the word. Not until after the Reformation did the towns begin to attract inhabitants of a superior social class who were not directly connected with trade. Defoe, writing in the early 1720s, commented admiringly on Shrewsbury as being 'full of gentry yet full of trade too', and Bury St Edmunds he commended as 'the *Montpelier* of Suffolk . . . it being thronged with Gentry, People of Fashion, and the most polite conversation'.[1] He said virtually nothing about the much smaller Hertfordshire towns and even the best could not have deserved praise in those terms.

It is difficult to make a fair comparison between the two principal towns, Hertford and St Albans, and those which drew favourable comment from Defoe. The proximity of London must have inhibited the development of a self-sufficient social life, yet St Albans, on the evidence of its architecture, was a particularly successful residential town relative to its small size. Hertford was perhaps less so, the advantages attaching to a shire town standing on the only navigable river in the county being offset by three things: its inconvenient position, tucked away in the south east of the county; the removal to the west of the Great North Road, so that it was no longer on an important highway; and the commercial supremacy of Ware. But it was the Reformation itself that gave St Albans the edge over any possible rival by releasing on to the land market former Abbey properties whose new owners quickly established administrative and commercial ties with the nearby town.

For several of the new houses – Sopwell, Tyttenhanger, Gorhambury, St Julians, Markyate Cell and New Barns – there is evidence of building activity. Not that the builders of these houses can really be regarded as inhabitants of St Albans; Sir Richard Lee and Sir Nicholas Bacon were first and foremost courtiers and as much residents of Whitehall as of the family seats they founded, but the permanent existence of their establishments and the periodic influx of people when the owner was in residence and entertaining must have brought enormous benefits. At the same time new houses were built within the town itself, although only one or two, such as Holywell House, were for gentry. Apart from a classical doorway (probably Elizabethan), which was preserved in a garden wall of 'Mr Kentish's Mansion' in St Peter's Street long enough to be recorded by Oldfield, all the evidence comes from the heralds' visitations. However, social change did not much affect town centres until after the Restoration; trade was the dominant force, as is shown by the architecture it engendered.

Commercial and administrative buildings

After the Dissolution the transfer of authority in St Albans from the abbot to the citizens necessitated the building of a town hall (see p 147). This is the long range running from Market Place down Lower Dagnall Street, which was built in the late 16th century, perhaps more precisely in the third quarter. The wider date bracket is established by the mouldings on the wall-posts and ceiling beams of the first-floor council chamber; the narrower one is suggested by the need and desire for such a building after the granting of charters in 1553 (Mary) and 1560 (Elizabeth I). Elizabethan town growth was epitomised less by the town hall than by the market house or market hall. It was not in itself a distinctive special-purpose building but rather an adaptation of an architectural type which included the guild or town hall and church houses. All are two-storey buildings combining an important upstairs room, used for committee meetings, with a ground-floor space put to humbler use.

Market halls cannot be shown to have existed as a class of special-purpose building before the 16th century in Hertfordshire. Early in 1588 the Corporation of St Albans concluded that the market house should be built and allocated £29 towards it out of the common stock, to which the Mayor was to add 40 shillings and 'the leads of St Albans church to be used about the same Market House'.[2] Building was still in progress in 1596; such dilatoriness in completion suggests that the Corporation did not consider the market house to be a matter of priority. However, most towns in the county were to be provided with comparable buildings in the course of the 16th and 17th centuries.

254 *Market House, Watford* (Buckler)

In 1650, a building of this kind at Tring was described as 'The old house called the Market House with the court loft over . . . containing two rooms or shops below stairs, with an entry and staircase up into the court loft used for keeping of the courts, bounded South with the Market Street and the churchyard North'.[3] Only at St Albans did the market house lack a first-floor courtroom, because a town hall with just such a room had already been built away from the market-place. Evidently, the general tendency to build permanent or semi-permanent structures within the market-place extended to the official market building itself, so that at St Albans in 1621–2 Thomas Goodridge, Mayor, was paying for a room or shop in the market house. That such shops were permitted to be built or were built by the Corporation to meet the needs of a particular trade is suggested by a reference in St Albans in 1651 to 'the stairs which go up to the cornshops of the Market House';[4] they were possibly the two shops 'being part of the lofts of the Market House'.[5] (A consequence of the predominance of corn in the Hertfordshire markets was the later rebuilding of many market halls under the new name of corn exchange.)[6]

As an architectural form, market houses generally conform to the type already described: a committee room standing on wooden columns (see p 147). Those at Berkhamsted, Bishop's Stortford, Hatfield, Rickmansworth and Watford [254] were all depicted like this by Buckler; the description of Tring quoted above is of just such a building, and the site of that at Ware, rebuilt in the 19th century, suggests that it, too, conformed to this pattern. Many of the smaller market-places are not known to have had a market house of this kind.

The fullest provision for market traders seems to have been at Hemel Hempstead, said in 1728 to be 'the greatest Corn Market in the County, if we judge by what is set down and sold in it. Here are Eleven Pair of Mills within Four Miles of the Place, which bring a Trade into this Part of the County, and furnish the City of *London* with a great deal of Meal . . . and indeed without them the City, at Times of Drought or Frost, when Water-Carriage fails, could not sub-

sist'.[7] It had the largest market buildings in the county, nor were they only for corn. The twelve butchers' stalls had increased to fifteen by 1708 and there is reference to the 'Womens Markett house containing three Bayes' and used, it may be supposed, for selling minor produce of the farm such as vegetables and poultry; under it was a 'work house . . . for a Tallow Chandler'. Also mentioned are several houses on the edge of the churchyard, which probably incorporated shops, and over the way to the vicarage was a two-storey gatehouse, perhaps for the market ('piepowder') courts.[8] It is not easy to relate all this to the range of timber-framed buildings at least thirteen bays long – corn lofts standing on wooden posts – which existed in the 1830s; they were interrupted by a brick town hall of 1825 set over the gate from street to churchyard.[9] It was all rebuilt in 1868 as a market with corn stores above.[10]

In addition to a market house some towns had a market cross, providing a number of stalls and serving as a market hall without an upstairs meeting-room. One was at St Albans and another at Ware is mentioned in 1669 as being, along with the market house and town house, in such decay that merchants were 'not able to sit dry with their goods'.[11]

The development of the town centre

By the middle of the 16th century several of the market-places had been reduced by encroachment to more or less the size they are today. Hitchin and St Albans are instances where the space in the market-place available for building changed little from the mid 16th to the mid 19th centuries,[12] and in these places evidence of more intensive development can be found. These new ways of exploiting the most sought-after sites take various forms: development around small courtyards, filling up the narrow plots ever farther from the street front, and building higher. This greater density is the result of the greater size, height and durability of buildings that together constitute a principal difference between the Elizabethan and earlier periods.

255 *Market Place, Hitchin: Nos 2/2A are to the left; No. 4 is the gabled building*

256 *No. 4 High Street, Hitchin: interior showing a first-floor bay window overlooking a courtyard*

Near the north-west corner of Hitchin market-place a group of buildings (Nos 2/2A Market Place) developed around a small courtyard, so small that it might be called a big light well [**255**]. The oldest surviving parts appear to be the south range facing the market-place and the east range, both of two storeys, which were built in the late 16th century; the front range, if not the others, must replace something older. Not far away, and not very different in date, 4 High Street [**256**] shows another way of gaining valuable space on a plot not wide enough to allow building around a courtyard. Here, both the front range and a wide one behind it are of two storeys and attics.

How this and other storeyed town buildings were heated at this period is uncertain; a chimney-stack at the north end, now removed, was probably original, whilst a first-floor room in the back wing which had a bay window must surely have had a fireplace. Since the adjoining room overlooking the street also had a fireplace and the staircase served both, it may be that hall, parlour and a service room were all on the first floor, with bedrooms above and a kitchen somewhere below – beneath the hall, perhaps. As for the range farthest from the street, it can be assumed to have had some commercial purpose such as a warehouse, there being no sign of a domestic function. Furthermore, No. 4 provides an early vernacular example of utilising the roof space; the combination of second-floor walls only about 3 ft (1 m) high, with dormers or dormer windows made possible a reduction in height from the three full storeys that had been usual for early 16th-century houses in the centres of many English towns. This older type exists only a few yards away at the building, now Nos 1 and 2, which has every appearance of being late medieval and of three storeys from the first; but inside much is obscured by modern fittings and evidence of both date and function is lacking.

Elsewhere, two storeys remained usual for town buildings and the roof space was generally left open and unused at least until 1600. Baldock shows the same kind of develop-

ment away from the street as Hitchin but without the extra storey. The older parts of Oak House, 22 Whitehorse Street [**257**], lie well behind the 18th-century street range which replaced something older, by inference late medieval, to which the 16th or early 17th-century blocks behind were added. The rearward part was jettied towards a narrow courtyard entered by a gateway from the street, implying that the street frontage was put to some different use, presumably as a shop, while the jettied elevation served as the true front of the house. Despite differences of plan and structure between this house and Nos 2/2A Market Place, Hitchin, they have one significant feature in common: the principal domestic accommodation lies away from the street and is reached through a yard at the side. This feature, common enough in the greater medieval towns such as King's Lynn,[13] rarely appears in the market towns of Hertfordshire before the Reformation.

The significance of covered gateways

Many English market towns still possess wide gateways with a room or rooms over them. Often the gateway is quite high so that the floor level of the room over it is above that of the buildings on either side. In Hertfordshire, several covered gateways are later than the building they adjoin, for example, the one at 105 Bancroft, Hitchin, which occupied the site of the service end part of the hall of the house fronting the yard. Similarly, at 4 High Street, Hitchin, it is virtually certain that there was a covered entrance at the north end, and the irregularity of the plan argues that it was a later addition. The difficulty of reaching the room over the gateway except by going through another room, or through a passage awkwardly cut out of a room, is a frequent sign of late addition, as at 75 High Street, Hemel Hempstead.

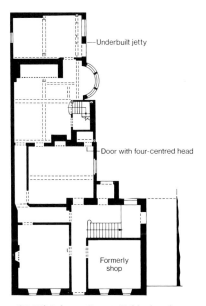

Underbuilt jetty

Door with four-centred head

Formerly shop

257 *Oak House, 22 Whitehorse Street, Baldock: plan*

258 *Dean Incent's House, Berkhamsted*

The significance of covered gateways is that they often mark a change in the use of the yards to which they lead. That is self-evidently true of the many cut through an old building, for such a change probably indicates the first use there of wheeled vehicles to transport goods.

Nothing is known about the function of the rooms over gateways. In general they seem not to have been very important, and the suggestion occasionally put forward that they were intended for a gatekeeper is improbable because hardly any have a staircase leading directly to the yard. A room over the entrance may have compensated to some extent for the loss of part of a house.

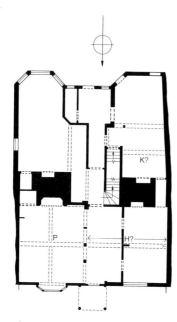

259 *Dean Incent's House, Berkhamsted: plan*

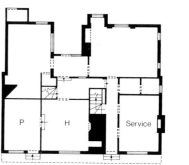

260 *No. 130 Fore Street, Hertford: plan*

Types of plan

One change from late medieval practice is the discontinuance of unheated buildings. From the late 16th century onwards, one or two chimney-stacks were universal, sometimes sited at the end gables and sometimes on the rear wall, and where no datable detail is visible the stacks reveal their date by their size and relation to the original rooms.

Two-room ground plans appear to have been fairly common, no doubt because that was all that could be accommodated in the street frontage of most plots. With a single chimney-stack at the gable end, this type is found in the late 16th century at Hitchin (7 Sun Street), and, with an internal stack, at Hemel Hempstead (74/76 High Street). A fairly large example can be inferred at the Guild House in Water Lane, Bishop's Stortford. A yet larger version, with two and a half storeys, at 16 Market Square, Bishop's Stortford, was built in the early 17th century. In rural buildings of this period, a chimney-stack sited at the rear, rather than axially, may mark a socially superior house, although in an urban context site restrictions may have been the deciding factor.

Where space was less of a consideration an enlarged three-room plan might be used. The house known as Dean Incent's, 129/131 High Street, Berkhamsted [**258**, **259**], has an axially placed chimney-stack to provide fireplaces for the hall and chamber over it, with the medieval open hall relegated to the status of a kitchen. The street range was built late in the 16th or early in the following century. A similar plan without the rear kitchen appears to have existed at 18 Melbourn Street, Royston. In both houses the siting of the staircase conforms to rural vernacular practice of the late 16th century, being next to the chimney-stack, and in houses lacking an old staircase it can reasonably be assumed to have been in close proximity to the hall stack.

A somewhat later form of enlargement at a higher social level is found at 130 Fore Street, Hertford [**260**], thought to date from 1649. Again, the two front rooms are slightly different in size, the hall being wider than the second room by the width of a cross-passage, but here both have fireplaces and so do the adjoining rooms in the two short wings. This must surely have been a residence and nothing more, and is the earliest such building to be noticed.

261 *Nos 3–13 Fore Street, Hertford: No. 13 has its principal front facing the market-place (to the right of the photograph)*

The process of renovation

If the years between the Reformation and the Civil War produced few identifiable plan types, it may be because the previous hundred years had provided many towns with a stock of buildings needing no more than slight modification to bring them up to contemporary standards. The essential change was the insertion of a floor and chimney-stack in a hall open to the roof. Although this work transformed the interior space, the effect on the existing timber frame was relatively small in two-bay Wealden houses and any others which had a hall equal in height to the two storeys of a chamber bay, such as 20 Baldock Street, Ware. Where the hall was too low for a normal upper storey to be inserted, it had to be either heightened or totally rebuilt.

Building for investment or speculation

The most distinctively urban building is to be found in 3–13 Fore Street, Hertford [**261**], a long three-storey timber-framed block well known for the scrolled pargetting in bold relief which dates it to the decade or so after the Restoration. It is remarkable as a row of large town tenements, probably built as an investment in order to raise money from the rents, but until the history of the property has been established the possibility cannot be excluded that it was built as a speculation, with the intention of selling off the individual tenements.[14] Like so many of its medieval counterparts, this development takes advantage of a corner site, standing at the junction of Fore Street and Market Place and extending most of the way to an important road junction. A

159

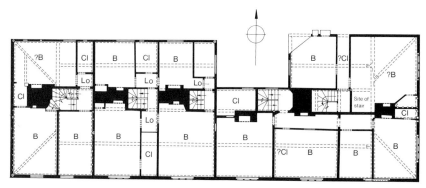

262 *Nos 3–13 Fore Street, Hertford: first-floor plan*

consequence of such siting is that the individual units cannot all be of the same size or have the same plan [**262**]. Other variations in size may arise from a wish to provide premises at slightly different rents.

In the reconstructed plan, which discounts 19th-century alterations, five tenements each had, on the second floor, two heated rooms and two others which varied in size from what might be called a dressing room to something no bigger than a closet, whilst the largest tenement at the west end had a further closet beside the chimney-stack. All rooms were entered through a lobby, making the staircases exceedingly dark, despite the likely use of grilles over the doorways. We do not know if the front ground-floor room, which must certainly have been a shop, had a fireplace. The back room in each of the five double-depth tenements was probably a kitchen, and on the floors above were four heated chambers. A total of six hearths was quite considerable for a town house and with the shop and cellars and the various small rooms made a commodious residence and workplace. Nothing remotely like this meets the eye in any other Hertfordshire town.

Houses, shops and workplaces

It is a curiosity of architectural history that quite a lot is known about shops in the 15th and early 16th centuries, and again from the late 18th century onwards, but that the interim is largely blank except for the customary reference to the famous early 18th-century shops in Artillery Lane, Stepney, London.[15] No doubt the majority of craftsmen continued to produce on the premises the goods they sold, so that the earlier notion of a shop as a workshop persisted. Retail shops are thought not to have appeared until much later.[16]

So far, no shop fronts of the late 16th or early 17th centuries have been identified in Hertfordshire. A drawing of an 'Ancient House' in Berkhamsted [**263**] shows, in the left-hand wing, what appears to be a shop, with a doorway in the middle and an unglazed window on each side; a position comparable to that of the alleged shop at Yew Tree Farm, Much Hadham (see p 32). If the drawing is correctly interpreted, it is understandable that shop windows have not been noticed because the evidence of mortises would almost certainly be ambiguous. An open-fronted shop required some shelter. A few flat canopies of later date remain in Hertfordshire, or have remained until recent years: one at 10 High Street, Bishop's Stortford [**264**], is probably older than the early 19th-century glazed shop windows it covers;[17] another projects in front of 31/33 High Street, Hemel Hempstead, covering more recent bowed fronts; and a third can be seen nearby at the adjoining shops, Nos 75 and 77. All these examples show the continuance of a form of shop canopy first used in the late 16th century. For the shops themselves, as distinct from their fronts, little evidence has been found.

The apparent contrast in Hertfordshire between the unheated lock-up premises of the late Middle Ages and the combined house and shop found from the late 16th century onwards is certainly misleading. The abbey of Tewkesbury built a long range of small houses in the town, each with a hall from which a shop was partitioned off at the front, and a chamber above.[18] No doubt functionally similar buildings were erected in Hertfordshire towns, however financed; Nos 22/24 St Andrew's Street, Hertford, may have been like this.

Conversely, little is known about the beginnings of purely retail shops, entirely divorced from the process of manu-

263 *'Ancient House', Berkhamsted* (Oldfield)

264 *No. 10 High Street, Bishop's Stortford: the flat canopy can be seen over shop windows (beneath projecting shop sign)*

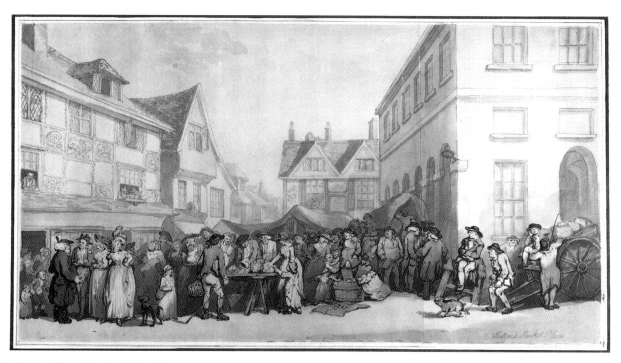

265 *Market Place, Hertford: No. 13 Fore Street, with a covered canopy over the shop front, can be seen to the left of the picture* (Rowlandson)

266 *No. 4 Market Place, Hitchin: first-floor plan*

facture. At first, they may have been hardly distinguishable from the craftsman's shop. In 1800 the range at 3–13 Fore Street, Hertford [**265**], still had the original medieval-style coved and tiled pentise roof.[19] A simpler version of the same form persisted for a long time and still exists in Hemel Hempstead, at 84 High Street, where it is no more than a single-pitch roof carried on brackets and projecting no farther than a jetty, in order to throw rain clear of an open shop front. It is an inference that this building was a shop, or two shops, but the Fore Street range must certainly have been intended as shops, if only because the comparatively crowded site would have been unattractive to anyone but a shopkeeper needing a good central position in the town. The same is true of 4 Market Place, Hitchin [**266**]: a house in that position must always have been a shop even though no structural evidence of it remains. Built in 1675, its plan is as near to being completely known as is likely for any house in the middle of a town, and shows no evidence of its intended function. Nevertheless, the front ground-floor room has unusual proportions, long in relation to its width, and it may be that a small part nearest the street was lightly partitioned off or perhaps only differentiated functionally as a shop from the rest of the room. Alternatively, the whole room could have been used for the display of the luxury goods that were by then coming into country towns. But if a light partition existed it may be compared with the stud partition at 22/24 St Andrew's Street, Hertford. Inference allows No. 2 St Andrew's Street to be identified as a shop, for only by assuming that the existing one had a predecessor does the plan, with the house door at one end, become intelligible. If the building has been interpreted correctly, it combined a residence on the first and second floors for the owner or landlord with a shop and quite small living accommodation for the tenant shopkeeper on the ground floor.

Small size continued to be a characteristic of shops into the 18th century. Encroachments could easily be made on the street because the space required was often little more than the overhead projection of a jetty or double jetty, or perhaps that used to display wares in the street itself. Some

of the small buildings in Hitchin market-place that were swept away in the mid 19th century (see p 136) were presumably like this, and one such structure, probably more than one shop originally, still survives in modern form near the north-east corner. Others existed in St Albans on three sides of the Clock Tower, and one a little to the east survives as part of The Old Boot public house.[20] They must have been typical of a prosperous 17th-century town. Many were removed in 18th and 19th-century town improvement schemes.[21]

Some early 19th-century shops, for instance, 5 Old Cross, Hertford, were not much bigger than their medieval predecessors and developed by extension at the rear rather than by much increase in the size of the trading part. It is likely, though, that by the early 19th century we are no longer comparing like with like in the neighbourhood of Old Cross, and that concurrently with the development of the retail shop this area had gone into a decline, with the best shops being established in Fore Street, leaving the ancient market to less profitable and less fashionable trades.

Houses as residences, not workplaces

Prior to the Restoration most town houses of Hertfordshire incorporated a workplace – a shop or workshop – and provided accommodation for a family, including apprentices, journeymen or other employees of the head of the household as well as his wife and children. In the second half of the 17th century this situation changed and, for the first time, houses were built as residences with no obvious provision for a trade or business. It cannot be assumed that no occupation was carried on in or from this new style of house and indeed the contrary was probably true, with the owners being professional people[22] whose work could be performed in a house hardly distinguishable, in its larger examples, from a minor gentleman's residence. Nor can such professional men's houses easily be distinguished by

267 *Bridgeman House, 37 West Street, Hertford: from the north*

their plan from those of merchants, save by the lack of cellars with a wide external entrance, or of space for a warehouse at the rear, features characteristic of merchants' houses.[23]

In the 18th century houses that were primarily residences were built in every town of any size. Their comparatively uniform appearance was governed by the rules of taste disseminated, in the second half of the century, through pattern books cheap enough for a provincial builder to acquire, but their plans frequently do not conform to types. Indeed, the restrictions imposed by town sites, coupled with the usual preference for modifying an existing building rather than rebuilding it, will always limit the possibilities of establishing types in the sense that they are now known in rural vernacular houses. Only in the late 18th century, with the enormous growth of towns, does this situation change.

House plans found in towns

Lobby-entrance houses

If the first house identifiable as purely residential is 130 Fore Street of 1649, Bridgeman House, also in Hertford (37 West Street) [267], cannot be much later. Perhaps it is properly described as a house in a town rather than a town house, for although it stands in West Street it is of a type familiar in rural contexts. In plan [268], with two rooms separated by an internal chimney-stack and a lobby-entrance, it does not differ from many a 17th-century farmhouse except in lacking ancillary rooms such as a brewhouse and dairy and it is not impossible that these once existed. But lobby-entrance houses can also be found in true urban contexts. At St Albans, 32 St Peter's Street had this form of plan until the early 19th century when it underwent a characteristic transformation to improve circulation, by driving a tunnel through the stack between the fireplaces. At Bishop's Stortford the lobby-entrance appears in the centre of the town, at 17 North Street, and probably in the adjoining house, No. 15, too. The complete removal of the stack from the ground floor of No. 17 North Street demonstrates that

this type was so much at risk from demands for space and ease of circulation that other examples may have vanished with hardly a trace. The lobby-entrance precludes the existence of a shop at the front, so the question arises of how the local owners and builders acquired their ideas about the kinds of plan suitable to town conditions.

In larger towns, such as Colchester and Cambridge, solutions had long been found to all the problems of urban housing faced in Hertford and St Albans, yet they were either not known in Hertfordshire or it was not thought worthwhile to seek them out. It is scarcely possible that in the middle of Bishop's Stortford, in North Street, a site could have been so un-urban as actually to need a rural plan type, and the same is true of St Peter's Street in St Albans. Such a conservative approach reinforces an observation derived from vernacular building studies: ideas relating to ornament and decoration travel fast; new structural techniques are slower but do travel; and forms of plan are transmitted only with considerable difficulty. It may be that urban vernacular building throughout the 17th, and well into the 18th, century continued to be bound by tradition. This would account for the adoption of a rural model to a town site where, for whatever reason, the urban types used locally were inappropriate.

Lateral-chimney and related plans

The 'Ancient House', 3 High Street, Stevenage [269, 270], was essentially a range of three large rooms, each with a chimney-stack and fireplace on the rear wall; the north end stack may have served a kitchen. Two features suggest that it may be older than its front: the curiously inconspicuous siting of the main staircase and the inclusion in the elevation of a small stair turret. The motif of narrower end bays appears in the coeval Little Cassiobury, Watford, but in plan [271] 3 High Street is like nothing else. Its antecedents, which are imprecise, include the earliest part of The George Hotel, Bishop's Stortford, and 34 Bancroft, Hitchin; farther back still, there is Redcoats (Wymondley).

The first two analogies are clear, the third is inferred. Inference of this kind can perhaps apply to other houses which have two or three chimney-stacks aligned parallel to the street front but otherwise are quite dissimilar to the Stevenage house in plan. Two such exist in Hertford. The first and more probable example is 4/6 St Andrew's Street, where two large stacks now within the building look as if they had been built on an outside wall. The second is problematic; 130 Fore Street, Hertford, is built on a narrower plot and therefore extends backwards to achieve the same size as 3 High Street, Stevenage, did a generation later. Can its two-room front range, with two chimney-stacks, be regarded either as an improvement on the two-room plan with one stack or as a reduction of the three-room plan at The George Hotel, Bishop's Stortford, to fit a cramped site? Probably the latter, but it is hardly possible to decide between the alternatives. Yet the point, however difficult it

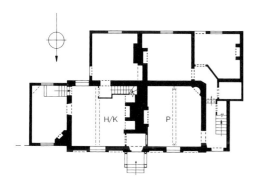

268 *Bridgeman House, 37 West Street, Hertford: plan*

269 *'Ancient House', 3 High Street, Stevenage: from the north west*

270 *'Ancient House', 3 High Street, Stevenage* (Oldfield)

may be to resolve, is not a purely academic exercise in typology, for it concerns the relation of plan types and individual features to the social class of the owner, and whether there are urban counterparts to distinctions of the kind which clearly existed in the countryside.

Polite architecture in towns: the beginning

By the 1660s the taste for exposed timber framing had been replaced by three modes of surface treatment. The most striking fashion, for bold plasterwork in large scrolls and swags, is represented in 3–13 Fore Street, Hertford, and at Ashwell, on what appears to be a piece of infilling (55 High Street) [**272**] dated 1681. Another way of modernising the appearance of timber houses was by plaster rustication, a treatment recorded in drawings of houses in Hertford market-place and Baldock. A third, and simpler, way of embellishing a plastered building was to create a panelled effect by the use of incised lines. Two of the more striking examples were 3 High Street, Stevenage, and the 'Ancient House' at Baldock; two which survive, 51 St Andrew's Street, Hertford, and The Elms, Bell Street, Sawbridgeworth, are less elaborate and represent a shift in taste away from the boldly modelled effects sought after in the time of Charles II.

By the later 1670s, a different type of elevation had made its appearance: 40/42 St Andrew's Street, Hertford [**273**], is an early example of the new appearance influenced by London models after the Great Fire. The influence lay in the adoption of brick for a house of modest size and also in the kinds of doors, windows and other architectural details used, rather than in the plan. The typical London house

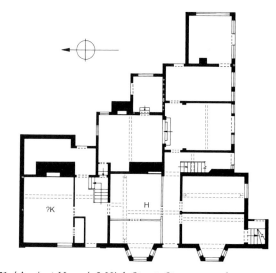

271 *'Ancient House', 3 High Street, Stevenage: plan*

built after the Great Fire had a three-bay elevation, whereas 40 St Andrew's Street was half as wide again as many a city site; separation of the entrance from the principal ground-floor room was, in provincial towns, a later refinement. The resulting double-depth plan on three storeys produced a house of twelve rooms which in all but appearance is really quite far removed from most of its London contemporaries. Intensive development of an urban site is better represented by the post-Restoration development in Fore Street.

No parallels are at present known for this combination of plan and elevation, although 6 St Peter's Street, St Albans, had a generally similar appearance, because its restricted site did not permit anything grander, and caused the front range to be only one room in depth. Development of this kind, adding a fashionable front block to an older house, may have occurred at 214 High Street, Berkhamsted, where only the first-floor room overlooking the street remains encapsulated in a large shop. All four bays of the front are

272 *Nos 53/55 High Street, Ashwell: No. 55 has a plastered exterior*

taken up by the one room into which, at the back, the chimney-stack and staircase protrude. Although there are other four-bay elevations in Hertfordshire, such as 33 High Street, St Albans, they are not common, for the future lay in adapting the five-bay elevation to a variety of situations and thereby achieving a more perfect symmetry.

A standard elevation develops

In the latter half of the 17th century, Hertfordshire saw country houses great and small built with a concern for symmetry and regularity hitherto unknown. The dialogue between architect and patron, which seems to have been customary in the evolution of country house designs, must have gone on in towns between builder and client. But architectural display was not as compelling a motive for building in towns; furthermore, economic considerations do not provide the key. The visual contrast presented by Fore Street in Hertford and High Street in Ware towards the end of the 17th century is still apparent, despite the changes of the last two hundred years, and, since Ware continued to flourish, different levels of prosperity cannot be the sole reason for the difference.

It is in Hertford and St Albans, and to a smaller extent in Baldock and Hitchin, that the new kinds of house are best represented, although all towns in the county can show some examples. The most common architectural formula includes a front of five bays and two or three storeys and, even when accompanied by almost identical details, it rarely produces a sense of repetition as can, for example, the corresponding Palladian formula for minor country seats. This is largely because it was applied to sites of a predetermined size within which certain conditions such as access to the rear might be imposed, so that the builder's desire to adhere to a system of proportion had to be reconciled with his client's need to utilise space to the best advantage.

Houses for professional men

The design problem confronting builders towards the end of the 17th century was how to combine a symmetrical front and a new and more spacious staircase with some increase in the number of rooms and the preservation of distinctions between them. Symmetry made it impossible henceforth to establish by external features which were the principal rooms on ground and first floors; the new kind of staircase had to be easily seen if its desired effect was to be achieved; and the rooms flanking the staircase had to be as high as the main ones at the front of the house. Lastly, the people who lived in the more important town houses began to concern themselves more about gardens, no doubt following at some remove the growth of this interest among the landed gentry.

The gardens themselves have disappeared, but their importance can be inferred from the increased concern for a tidy rear elevation, which sometimes could be superior, architecturally, to the front. This was certainly so at The Hermitage, Hitchin [274]; the front which faced Bancroft, a jumble of plastered timber-framed buildings of several periods of construction, contrasted remarkably with the symmetrical brick elevation of five bays, the middle one with pilasters and pediment, which faced a garden renowned for

273 *Nos 40/42 St Andrew's Street, Hertford: from the south east*

274 *The Hermitage, Hitchin (demolished): view of the garden and garden front (photograph by T B Latchmore)*

a box hedge 50 yds (46 m) long and 50 ft (15 m) high. The rear elevation was probably of the early 18th century. The only real front gardens were found in exceptional houses such as Hitchin Priory or newly built houses on the fringe of town, like Lewesford House, 42 Tilehouse Street, Hitchin.

Solutions to design problems varied in detail, but nearly all those which relate to a five-bay front – to what might be called an average house of the more prosperous citizen – entailed abandoning a room as the point of entry in favour of a narrow entrance-hall leading straight through from front to back. The usual place for the staircase was in a widening of the passage in the rear half of the house, thus enabling a visitor on entering to see the balustrade, one of the principal modes of architectural display. Dimsdale House, 16 Bull Plain, Hertford [275], a doctor's house from the first, is like this; but for the encroachment of the staircase, it would have four virtually equal-sized rooms on each floor, all with fireplaces.

275 *Dimsdale House, 16 Bull Plain, Hertford: from the south west*

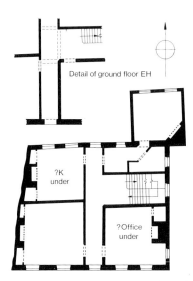

276 *Nos 99/101 Fore Street, Hertford: first-floor plan with detail of ground-floor entrance-hall*

It is difficult to decide how typical Dimsdale House was. It has a well-lit basement intended for work, not merely for storage, and until recently had a flat, lead-covered roof spanning the space between the two parallel ridge-pieces, from which to admire the view and take the air in summer when the house became uncomfortably hot.[24] These two architectural features distinguish it from other houses of its kind, to most of which it was slightly superior. But Dimsdale House is also unusual in having such equal-sized rooms. Most squarish five-bay houses from the end of the 17th century onwards have at the front two rooms of unequal size, with corresponding adjustments at the back. For instance, 99/101 Fore Street, Hertford, presents a generally similar appearance to Dimsdale House, yet the ground plan, which can be inferred from the first-floor plan [276] and surviving doorways, indicates that the builder may have been presented with a problem. The starting points for analysis are that one front room is larger than the other and the staircase is set at right angles to the entrance, not facing it. Among the minor differences is the position of the doorways, which do not open from the entrance-hall into the middle of each of the front rooms; instead, a doorway into the larger room is at the front end of the hall and that into the smaller room is at the back, near the foot of the staircase. These positions are intelligible if the front rooms were used for commercial purposes, perhaps a general office in the larger one and a private office, counting-house or study in the smaller. Entrance to the larger room was near the front doorway for clients and was differently placed from that to a reception room. Access to the supposed office was as private as could be. The position of the staircase, concealed from the entrance, is not uncommon, perhaps because the supposed use of the entrance-hall by business clients made the customary position inappropriate. No other house revealed a similarly significant siting of doorways into the front rooms.

One factor complicating the interpretation of early 18th-century houses and already mentioned in connection with Dimsdale House is the way the first floor was used. Was it no more than a series of bedchambers, or was there a principal reception room at the front of the house? It is rarely possible to infer the latter from the fittings and decoration although 214/216 High Street, Berkhamsted, is a likely instance; and 6 High Street, Bishop's Stortford, may also have had a first-floor reception room as built, occupying three of the five bays of the front. A further problem in houses like this that have undergone antiquarian restoration is that the date of building may be more difficult to determine than with a similarly treated house in the country. Do the present 'Queen Anne' fittings of the Bishop's Stortford house necessarily represent what was there originally?

The forms of plan

The five-bay elevation could front a variety of plans, not all as imposing as their street frontages might indicate. At the early 18th-century brick houses of 3 High Street, St Albans, now no more than the handsome pilastered facade of a good-sized double-pile house, and Holford House, 9 High Street, Baldock, the rooms fail to meet the expectations raised by the exterior. The contrast is even more marked at 28 St Andrew's Street, Hertford [277], where it would be

277 *No. 28 St Andrew's Street, Hertford*

278 *No. 68 High Street, Stevenage: from the south east*

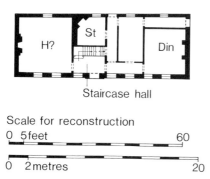

Staircase hall

Scale for reconstruction

0   5 feet   60

0   2 metres   20

279 *No. 68 High Street, Stevenage: reconstruction plan*

principal rooms are square or nearly so, the Stevenage house has one room bigger than any ground-floor room in the other two, and must have been used in a quite different way. No first-floor drawing room here: the big room surely served that purpose, the room at the opposite end was the dining room, and behind the staircase was what might have been a study or office. Perhaps that was where the owner-builder's professional business – something that did not require clients to enter the house – was conducted and, whatever it was, he was a man of somewhat lower social status than the Dimsdales and their like, despite the grand house front.

The long one-room-deep house appears in more modest form and considerably earlier at 51 St Andrew's Street, Hertford, a timber-framed house of five bays. Other kinds of one-room-deep house, such as 13 Tilehouse Street, Hitchin, and 33/35 Hitchin Street, Baldock, comprise a range of three rooms with a staircase projection at the back, but neither has enough of the original fittings left for the date or plan to be securely established.

Not much larger are houses that might be described as being one and a half rooms deep, in so far as the rear rooms are small and, like the staircase, are of only about half the width of the principal room facing the street. No. 34 Bancroft, Hitchin, already mentioned as a house of gradual growth, did not achieve this form until the middle of the 18th century. About that time the former Brewery House, High Street, Baldock [**280**, **281**], replaced part of a row of timber-framed buildings; its plan shows in a general way what a new-built house of this type was like.

interesting to know what proportion of the total cost went on the cut and moulded brickwork of the front.

Holford House, with its smaller front rooms, exemplifies rather more clearly than 101 Fore Street, Hertford, what was evidently an alternative form of plan to the type represented by Dimsdale House with two equal-sized front rooms. No. 16 High Street, Baldock (Goldcrest Hotel), is of the same type as Holford House. Such smaller front rooms were probably intended as offices for the professional men – mainly doctors, surveyors and lawyers – whose numbers increased so markedly in the first half of the 18th century.

Houses looking as if they might have been built for the near-gentry professional man are naturally less common in the smaller towns. A likely candidate in Stevenage is 72 High Street, but more interesting is 68 High Street [**278**, **279**], which presents a contrast between exterior and interior, with an impressive seven-bay front behind which are only two principal ground-floor rooms and two minor ones, with a similar number of bedrooms. Inevitably, given the modern alterations, the original plan is to some extent conjectural, yet, unless some unperceived major change has taken place, the building can never have embodied a shop. Hence it presents a remarkable contrast with both Dimsdale House and Holford House, for although in all three the

Tradesmen's houses in the 18th century

It has not been established whether Brewery House was built for a brewer or if, as was the case at Watford, the brewery was established behind the house at a later date. If the former, it was in some sense a tradesman's house, although the possibility of a local equivalent to Mr Thrale, whose involvement with brewing was not of a day-to-day kind and did not impair his standing in the eyes of Samuel Johnson and his circle, should not be overlooked. But the status of this kind of house can better be judged by comparison with what can only be tradesmen's houses, built in brick and in a fashionable style but still, like the earlier ones around Hitchin market-place, designed to make the most of a narrow plot because that was the best place for their owner's business.

The many buyers and sellers of corn drawn to Hemel Hempstead by the corn market were potential customers for other kinds of goods and it was by catering for their needs that those who lived and traded on the east side of the market-place were able to rebuild their premises in handsome style. Nos 81 and 83 High Street were built earlier,

280 *Brewery House, High Street, Baldock*

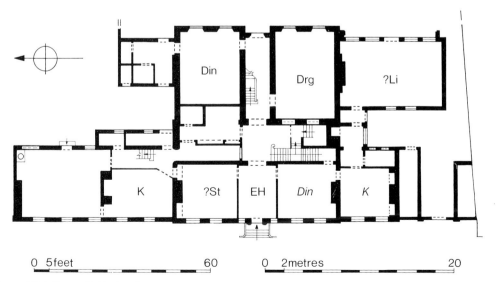

0 5feet   60   0 2metres   20

281 *Brewery House, High Street, Baldock: plan*

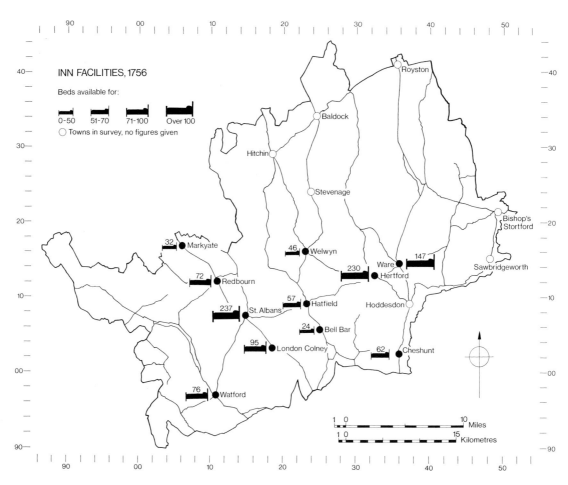

282 *Map depicting the number of inn beds available in Hertfordshire in 1756*

perhaps *c.*1710, as a semi-detached pair, five bays in width, with a carriageway in the middle. In ground plan they were identical, with two rooms heated by corner fireplaces and, between them, a staircase, reached from the carriageway as well as from both rooms. No. 83 has an identical plan upstairs whereas No. 81 extends over the carriageway, giving it a large first-floor room of three bays and two bedrooms on the second floor. The shop canopy extends in front of both houses and it can be assumed that the front room was given over to trade, the back room was the kitchen and the front room upstairs a drawing room – in No. 83 a rather grand one.

A very different and more modest form of development at 63 High Street testifies to a steadily growing prosperity over quite a long period. What seems to have happened here is that the plot represents only about half the width of the original house, and that, about the beginning of the 18th century, a division into two separate buildings, which may by then have been of long standing, was translated into a more definite architectural form. Such alteration of plot boundaries by subdivision and encroachment testifies to the growth of the town while making the architectural historian's task difficult.

170

The development of inns

The several main roads radiating from London ensured that Hertfordshire was well provided with inns offering accommodation to travellers. Variations of route from time to time caused the decline of some places and the rise of others, and the inns with them [**282**, **283**]. Pre-eminent among the latter was St Albans. Inns providing for visitors to the great medieval abbey gave the town a lead which it maintained well into the 19th century, and as early as 1577 it had over 20 per cent of the inns in the whole county. By 1686, St Albans provided 719 beds and stabling for 1,411 horses.[25]

The purpose-built inns in Hertfordshire were distinguished by the galleries or staircases giving access to groups of rooms. The earliest is the former Crown and Anchor, now 37 Holywell Hill, St Albans [**284**]. It stands at the corner of the old London road (now Sopwell Lane) and Holywell Hill, and was probably built in the second quarter of the 16th century. What remains is principally a jettied range extending for 120 ft (36 m) along Sopwell Lane, which has preserved along most of its length a covered gallery from which the eight or nine chambers were reached. The outer wall was originally open in its upper half to give light

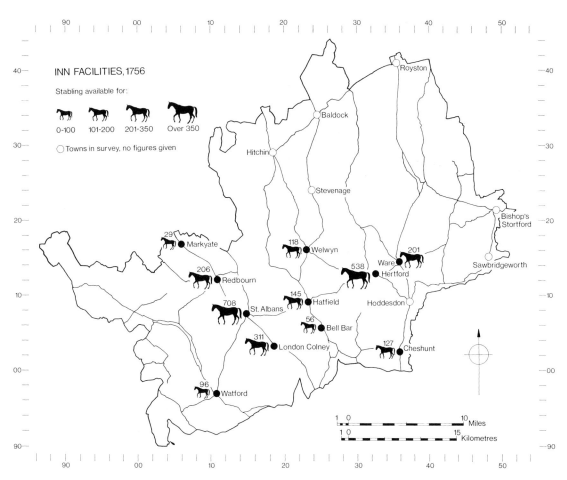

283 *Map depicting the amount of inn stabling available in Hertfordshire in 1756*

to the passage and indirect light to the rooms, each of which had a large window on that side. But not all of this long range was given over to lodging chambers, for on the ground floor is an internal chimney with a stone fireplace of a width and quality which suggest that it served the principal room of the inn, the hall; this was entered in the usual way, by a cross-passage. A binding-beam and bearers in the hall are moulded whereas the beams on the opposite side of the stack are plain, and the fireplace, too, in so far as the evidence remains. The hall was entered by a cross-passage at the lower end, the fireplace, with a staircase beside it, corresponding to the upper end. Beyond was the kitchen, and presumably other service rooms. Two rooms upstairs also had good stone fireplaces. Evidently it was an inn of quality, combining in one range all the principal rooms, whatever may have existed farther to the south along Holywell Hill. Access to the chambers was by a staircase placed beside the hall chimney-stack and probably reached directly from the yard as well as from the hall itself, from which it was easily overseen.

The Crown and Anchor is much the most complete of Hertfordshire late 16th-century inns. Not many years later, The Sun at Hitchin was established and seems soon to have become an altogether larger establishment, but it is with inns as with farmhouses: those that prosper most tend to be rebuilt most, and the whole of the original street range has been lost in the cause of improvement. Only a timber-framed range on the south side of the courtyard, well away from the street, establishes the existence of a sizeable earlier inn.

As trade grew, older inns were enlarged and rebuilt. The Bell at Hertford was expanded in the late 16th century, as was the White Swan (28/30 Fore Street), where a corner block jettied on two sides was added. Although the ground-floor arrangement is lost, no doubt it corresponded to that of the first floor, having one large room with a fireplace and a smaller one at the corner. If this were so, it resembled the Crown and Anchor, the big room being the hall and the small one the buttery or bar, and in much the same way there was probably a staircase beside the stack, in a small projecting turret of its own. Such a plan implies a difference from the Crown and Anchor in the point of entry, which here must have been at the same end as the staircase, not the opposite end.

A less important inn than these, but more interesting for its structure and plan, is the late 16th-century purpose-built

171

284 *Nos 37 Holywell Hill/2 Sopwell Lane, St Albans: former inn gallery*

285 *No. 27 Leyton Road, Harpenden*

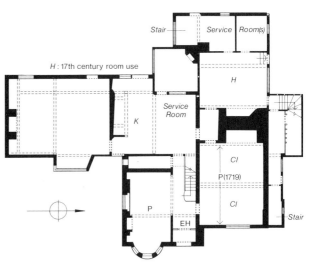

286 *No. 27 Leyton Road, Harpenden: plan*

Old Bull at Harpenden (27 Leyton Road) [**285**, **286**]; its location near the common suggests a connection with the fair as well as with the needs of travellers. The form of this little inn is highly remarkable and throws light on how some larger ones were organised. The plan in its present state is that of an internal-chimney house with lobby-entrance and staircase beside a chimney-stack. It appears that the present staircase is an addition and that three of the four rooms grouped around the stack were each subdivided into two, the fourth, at the rear, being the hall. Two staircases each gave access to two rooms, either by means of a lobby in one room or by providing a landing at the top of the stairs from which two doors could open. The only fireplaces were the two on the ground floor (see [**306**]). Lighting must have presented some problems in three of the rooms around the chimney-stack – the two inner ones on the first floor and the inner ground-floor one at the front; indirect lighting must have been used on the staircase side. The means of access is the same as that in a college where the rooms are reached from a series of staircases.

Architecturally, the second half of the 17th century was the heyday of inns in Hertfordshire. Ware has two of considerable interest. The French Horn certainly incorporates work of an earlier period but about the middle of the 17th

century a grand new staircase in the heavy, derived Jacobean style [**287**] was inserted to serve a new block of taller rooms as well as those in the older part which were reached from the half landings. But the most remarkable feature about this inn was its siting, for before part of it was sliced off in the 19th century to widen the junction of the two market-places, a corner of the French Horn had projected out, as a continuation of the building line of East Street, to reduce the road width at its narrowest point: no inn was ever better placed to attract custom. The second inn is now divided into several occupations, going under the numbers 14, 16 and 18 Baldock Street. Its interest lies in the fact that it preserves many of its original arrangements despite these alterations. Here the importance of the relationship between the yard and the staircases is particularly obvious, especially the staircase serving the long back wing away from the street front, which had to be reached easily by the dismounting traveller.

One of the largest inns, formerly The Swan at Stevenage (now The Grange, 5 High Street) [288], seems to have been quite large already by the early 17th century. Subsequently, a virtually independent block of rooms, served by its own kitchen, was added beyond the putative Assembly Room at the far end of the south wing from the street range. This block had its own entrance from the courtyard into a staircase-hall, giving access to three ground-floor and five first-floor rooms. In the much smaller inn at Baldock Street, Ware, there is a similarly placed staircase, although here the corridors run the full length of the wing on both floors. This block may have had rooms for public meetings and other social events.

Lying at the end of town, on a large plot of ground, The Swan at Stevenage was in an unusually favourable position. By contrast, the long-established inns of medieval origin were all in town centres where enlargement to meet the growing number of travellers in the late 17th and early 18th centuries meant cramming as much as possible on a restricted site. The Bell (now The Salisbury Arms) at Hertford developed residential wings down both sides of its long tapering courtyard and closed the end with open sheds under which carts and waggons and private carriages could be sheltered overnight. At Hitchin, The George and The Swan were both free to develop in the same way but The Bell's neighbour, the White Swan, where only a fairly

Former gallery

Straight joint

```
0   5feet                    60
0   2metres                  20
```

K

Assembly Room?

H

Straight joint

287 *The French Horn, Ware: staircase*

288 *The Grange, formerly the Swan Inn, Stevenage: ground and first-floor plans*

173

289 *The Swan, Berkhamsted: development plan*

restricted frontage was available, appears to have been less able to respond to growing custom.

Most inns in town centres developed more or less awkward plans because of site restrictions. The Swan at Berkhamsted [289] seems to have been governed by the existence of an early 15th-century open-hall house which first extended along the street front in both directions, then developed a wing, and finally had galleries added to produce for the first time what is recognisably an inn plan. The

position and width of the presumptive hall (for very little remains of it) necessitated the formation of a second and very narrow courtyard and so produced a plan less compact than was usual by the late 17th century. At about the same time, balustraded galleries were added at The George, Hitchin, and its namesake at Bishop's Stortford, where the gabled south elevation marks the provision of a third storey with semi-attic bedrooms.

The King's Arms, Berkhamsted, is an example of an inn built as such in the late 17th century on a narrow site so that the carriageway was at the north end of the frontage and a long range of rooms ran down only one side of the yard. Like a number of others, this inn had a second entrance into the yard from a side street.

By the beginning of the 18th century Hertfordshire towns were so well provided with inns that it is difficult to discover one of any consequence that was newly built much after 1700. Refronting went on but otherwise the principal development was the addition of an assembly room or ballroom. A very large one was built at The Sun, Hitchin, in 1770 as a meeting-place for the hunt ball and other grand occasions, whilst The King's Arms, Berkhamsted, acquired one early in the Victorian period. Significantly, the latter must have replaced some bedrooms, for by the late 1830s the coaching trade on that particular road had fallen off sharply, following the opening of the London and Birmingham railway in 1837. Within a very few years the new mode of transport had produced a new kind of building, the railway hotel,[26] which sent the town inn into a decline. Coinciding with the growth of residential suburbs, which drew people out of the town centre, the development of the railway hotel provides a symbolic full stop to the story not only of the inn but of the residential town itself.

Appendix

Structure and materials

The primary concern of the present survey was to study the way in which houses were used, rather than to make a detailed study of structure and materials. What follows, therefore, is not a systematic survey but rather a commentary on the material that came to notice and a discussion of some problems that emerged.

Roof construction

Aisled halls and passing-braces

Few forms of roof construction not already familiar to students of the subject were found. At the 12th-century Burston Manor, St Stephen, a hitherto unrecorded form of passing-brace was discovered which is unusual in three respects: the braces are of considerably larger scantling than the common rafters; they taper towards the top; and they do not extend to meet the common rafter in the opposite slope of the roof [290]; instead, they stop where they meet on the vertical axis. Passing-braces of the orthodox kind are halved or lapped across other timbers so that the tight fit of the joints prevents distortion of the structure in the vertical plane.[1]

The particular point of interest about Burston Manor lies in the position to be assigned to it in the development of such roofs. It can be argued that it has an early place in the typology of passing-braces because, first, it is as old as any application of this system of construction anywhere, the only one of comparable age being above the nave of Lisieux Cathedral where it is dated before 1181; and secondly, it resembles a few other roofs in looking like a tentative step towards the full development of the passing-brace system.[2] The only known parallel is in Surrey, at The Forge, Dunsfold.[3] An alternative view, according to which passing-braces were developed abroad and were already archaic in such applications as Almshoe Bury, Ippollitts,[4] would give Burston Manor a quite different significance – an early attempt to break away from the system, perhaps.

At Thorley Hall [291] the mortises suggest that in the original aisled hall phase there were three braces instead of one, and that only the lowest one was truly a form of passing-brace, where it crossed the aisle tie-beam. A recent dating of the reconstructed upper part of this roof – which

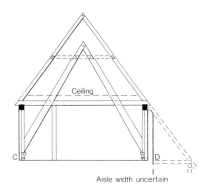

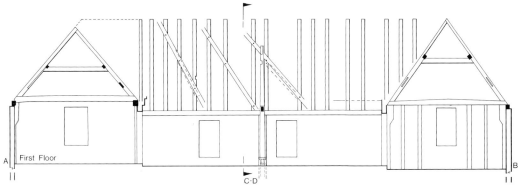

290 *Burston Manor, St Stephen: long and cross-sections of roof and first floor*

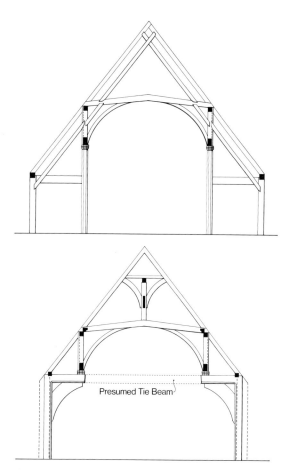

291 *Thorley Hall: cross-section of original building with reconstruction above*

292 *Place House, Ware: moulded crown-post of open truss in hall roof*

Presumed Tie Beam

has a crown-post – to the early 14th century implies that the first phase must be considerably earlier, probably no later than the middle of the 13th century. It seems unlikely that carpentry joints, on which the early 14th-century date is founded, provide greater chronological precision than other typologies, and hence a considerably later date can be envisaged for the Thorley Hall crown-post and consequently for the earlier structure on which it stands.

Passing-braces continued in use until at least the end of the 14th century. At Croxley Hall Farm, Rickmansworth, which was once a possession of St Albans Abbey, is a large aisled barn combining a main-span roof with crown-posts and passing-braces rising from the outer walls to the nave tie-beams. This is likely to be the 'new great barn built at Crokesle' some time between 1396 and 1401.[5] A different combination of passing-braces and crown-posts is found at The Swan, Berkhamsted, in the roof of the cross-wing; it may be of about the same date. Nor is this the end of the passing-brace story; in a reverse-curved shape, which must be their very latest manifestation, they occur in a barn at Aston Bury Manor which is not at all closely datable but must, from its formal relation to the house, be comparatively late, perhaps 16th century, or even mid 17th century like the house itself.

176

Hertfordshire has another important aisled hall: Place House, Ware [**292**]. The hall itself is lofty and well finished, with moulded capital and base to the freestanding octagonal posts and a moulded cornice running completely around each bay. Its date is a matter of argument, between about 1295 and some thirty or forty years later. Everything hangs on the evidence of the mouldings, for which parallels are hard to find. (Precisely dated wood mouldings before the 15th century are so scarce that they do not afford a chronology, and do not appear to follow exactly the same forms as stone mouldings after the 12th century.) The date matters because it limits the transition, in work of comparatively high quality, from the passing-brace roof as represented at Almshoe Bury to the crown-post roof; and whether this change is accomplished in a period of fifty or nearer a hundred years is of some importance.

Mono-span derivatives of aisled halls

The desire to remove the posts from the hall to give an unencumbered floor space took several forms, one of which was to set the aisled construction of the open truss upon tie-beams. This device, an alternative to hammer-beam or base-cruck construction, is common in Suffolk and other parts of East Anglia and is thinly represented in Hertfordshire. Wymondley Bury and 125 High Street, Hemel Hempstead, are early examples from the first half of the 14th century. The only other one known, which stood near Wheathampstead and was demolished long ago, looks from a drawing to have been considerably later, perhaps early 15th century [293]. Thorley Hall was converted to this type in the 14th or 15th century when the aisles were narrowed and the posts cut away to stand on a tie-beam.

Secular hammer-beam roofs are not common anywhere and in this county are confined to a single example, at 103/104 Queen Street, Hitchin.

Crown-post roofs

Hertfordshire is the only county for which a detailed study of crown-post roofs exists.[6] As always, dating criteria are difficult to establish and typology is as uncertain a guide here as in other fields; one tightly dated scheme based to a considerable extent on Berkshire has been proposed[7] but proves to be no more applicable to Hertfordshire than earlier generalisations.[8] Furthermore, even the function of the crown-post roof is a matter of argument, and it may be well to start with that.

Essentially, the crown-post provides one means of stabilising couples of common rafters which were spaced, in early examples, equidistantly along a roof. Each post is jointed into a collar-purlin and into the collar-beam forming part of the couple, and by this triangulation of timbers the roof is made perfectly stable at three or more points and incapable of deformation unless the joints fail. The rafter couples between these points stand independently and are linked to each other and to the crown-post trusses only by tiling laths; their individual stability depends, in a mass-walled building, on the triangulation afforded by ashlar-pieces and sole-pieces at the foot of each rafter, and, in a timber-framed building, on the use of braces to prevent spread. Occasionally a carpenter emphasised lengthwise stability by pegging the collars to the collar-purlin, as at Hoo End Grange, St Paul's Walden, but this is rare. In principle it does not matter whether the central purlin and its braces are below the collar-beams or above them, as French examples demonstrate, but since for aesthetic reasons the

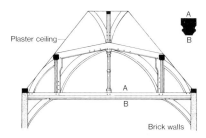

293 *Cottage at Gustard Wood Common, Wheathampstead (demolished): cross-section of roof*

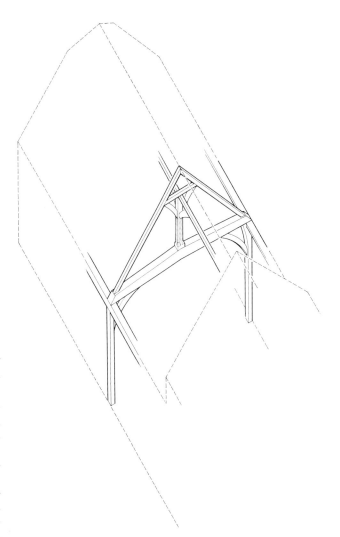

294 *Stebbing Farm, Stevenage: axonometric drawing of open truss in hall*

crown-post itself was developed in England as a decorative feature it became usual to put both bracing and purlin below the collars. Viewed in these structural terms, the crown-post provided, at the time of its inception in the early 13th century, a more efficient means of providing points of stability than the alternative method of the passing-brace.[9]

Few buildings are sufficiently closely dated to provide a chronology for crown-post roofs. Place House, Ware, marks the beginning of the series in the early 14th century, and not much later a crown-post roof in Sandon church can be dated by a contract of 1348 for the rebuilding of the chancel walls.[10] To the middle or third quarter of the 14th century belongs one of the buildings of the house of Grey Friars at Ware founded in 1338; the roof of this building, now called The Priory, combines crown-posts and scissor-bracing. Already mentioned is another combination of two techniques, using crown-posts in the main-span and passing-braces linking nave and aisles, which is dated to the closing years of the 14th century at Croxley Hall Farm. The date between 1406 and 1420 proposed for Bramfield Bury is not accepted here; and the latest firm date for a crown-post roof is 1442–3 when Stebbing Farm, Stevenage [**294**], was built.

In broad outline the typology of crown-post roofs is simple: nearly all early examples have braces rising in four directions, two to the collar-purlin and two to the common rafters, whereas nearly all late examples have only the two braces to the collar-purlin. Place House is exceptional in having both. The rare use of crown-posts in conjunction with other forms of structure is characteristic of the middle or second half of the 14th century as, for example, The Swan, Berkhamsted, or No. 22 George Street, St Albans, although neither can be closely dated. Even the building called The Priory at Ware could be years after 1338 since nothing is known about the sequence or completion dates of the friary buildings.

Roofs with side purlins

The earliest English roofs have no lengthwise stiffening in the form of purlins.[11] In what tends, in roof studies, loosely to be called south-east England, a region extending from east Hampshire to south Suffolk and embracing Hertfordshire on the way, the crown-post and collar-purlin roof provides the first form of longitudinal stiffening to have been widely adopted. It was developed in the course of the 13th century and continued in use at least to the end of the 15th century. Before then, forms of roof had come into use which employ not a central purlin but side purlins and embody a different structural principle from the earliest purlin roofs known in the West Midlands and north of England. These purlin roofs have side principal rafters into the backs of which purlins supporting the common rafters are laid in trenches to about half their depth, the earliest and certainly one of the grandest of the kind being the roof of the Guesten Hall of Worcester cathedral priory.[12] In this type, lengthwise rigidity is achieved in the usual way by a triangular formation of timbers, using windbraces jointed into the principals and purlins.

In south-east England, of which Hertfordshire may be considered the microcosm, purlins had quite different beginnings and were possibly conceived as having a different function; they were supported by raking struts standing on tie-beams or other timbers and could not stay in position independently of the pairs of common rafters with which, at the points of support, they formed a rudimentary kind of

295 *Clintons, Little Hadham: hall roof*

296 *Redbournbury: hall roof*

truss. Alternatively, the purlins were supported directly by principal rafters of scantlings hardly larger than the common rafters.[13] In this first stage of development purlins were not always braced to their supporting struts or principals and consequently cannot have provided longitudinal rigidity. Their purpose was the more limited one of preventing the common rafters from sagging at their midpoint and in a main-span roof they were a substitute – perhaps a cheaper one – for collar-beams to each rafter couple.

These beginnings are not represented in Hertfordshire. In the succeeding stage a quite different kind of truss is used. At intervals the lower part of a common rafter is increased in thickness so that a collar-beam can be tenoned into it, above which it reverts to a normal scantling; the purlin is housed in a notch cut in the collar-beam and can be thought of as being clasped between collar and rafter, hence the clasped-purlin roof. In this system, as in the preceding one, the collar-beams necessary in collar-rafter and crown-post roofs are dispensed with, although that clearly was not the prime intention of the design; rather, it was to have, by means of windbraces, the triangulation which provides lengthwise rigidity and is invariably found in such roofs. When this kind of roof first appeared in the houses of Hertfordshire is hard to say.

An alternative form of construction to the same end was to tenon the purlins into principal rafters which themselves, unlike those of the Guesten Hall type, doubled as common rafters in so far as they bore the tiling laths directly. It is because the truss is not independent of the common rafters that this type still shows its affinity to the earliest strutted-purlin roofs. The earliest dated example at present known is the roof of Westminster Hall, built in the later 1390s, where such purlins are used both above and below the arcade plates, and the earliest domestic example in Hertfordshire may be Clintons, Little Hadham [295]. Whatever uncertainties attach to the hall roof there, its traceried spandrels suggest the stylistic influence of Westminster Hall and its mouldings are consistent with a date in the first half of the 15th century. Clintons, though small, had craftsmanship of a high quality lavished on it. Unfortunately, no domestic roof comparable in importance to those of Burston Manor or Almshoe Bury survives from the 14th or 15th centuries, for it is in such buildings as Rye House, Stanstead Abbots, or Hunsdon House that the early important examples might have been expected.

Aesthetic preference may have dictated choice in some of the comparatively small roofs considered here. Two principal objectives can be discerned: one is the creation of a lofty upper space in which whatever decorative effects are sought are confined to the two planes formed by the rafters; the other is to exploit the visual possibilities afforded by transverse structural members and ornament. Although the two aims are not mutually exclusive, they provide one means of ordering the bewildering variety of roofs. Thus the roof of Redbournbury [296], which has arch-braces between and curved windbraces within each bay, combines the clear definition of three uniform spaces with the sense of progression which would have been clearer seen from the ground than now. Betlow Farm, Tring Rural, shows a generally similar intention, modified slightly by the desire to emphasise the open truss. In contrast to these are such roofs as Clintons, Little Hadham, or Ayot Place, Ayot St Peter, where traceried spandrels relieve the bulk and prominence of the structurally sounder tie-beam by their effect of lightness. The tie-beam was preferred to a collar-beam for its greater resistance to outward thrust, and although windbraces might be used, the emphasis in such a roof remains firmly in the vertical planes. In John

O'Gaddesden's House, Little Gaddesden, where only the alternate trusses have tie-beams, elaborately carved solid brackets provide an effect of richness rather than the lightness fashionable earlier.

Between the very plain roofs and those enriched with carved ornament come those relying on mouldings for their effect. Much the best of them is The Brotherhood, Hitchin, in which all the roof timbers except the common rafters are worked, some simply, some quite elaborately. The general effect, to which moulded wall-posts with capitals and bases contributed, was one of movement and a strong play of shadows varying as the light moved around this great upper chamber.

All the buildings so far mentioned are of some importance and of good quality, even Betlow Farm which is the lowliest of them. It is difficult to discern from them why tenoned purlins were used in preference to clasped, although where two purlins and their accompanying array of windbraces were desired, the latter would not serve; Oxhey Hall, Watford Rural [297], where a panelled effect

297 *Oxhey Hall, Watford Rural: roof of the lodgings range*

was sought throughout, is a case in point. It is as if tenoned purlins were considered to be superior in some way, yet both Redcoats, Wymondley, and Langley Lodge, Kings Langley, buildings of unquestionably high quality, have clasped purlins.

Cruck construction

Cruck construction, on which an extensive literature has appeared in recent years,[14] has only been found in a few parishes on the western fringe of the county and its distribution is more interesting than the houses themselves, which are structurally unremarkable. Crucks are of two types. Four houses – Grove Farm, Tring [298], Moor Cottage, Great Gaddesden, 6/8 Church Street, Bovingdon, and Searches, St Stephen – have the kind of cruck blade that terminates a little way above the collar-beam. Two houses have (or had) full crucks rising to the ridge of the roof; they are Westwick Row Farm, St Michael, and a now demolished cottage which formerly adjoined the King William IV public house in Kings Langley, one truss of which has been preserved by securing it to the wall of a house in Sarratt. At 15 Akeman Street, Tring, is what looks more like an upper cruck than any kind of true cruck. One base cruck, at The Court House, formerly the Old Post Office, Offley, supports a crown-post roof. The base-cruck house is 14th century; the others are unlikely to be older and are more likely to be of the 15th or early 16th century.

Timber framing

All over Hertfordshire the framing of load-bearing walls comprises upright timbers, or studs, which are tenoned top and bottom into sills and plates; the differences between one kind and another relate to their spacing, the scantling of the timber and the ways in which braces are used to prevent lengthwise deformation. The task of describing and classifying the variant forms is complicated by the many gradations of spacing, the deliberate concealment of braces externally, for aesthetic reasons, and their concealment internally by plaster and panelling.

Close and not-so-close studding

For the best work, close-studding was the rule. It has been defined as narrow panels divided by studs, the panels being 'seldom much more than twice the width of the studs'.[15] Tudor Cottage, Albury, shows what the best vernacular work of this kind was like in the mid 16th century. Church Farm, Holwell, is also 16th century and in both houses the braces are deliberately concealed in order to produce a perfectly uniform external effect.[16] But there is a difference in

298 *Grove Farm, Tring: open cruck truss in hall*

the quality of the work. At Tudor Cottage, the studs are well finished internally with sharp arrises and the braces are flush with them, neither of which applies at Holwell. Both conform to the quoted definition but some walls framed only with studs and braces are hard to bring within it.

The panels between studs were filled, not with the well-known kind of basketwork commonly associated with wattle-and-daub infilling, but with roughly trimmed staves of wall height fastened by withies to three or four short horizontal staves or wattles sprung into an augured hole in one stud and a groove tapering towards the top in the next one. A partly cut-away panel at The Horns, Datchworth, shows the tapering of the horizontal staves to fit the augured hole. At Tudor Cottage this produced much the same flush-walled effect inside as outside, with only the truss posts intruding into the rooms. In less finished buildings the braces might protrude from the wall surface as well but, even where they were not halved into the studs, a flush face could be achieved by additional internal cladding. Nos 177/179 High Street, Watford, yielded interesting information on this point. There, the close-studding and its flush infill had received a covering of broad, well-cut laths, long enough to reach from the principal post to an intermediate post and nailed to every stud and upright stave, upon which the plaster was placed. The resulting surface was flush with all the main wall timbers except the principal post.

The Watford method of building was evidently cheaper than the Albury one and it shows the way wall construction was developing. By the middle of the 17th century, wall-posts and tie-beams did not always coincide, and the wall had become a series of good-sized intermediate posts with smaller square studs between them, like an opened-out version of 177/179 High Street, Watford; No. 62 Blanche Lane,

Potters Bar, is like this in part. This kind of construction can be found in houses and barns for most of the 17th century, and those examples in houses were intended to have a flush finish.

Methods of bracing

Bracing was introduced into timber-frame construction because the joints alone were insufficient to prevent distortion under weight or wind pressure. The most effective and by far the most common way of achieving this was to form a triangle of timbers at corners, the whole being held rigid by mortise-and-tenon joints. This could be of two kinds, one downwards from post to sill and the other upwards from post to plate, both with curved or straight braces.

Down-bracing was the norm in late medieval Hertfordshire; the braces were invariably curved and often approximated to a quadrant. They commonly formed part of the external framing at the gable end of cross-wings, where the resulting pattern is called Kentish framing; the name, like Wealden house, is justified by convenience and little else. Down-curved braces generally are known as tension-braces; upward braces, of concave curvature are more reasonably called arch-braces. The size of tension-braces was governed partly by aesthetic considerations and partly by the need to accommodate windows; thus the wish to achieve a bold effect in a wing by having the braces rise from the middle of the sill nearly to the top of the posts would not permit a window of more than two lights unless the wing were unusually wide.

By the beginning of the 17th century long, straight down- or tension-braces had become common. Upward bracing is less common and appears to have both a shorter time span and a restricted geographical distribution. The best example, and one of the earliest, is King John's Farm, Chorleywood, of the early 16th century; Oak Cottage, Flaunden [299], and a rear range at 177/179 High Street, Watford, are of similar date. All have bold curved braces. Later, upward braces are straight, appear in minor buildings and persist to the end of the 17th century. Yew Cottage,

299 *Oak Cottage, Flaunden*

182

300 *Yew Cottage, Abbots Langley: from the north*

Abbots Langley [300], the timber frame of which was never intended to be exposed, is the latest example noted, of about 1700.

A third way of stiffening wall framing, known as stud-bracing, is a technique with definite East Anglian links. Its distinguishing characteristic is that a brace terminates on a post or stud at both ends, thus contradicting the otherwise universal principle of triangulation. Yew Tree Farm, Much Hadham [301], incorporates both downward and stud-bracing and Tudor Cottage, Albury, has only the latter. In Hertfordshire it appears to be largely confined to the 16th century.

Ornamental panelling

Framing in eastern England is essentially composed of vertical timbers, whereas in western England it usually incorporates horizontal timbers to form a panelled effect. Hertfordshire timber framing is of eastern character, with one or two specifically East Anglian elements. It is all the more surprising, therefore, that the western fringe of the county can show a few examples of a kind of ornamental panelled framing that would not be out of place in the Marches of Wales; Oxhey Hall, Watford Rural [302], for example, has retained one room in the most florid western style of the late 16th century. Other buildings where ornamental panel framing has been recorded include Gaddesden Hall, Great Gaddesden, and The Abbot's House, Abbots Langley.

Tapered wall-plates and barge-boards

Certain previously undocumented details of timber-framed construction were developed to minimise the effects of the weather on the exposed ends of horizontal timbers. At Howell's Farm, Weston, Yew Tree Cottage, Aston [303], and Hyde Lane Farm, Abbots Langley, the ends of wall-plates are tapered off where they project beyond the gable-end wall. It is not perfectly clear why the plates should have extended like this. They may have supported the lower ends of barge-boards, although the only clear indications of how barge-boards were supported occur at Burston Manor. There, in an early 17th-century gable, short lengths of timber extend from the nearest common rafter to the principal rafter of the end truss, into which they are trenched. They were for barge-boards, no doubt, which can only have been supported at the lower ends by the projecting wall-plates. This provides an adequate reason, in roofs with clasped or tenoned purlins, for extending the plate beyond its natural termination at the end truss; either two or four major timbers needed protection for the exposed end-grain. This holds good for Burston Manor, Hyde Lane Farm and Yew Tree Cottage, but not for Howell's Farm, which has a crown-post roof and for which no explanation can be offered.

Posts and beams with enlarged ends

The technique of enlarging the head of a post to provide a housing for a horizontal timber, whether a wall-post to take a wall-plate, a crown-post to take a collar-purlin, or any similar application, is very widespread. Such a head is often called a jowl, although the reason for the name is unclear. In Hertfordshire, from the early 14th century, principal posts

supporting roof trusses are almost invariably thickened. Place House, Ware, has them in slightly different forms in the screens truss and the open truss. The reason for thickening a post is clear; the intention underlying the thickening of the ends of bearers on the underside is not. It occurs at Howell's Farm, Weston, Fabdens in Standon, Rumbolds, Cottered, and in several other houses. The examples quoted are late medieval, and probably the practice did not continue much after the middle of the 16th century. The general intention is evidently to provide extra strength where the bearer joins the post, perhaps by increasing the size of the tenon.

Mixed construction: brick and timber

Brick was first used as a substitute for stone or flint to provide an equally solid and durable form of mass walling. So far as is known, it was used in that way for the best buildings, until about the middle of the 17th century, when various forms of mixed construction, combining brick and timber, came into use, first at manorial level and later for humbler houses.

Aston Bury Manor is a good example of this technique. The house appears from the outside to be wholly of brick, with the exception of some patches of flint at the rear on the

301 *Yew Tree Farm, Much Hadham*

302 *Oxhey Hall, Watford Rural: interior view*

ground floor. These have been regarded as the fragmentary survival of an older building but the fact that they fit perfectly into the existing structure, without any difference of alignment or wall thickness or traces of earlier openings, casts doubt on the notion. This curious feature notwithstanding, the ground-floor walls are entirely of mass construction. On the first floor the external brickwork rises unbroken by any other material but the walls are considerably narrower than below, and internally a skeletal framework of timber can be seen to reinforce a mass wall which was evidently felt to be inadequate to bear the attics and roof. Although the brickwork is more than an infilling, the framing, which is jointed to the partitions and to the tiebeams of the attic storey, was intended to ensure the stability of the building: this it did, and does, as effectively as thicker walls wholly of brick, and probably with some saving in cost. That some uncertainty was felt about the stability of brick, despite its earlier use on the grand scale in country houses, is perhaps shown by the curious buttresses to the gable walls at Aston Bury and Upp Hall, Braughing.

A more conventional combination of brick and timber occurs at Hammond's Farm, Pirton, again about the middle of the 17th century. When the major part of the house was rebuilt and enlarged, brick was used, at a good thickness, for the ground-floor walls, whereas the first floors are of

303 *Yew Tree Cottage, Aston: interior showing tapered end of wall-plate (at left-hand side)*

orthodox timber framing with brick nogging – one of those rare cases where an infilling of brick is undoubtedly original. Another is the rear wing of Rook's Nest Farm, Walkern, of much the same date.

A common combination of the two materials uses the brick for show, to provide a good, up-to-date front, and tim-

184

304 *Nos 65/67 High Street, Hemel Hempstead: the plastered side wall can be seen*

ber framing for the rest. This practice probably began in the late 17th century. Houses in Hemel Hempstead High Street like this include Nos 65/67 [**304**], which is of that period, and others which are slightly later. An estimate made in 1720 for rebuilding the dwelling house of James Martin of St Albans, farrier, provides for the front and rear walls to be of brick and the sides next to the adjacent building to be of timber.[17] The technique persisted for a long time, being used at the Blue Boy public house in Fore Street, Hertford, towards the end of the 18th century and in 29 High Street, Ashwell, as late as 1830–40.

Hearths and chimneys

Only at Redbournbury were the remains of a louvre above the open hearth noticed; on each side of the roof two rafters are tenoned into trimmers which have a horizontal upper face to support some form of smoke outlet. This could have been no more than a small gabled roof carried on short posts a little way above the main roof to enable smoke to escape without letting in rain.

Where a central louvre did not exist, smoke escaped out of the roof through an open gablet above a hipped roof. It is often hard to discover how smoke was conducted to that point without entering the upper chambers above which such gablets stand. A rare survival at Fabdens, Standon [**305**], shows one way of doing this. The partition at the upper end of the hall is carried up only as high as the collar-beam; from there a boarded ceiling runs on the collar-beams to the vertical plane of the gablet and at that point a small wattle-and-daub partition closes off the space between ceiling and gablet, so that smoke is excluded from the solar or upper chamber. Constructions like this have been observed in Suffolk and Surrey.[18]

Timber chimney-stacks

Examination of vernacular open-hall houses showed that upper floors inserted in halls are frequently earlier than the existing brick chimney-stack which, in theory, should be of the same date. The floor is commonly late 16th century and the stack about a hundred years later.

Timber chimney-stacks could serve one fireplace, or two back-to-back, but not, apparently, fireplaces on different floors. This is an important limitation. At 27 Leyton Road, Harpenden [**306**], there is sufficient space for a separate flue leading from a first-floor fireplace, but none was ever inserted, and although a considerable number of houses produced evidence of vanished timber chimney-stacks, there was no suggestion in any of them that a first-floor room had ever had a fireplace. At Harpenden, the frame of the chimney-stack is integral to the house but not to the upper-floor framing, which demonstrates that timber stacks could be removed without leaving any of the mutilations which are the normal sign of alteration to timber-framed buildings.

Most of the evidence for lost timber stacks, which must have been very common, is presented by beams, the most

305 *Fabdens, Standon: boarded and wattle and daub flue*

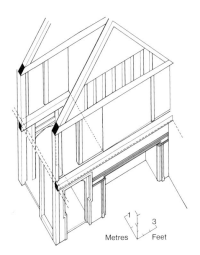

306 *No. 27 Leyton Road, Harpenden: axonometric drawing of timber chimney-stack*

important being a binding-beam chamfered towards the room, and in whole or in part square towards the chimney-stack. Sometimes the evidence is less straightforward because chimneys could be built with fireplaces which had the lintel and jambs worked in timber, like one at 177/179 High Street, Watford, and it has not proved possible to distinguish with certainty between them and fireplaces forming part of timber stacks. What seems clearly to have been a timber stack occurs at Town Farm, Standon, where the fireplace opening has an unusually high and slightly cambered lintel. At Hill End Farm, St Michael, the beam forming the fireplace lintel extends beyond the opening, whose size is indicated by mouldings which returned down the jambs (now rebuilt in brick), and this resemblance to the Harpenden house argues strongly for an original wooden stack.

So far as is known, no chimney-stack with more complex flues than two set back-to-back was ever built in timber, and this was a pressing motive for the adoption of brick chimneys. In the late 17th century, upstairs rooms either came to be used as bedrooms for the first time or a higher standard of comfort in general was demanded; whichever of these two factors caused the change, there was a demand for fireplaces. This is when and why brick chimney-stacks were introduced into the vernacular buildings of Hertfordshire on a large scale.

Brick chimney-stacks

All the indubitably early chimney-stacks mentioned above have wide and deep fireplaces and all are vernacular. They resemble a very large cover placed over an open hearth, the heat from which was never intended to be so great as to affect the structure above it, whether that was of timber or of brick. Excavation of medieval houses reveals that their hearths, as shown by marks of burning and deposits of ash,

usually covered an area considerably larger than was required for the fire at any particular time.[19]

Early brick stacks usually batter inwards above the lintel on three sides, course by course, to improve the draught, only the back remaining vertical; the characteristic appearance this produced is one of the features distinguishing Elizabethan from Restoration stacks at vernacular level. Subsequently, the need was felt to improve the appearance of the stack where it passed through a first-floor chamber. At Cromer Farm, Ardeley, the face of the stack above the hall fireplace was made vertical and its inward taper on both sides was masked by a series of decorative brick steps [**307**], of a kind observable in the parlour stack of the Old Rose and Crown, Braughing. At Ashmeads, Little Hadham, the internal stack has similar decoration on the parlour side. None of these examples is easy to date; a fireback inscribed with the date 1630 may be relevant to the Cromer example but otherwise their timespan may extend for a generation either side of 1600. About the middle of the 17th century considerable improvement in design, perhaps connected with the kind of fuel used, led to the adoption of grates (see p 191) and the need that was evidently felt for first-floor fireplaces led to the building of much smaller stacks with straight sides from the ground to the base of the shafts and incorporating at least three flues. The difference between

307 *Cromer Farm, Ardeley: stepped chimney-stack*

308 *Rye House, Stanstead Abbots: chimney-shaft on gatehouse*

these and earlier stacks is easily observable in plan. Instead of tapering gradually, the late 17th-century stack rises vertically on all four sides to a point above the first-floor fireplace lintel and often about the height of the wall-plate, then narrows sharply on the short sides and a little on the long sides to about the height of the collar-beams in the roof; above that, the stack again rises vertically to a moulding above which rise the shafts, usually four in number. It is a shape entirely distinct from that of 16th-century work.[20]

A short-lived but distinctive development in the mid to late 17th century was to put small windows in the upper parts of chimney-stacks. This curious way of combining heat and light, in a part of a room where it was not always easy to have both, appears at Aston Bury Manor, Kimpton Hall and Beeches, Brent Pelham.

The dating of chimney-shafts

The dating of that part of the chimney appearing above the roof is problematic, largely because of the difficulty of gauging how long any given type or feature persists (see p 11). The oldest shaft in Hertfordshire is one at Rye House,

Stanstead Abbots [**308**], with a spiral motif and decorative cap, and the plain, diagonally set shafts at Redcoats, Wymondley, are probably the second oldest. From the early 16th to the early 17th century there is a gap in the Hertfordshire evidence. The larger Elizabethan and Jacobean houses have all been demolished, rebuilt or restored and the clusters of chimneys at Hatfield House are too grand to be comparable. What principally remains from the late 16th and early 17th centuries are many chimneys with square shafts set diagonally – that is, provided they are correctly dated. Because the type is simple and does not incorporate datable mouldings, and because the fireplaces in such a chimney-stack often themselves lack closely datable features, it has been assumed, not unreasonably, that the stack is of the same date as the beams carrying the first floor. In Hertfordshire this situation often arises in connection with altered late medieval houses, and, in houses incorporating from the first an upper floor throughout, at Redcoats, Wymondley, and Tudor Cottage, Albury. But, although the underlying assumption is reasonable, it may be wrong, as Tudor Cottage shows, and the problem is then to decide how long diagonal shafts were in use.

Allied to simple diagonal shafts are the variations arrived at by bunching them together or varying them with square or octagonal shafts. Conjoined diagonal shafts may appear in the early 17th century[21] but the dating is hardly secure before the second half of the century, as is also true of the combination of diagonal and square shafts; the latter appear at Abbots Langley manor house. Octagonal and square shafts are combined at Rawdon House, Hoddesdon. Dated examples in Essex and Cambridgeshire might solve this problem. Both types were introduced not earlier than the middle of the 17th century in response to the demand for upstairs fireplaces and hence the need for more flues. The increase in the number of hearths affected houses of all sizes, and begins, appropriately enough, a little before the time when the Hearth Tax was introduced.

In the middle and third quarter of the 17th century the elaborately carved and moulded shaft was adopted by the

309 *Mackerye End, Wheathampstead: chimney-shaft dated 1665*

middling or minor gentry, at a time when chimney development in the greater houses was taking a quite different form. Rothamsted Manor, Harpenden Rural, where such stacks are dated to 1651, is the largest house of the period in which they were used, and by 1663 they had appeared at Mackerye End [309], a lesser house, in the neighbouring parish of Wheathampstead. The most remarkable aspect of these late decorative chimneys is their use of archaic features such as the concave-sided cap with spiky projections and the very Perpendicular-looking bases to octagonal shafts. Both were in use at a much higher social level in St Osyth's Priory, Essex, by the middle of the 16th century;[22] this and a few similar instances have led to many such stacks being given far too early a date.

How and why did a form of ornament, especially the moulded base which had been the height of fashion in the early 16th century, persist far into the reign of Charles II? When Sir John Wittewronge began remodelling Rothamsted Manor, an example of advanced taste in chimney design was to hand of which he can hardly have been unaware: Balls Park, Hertford, had panelled chimney-stacks of 1640–2 which are shown clearly in Drapentier's engraving; Tyttenhanger House, Ridge, has similar shafts of the 1650s.[23] After the Restoration, plain square shafts with deep corbelled-out caps came into fashion and were used, in a fairly simple form, by Thomas Saunders of Beechwood for the almshouses built at Flamstead in 1669:[24] an example of gentry display not intended for gentry use. Other stacks of this kind at Brookmans, North Mymms, can probably be dated to 1680–2. This fashion was probably far more widespread than now appears, for two reasons. First, when the caps needed repair it was easy to reduce their height to the one or two corbelled courses which were usual by the late 18th century and necessary to strengthen the top of the shaft. Secondly, restoration of a manor house sometimes entailed replacing a comparatively plain shaft and cap by one encrusted with ornament. Vernacular counterparts to the heavy-capped stack include those of rectangular plan with a triangular fillet on each side, others with two or three square shafts joined by a common cap, and stacks of cruciform (King's Lodge, Abbots Langley) or L-plan which sometimes have a square fillet in the re-entrant angle.

In houses that have clusters of chimney-shafts it is often difficult to find as many fireplaces demonstrably of the same date. It seems to have been usual to provide one hearth, no doubt the one in the hall which was the largest, with two flues and two shafts, although this point is now quite difficult to check because later insertions of the 18th or 19th centuries are commonplace and in most houses any tell-tale joints are concealed. This conjecture may explain a feature of the first two Hearth Tax assessments in Hertfordshire, that in certain households the number paid for drops by one from 1662 to 1663 – a reduction quite contrary to the general chimney-building tendency of the period. The situation is not unique to Hertfordshire; it occurs in Warwickshire too, in respect of houses for which there is no mention of a hearth being stopped or pulled up;[25] and it is conceivable that the High Constable and Petty

Constable, upon whom the duty of assessment lay, had, in the difficult circumstances under which the first returns were required, been unable in some cases to do other than count chimney-shafts.

Fireplaces

Whenever a fireplace had a long lintel there was the problem of how to support the brickwork overhead. For late 15th or early 16th-century fireplaces with stone jambs and head a relieving arch was necessary, more particularly because the head was formed of two pieces of stone; the fireplaces at Redcoats, Wymondley, were like this; so, too, was the remarkable fireplace at The George, Hitchin [310]. Relieving arches appear in the early 16th-century brick wing at Clintons, Little Hadham, and evidently continued in use in conjunction with stone fireplaces for a long time. A fireplace at The Bury, Rickmansworth, has the simplest kind of arch with voussoirs formed of headers; and when, some years ago, The Priory, Wymondley, underwent a thoroughgoing restoration, a better-finished arch of this kind was discovered. Both examples are mid 17th century.

An alternative way of combining style and appearance at less cost was to use timber for the lintel and stone for the jambs. This is rare in Hertfordshire. Bear House, Ashwell, has a fireplace lintel unusual in its elaborate carving and

310 *The George, Hitchin: fireplace in rear wing. The original stone lintel has been removed*

311 *No. 21 West Street, Hertford: fireplace*

equally in being cambered – to resist the weight of brick-work, presumably – but it is set at normal height, unlike the cambered lintel at Town Farm, Standon. The remains of another such fireplace, though plainer, are in the hall of Dean Incent's House, 129/131 High Street, Berkhamsted; both this and the one at Ashwell are mid 16th century. Not that stone, always expensive, was needed even for the jambs. As was remarked above, the careful examination of 177/179 High Street, Watford, produced a fireplace opening wholly of timber, with moulded jambs and a four-centred arch so depressed as to be almost flat, and moulded spandrels, while a smaller one with more carving spanned the fireplace in the chamber over the hall. Another of about the same size is used at Pirton Grange.

How fireplace lintels of *c.*1600–50 in stone or brick were relieved of the superincumbent weight is uncertain. Above some good stone fireplaces all the brickwork is concealed and in vernacular buildings a heavy timber lintel was often preferred to stone. By the middle of the century, chimney design had become standardised: if the fireplace itself was of stone or brick, a beam of a scantling proportional to the width of the opening was set above it; this relieving beam sometimes just touches the apex of the four-centred arch of brick (or flattish triangular head formed of two stones), and is sometimes two to four courses above it. Where the lintel itself is of timber, it does not rest directly on the brick jambs but on planks about 1 ft (0.3 m) wide which run back into

the body of the stack. Occasionally, where the flank of a fairly small first-floor stack serving back-to-back fireplaces has been stripped of plaster, the planks can be seen to go right through to perform the same function for both lintels; this is observable in stacks at Oak Cottage, Flaunden, and 21 West Street, Hertford [311], of the late 17th century and early 18th century respectively.

One conjectural explanation applies equally to the common practice of seating binding-beams upon timber window lintels in stone-built vernacular houses; it is that the timber, normally being used green, tended to warp and crack as it dried out, and, had timbers of large scantling been set directly on the comparatively small surfaces of the jambs, or within masonry held together by clay mortar, such changes might have weakened the brickwork or rubble. Alternatively, the through planks were intended to distribute the superimposed weight of the stack in the event of localised settlement of one jamb or another, and to ensure that if settlement did occur, the whole structure sank consistently, rather than cracking.[26]

Stone fireplaces

So far as Hertfordshire examples tell us, stone was used for fireplaces from the late 15th century to the late 17th century. It was probably used earlier in large mid 15th-century brick houses although no trace of such work remains. The earliest ones were the best and then, as subsequently, were often vehicles of architectural display. The remnant of a four-centred arched head in the chamber over the hall at Redcoats, Wymondley [312], or the other upstairs fireplace which has dragons in the spandrels, are possibly the best now remaining. No other example of ornament applied to an arch is known, nor any carving of animals or mythical beasts.

In 16th-century fireplaces mouldings are the rule for a stone arch and its square-headed frame; carving is confined to the spandrels of the arch and is rarely more than fairly simple formalised foliage. The wider the fireplace, the more

312 *Redcoats, Wymondley: detail of first-floor fireplace*

313 *Salisbury Hall, Shenley: hall fireplace*

depressed the arch and the smaller the space available for carving in the spandrels; and since in houses of high social status the hall was always the largest room and had the largest fireplace, its inferiority in this respect corresponds to the growing importance of the parlour. At 37 Holywell Hill, St Albans, the hall fireplace is wider and has coarser carvings in the spandrels than the one in the parlour, and at Gaddesden Hall, Great Gaddesden, the spandrels of the large hall fireplace are plain, whereas those in the parlour have trails of foliage. The comparison is not possible in many houses because the hall fireplace has so often been mutilated or completely renewed.

Problems of dating arise yet again with stone fireplaces. Probably fewer than has been supposed are Elizabethan or Jacobean, and only those which have carving in the spandrels can really be assigned to these periods. Mouldings help to distinguish others. A fireplace at Maydencroft Farm, Ippollitts, has lost its original jambs but the depressed four-centred head remains, and by its comparatively bold mouldings, especially a sunk roll defining the frame, appears to be earlier than many that are similar in form. Few criteria are really reliable and one in particular which has found favour, that high stops to the mouldings of the jambs indicate a late date, may be generally true but admits of exceptions.

The middle of the 17th century was a period of enormous stylistic variety. One feature not found at any earlier period

is the angular depressed head which, instead of rising from the jambs through a curve, does so through a straight section. The ornament associated with these angular heads is so extraordinary that only the battered condition of several of them prevents their being classed as Victorian or Edwardian imitators.

Coeval, more or less, with these, is the hall fireplace at Salisbury Hall, Shenley [313], in which a very depressed, almost flat, arch within a square head is treated like a bolection moulding, and indeed, despite the vaguely Tudor air of the arch, it does conform to the canon by projecting beyond the surface from which it springs.

Brick fireplaces

Lacking the decorative possibilities of stone, fireplaces with the arched opening turned in brick have much less variety. An unusually early one is the fireplace in the hall of Cheshunt Great House. The most noteworthy point is how often, despite their supposed Tudor appearance, they occur in houses that are in every other respect of the middle or late 17th century. There is no reason to think that rebuilding has altered the essential appearance of the hall fireplace at Aston Bury Manor; its depressed four-centred head is appropriate to the mid century, as the three-centred head of the hall fireplace at Gaytons, Much Hadham [314], is to the last quarter. Chamfering is the usual extent of decoration but Wickham Hall, Bishop's Stortford, and The Old Rectory, Hormead, have mouldings of Elizabethan appearance in the jambs and head. A curiosity of carved brickwork is a fireplace at Guessens, Welwyn, which has three linked hexagonal sinkings on the arris of each jamb; these occupy only the upper half of the jamb. Many brick fireplaces, especially those in bedrooms, have kept their original plaster finish. Often brick jambs were used in combination with a chamfered timber lintel.

The use of fireplaces

Fireplaces in vernacular buildings occasionally provide, through their secondary features, some indication of how they were used. The better-finished fireplaces, however wide, were clearly too good for cooking. For that, the lintel had to have a certain height. On this basis, among the fireplaces inserted, with timber chimney-stacks, into halls in the late 16th century, the one at Ramridge Farmhouse, Kimpton, is disqualified, whereas another one at Town Farm, Standon, with a much higher lintel, probably was used for cooking. If this is correct, it provides a criterion by which the comparative social standing of the owners of generally similar houses can be distinguished. By the middle of the 17th century kitchen fireplaces are not uncommon, and where the original jambs remain they have low wooden shelves or seats, usually on both sides but sometimes only on one. No evidence was found of coeval ovens, which do not make their appearance until well into the 18th century.

Recesses of various shapes are often found in fireplaces and chimney-stacks. In the 16th and early 17th centuries they are sometimes above the lintel of the hall fireplace. A pair of small recesses standing well above the present lintel at The Old Rectory, Aspenden, have trefoiled heads which suggest by their somewhat Gothic appearance a religious association, and in other houses this idea has actually been put forward. At present there is nothing to corroborate it and it is more likely that they are smaller versions of the five triangular-headed recesses at 30 Tilehouse Street, Hitchin. These resemble the recesses usually found in 17th-century cellars, hardly any of which show signs of having had a door and so are not truly cupboards; the contemporary term 'keeping-hole' expresses their general function. Just as cellar keeping-holes vary in the shape of the head – square, semicircular, segmental, stepped or triangular – so do those above and within fireplaces. Ballslough Cottage, Kimpton, has two unusually large recesses with segmental or four-centred heads which were built later than the timber lintel and jambs below; they are probably late 17th century. Where one or two recesses appear at the back of a wide fireplace [315] they are commonly referred to as salt or tobacco holes, which indeed they may be, but in the absence of any genuine tradition it can only be said that they were for something that either had to be kept dry or was used in or near the fireplace; tinder is a possibility.

The shape of a fireplace in plan is important. During the 16th century hall and parlour fireplaces were of rectangular plan. But by the beginning of the 17th century it seems to have been usual for the parlour fireplace to be five-sided, presumably the better to throw out heat. When the hall fireplace was not used for cooking the same form might be adopted, a distinction clearly seen in the late 17th century at Walnut Tree Farm, Pirton.

Fire-grates

Little is known about the date when the iron fire-grate was introduced. The Oxford English Dictionary gives three early 17th-century references for 'grate' but no fireplace at vernacular level carried a hint that it had been designed for such a feature and all fireplaces in manor and country houses of that period have long been rebuilt. Rothamsted Manor, Harpenden Rural, and Bride Hall, Wheathampstead, hint at the presence of grates by the chequer pattern painted inside fireplaces; these simple patterns of black-and-white squares could surely not have survived if the fire had been laid directly on the hearth.[27] When Dutch tiles appeared in the late 17th century they were in all probability used in conjunction with a grate of some kind,[28] but, unfortunately, the modern fashion for collecting them casts doubts on how many are in their original position.

The precise meaning attached to the word 'hearth' is similarly obscure; in some contexts it appears to mean what is nowadays called a grate. Thus an early 18th-century inventory of Cole Green Park, Hertingfordbury, shows that the several kinds of fittings in use included: 'A large iron Hearth . . . and Back' in the Great Hall; brass hearths with brass hobs in the Day Parlour, the parlour to the garden and the one next to the Wardrobe; steel hearths in five rooms described as chambers or bedrooms; and four rooms including the nursery and My Lady's bedchamber with a stove grate. Several of these hearths or grates also had 'an iron back in the chimney' but the Damask Drawing Room, Library, Inner Hall and Long Gallery had no more than that. One fireback, dated 1635, can be assigned to its original fireplace in Cromer Hall, Ardeley. Iron was used for a practical purpose as well as for display, to replace the thin, hard, tile-like bricks used in preference to common bricks and laid in a herring-bone pattern where the fire was hottest. A cheaper alternative was the clay fireback, as at 2A Market Place, Hitchin.[29] Even allowing for inconsistencies of terminology, the Cole Green inventory shows no rationale in the location of the various fittings and the matter is complicated by uncertainties about the kinds of fuel used. The debate about the use of charcoal in braziers has already been mentioned (see p 145); in the early 17th century it was clearly used in conjunction with ordinary or sea coal, apparently in open hearths. Some forty years later, Pepys's note that 'the dining room smoakes unless I keep a good charcole fire'[30] is ambiguous in this respect.

314 *Gaytons, Much Hadham: hall fireplace*

315 *White Posts, Barley: hall fireplace*

Abbreviations

BL	British Library
BM	British Museum
Bodl	Bodleian Library, Oxford
CL	*Country Life*
DNB	*The Dictionary of National Biography*
HRO	Hertfordshire County Record Office
NMR	National Monuments Record
PRO	Public Record Office
RCAHM (Wales)	Royal Commission on Ancient and Historical Monuments in Wales
RCHME	Royal Commission on the Historical Monuments of England
RO	Record Office (County)
VCH	The Victoria History of the Counties of England

Notes

Author's Preface

1 Stone and Stone 1972.
2 Summerson 1959.

Chapter 1

1 Little is known about Johannes Drapentier (active 1669–c.1700); Thieme and Becker 1907–50,Vol IX (1918), 541.
2 Little Chesterford: Wood 1948, 19–21. Middle Farm, Harwell: Fletcher 1965–6.
3 Fox and Raglan 1951–4, Part II (1953), 72–4.
4 Beresford 1975, 36–40.
5 Beresford 1974.
6 Braziers are discussed in Faull and Moorhouse 1981 (Vol 3, 812–13), where two references to portable fire-stands in the house of minor tenants are cited. But it is not clear how a brazier intended for use in a storeyed house can be distinguished in a documentary reference from the large metal fire-stand called a brazier which was used in the open hall of Westminster School until 1850 (Turner and Parker 1851–9, Vol III, Part 1 (1859), 58 and plate opposite page 49).
7 See Inventory. The quotations are from Chauncy 1826, Vol I, 280, 281.
8 Sudbury Hall: Hill and Cornforth 1966, 162–73; Ham House: Hill and Cornforth 1966, 65–74; Chevening Park: Newman 1976, 210–12, and Hill and Cornforth 1966, 227; St Clere, Kemsing: Newman 1976, 350, and Hill and Cornforth 1966, 239.
9 Buckler II, 51.
10 Luppino (active 1790–1831) was a scene painter at Covent Garden c.1790 (note prefacing 'Sketches in Hertfordshire and Essex', St Albans Public Library).
11 James Wilcox (1788–1865) of Great Hormead was a wholesale linen draper and prolific amateur artist; a biographical note is prefaced to the catalogue of his sketches in the Museum of St Albans (formerly the Hertfordshire Museum).
12 That even the most convincing graphic evidence needs to be used circumspectly is shown by A Whitford Anderson's careful measured drawings of a hammer-beam roof truss at Thorley Hall, in which the crucial evidence of alteration provided by the mortises for passing-braces is omitted: see drawings in Hertford Museum.
13 John Oliver, cartographer and building surveyor; Chauncy 1826; Colvin 1978, 601.
14 For Oldfield (active 1790–1803), see EHAST 1940–2. Reference to his drawings is by volume and folio numbers.

Chapter 2

1 Bedal 1978, 58–9, lists late 13th and early 14th-century houses dated by dendrochronology. Many more have been discovered since.
2 Jones and Smith 1960. See now Blair 1987.
3 West 1970.
4 Rahtz 1979, 178–87.
5 Fyfield Hall: information from the owner, Mr Robert White; Nurstead Court: Turner and Parker 1851–9, Vol III, part 1 (1859), 281–2, and Smith 1955. See also Sandall 1975 and 1986.
6 Alcock and Barley 1972; outside the area there covered, aisled halls were built in considerable numbers; see now Sandall 1986.
7 This was established by staff of the RCHME office at Ashford. A reappraisal of the house is about to be published (Cherry forthcoming).
8 Beresford 1974.
9 See also Jones 1809, Vol III, 26, 79; Vol IV, 101. Comparable conjunctions of architectural evidence, adoption of a surname and the abandonment of gavelkind occur in Breconshire: Trebarried, Llandyfalle: Jones 1809, Vol III, 26, 29; Jones and Smith 1963–72, Part II (1964), 100–2; Newton, St David Without: Jones 1809, Vol IV, 171; Jones and Smith 1963–72, Part III (1965), 24–30; Neuadd, Llangenni: Jones 1809, Vol III, 147; Jones and Smith 1963–72, Part IV (1966/7), 18–20. For the continuing operation of gavelkind among the gentry (and not only in Kent) in the 13th century, see McFarlane 1973, 70–2.
10 Full report on the excavation of the preceptory forthcoming; interim report, Mayes 1967.
11 Frequently illustrated, eg, Lloyd 1931, 176–7.
12 Roberts 1974.
13 Biddle, Barfield and Millard 1959.
14 Lloyd 1925, 107. For references to earlier publications, see Wood 1951.
15 PRO, Star Chamber Proceedings, ST CH/2/8/66.
16 BL Harley Roll C31.
17 Wood 1965, 161, 172.
18 Jones and Smith 1958; Mercer 1975 (see index).
19 VCH *Berks*, Vol III (1923), 105; Wood 1965, 337.
20 Borenius and Charlton 1936; *King's Works*, Vol II (1963), 193; James and Robinson 1988.
21 Chauncy 1826, Vol II, 173.
22 The Old Deanery, Salisbury, built before 1274, is another: Drinkwater 1964.

Chapter 3

1 A point made by Mr R Machin (personal communication).
2 Inquisition *post mortem*, 23 September 1461 (PRO C140/2/28).

3 See below, Chapter 4, pp 63–4.

4 Steensberg 1952, 200–34 and 309–17.

5 Monks' Barn, Newport: RCHME 1916, 204; The Clergy House, Alfriston: Gravett 1981; Old Vicarage, Headcorn: photographs in NMR; Pilgrims' Rest Café, Battle: Mercer 1975, 209.

6 It may be unlikely that what was replaced in the 18th century still had earthfast posts, but the discovery of houses in Virginia so constructed and still standing shows that where some protection from damp was provided by outshuts the possibility cannot be dismissed out of hand; Carson et al 1981.

7 See, eg, Munby 1963, 137.

8 For example, The Old Post Office, Offley. Plummers, Much Hadham, looks like this (access refused).

9 A variant form of this development is at Kingston (RCHME 1968, 157–8, monument no. 5).

10 RCHME 1923, xxxv–xxxvi.

11 Beresford 1974.

12 Mercer 1975, 20.

13 Cf RCHME 1952, xxxviii–xxxix.

14 A rather grand example of such a stair, decorated with armorial bearings and datable to the 15th century, still existed at Vaughan's Place, Shrewsbury, in the 1820s when John Buckler drew it: BL Add MS 36378, fos 81, 82; Smith 1953. Clintons, which is a rather superior manor house, probably had a stairway treated something like this, and possibly The Holly Bush at Elstree had a humbler version, although the evidence is not as good as could be wished. For other examples, see Wood 1965, 328–30.

15 Smith 1975, 144; Jones and Smith 1963–72.

16 Alcock and Laithwaite 1973.

17 Alcock and Laithwaite 1973; Purton Green Farm, Stansfield, Suffolk, appears also to belong to this class and there are indications of this, for example, at the lower end of The Manor, Chalgrove, Oxon (personal observation).

18 Jones and Smith 1963–72; RCAHM (Wales) 1988, passim.

19 Some of these problems will be clarified by the excavation of house sites and deserted villages. A promising start has been made at Caldecote, where house foundations ranging in date from the 12th to the early 16th centuries have been examined: Beresford 1978.

Chapter 4

1 Evelyn Diary: 3 November 1633.

2 Smith 1971, especially Plate XXIVB. The explanation there offered for Lostock Hall may need revision in the light of the present work.

3 The earliest windows of this type were those at Somerset House of 1547–52; see Summerson 1953, Plate 10. They existed also at Little Court, Buntingford.

4 John Skinner 1772–1839: DNB. Drawings of Knebworth House in British Library, Add MS 33641, fos 208–9.

5 Cf East Riddlesden Hall, West Yorkshire: RCHME 1986, 206–7.

6 Girouard 1978, 88–100.

7 Summerson 1959a, especially page 112 and Plate XXVIIA.

8 OED 'Surveyor', paragraph 1 (d); a survey of St Albans Abbey dated 31 January 1548 mentions 'the surveying place between the Abbot's Hall and his kitchen . . . ' (PRO SC 12/8/39); see also entry for Hatfield House in Inventory.

9 For much of the information in this paragraph I am indebted to Dr Joan Thirsk, citing Fitzherbert, The Book of Husbandry, 132 ff.

10 Kirby Hall: Summerson 1953, 37.

11 Burghley House: VCH Northants, Vol II (1906), 524–6 and plan.

12 Summerson 1966.

13 Mercer 1962, 18, 26.

14 Summerson 1966.

15 Ware Park also had a three-quarter H plan by 1766 (Dury and Andrews 1766); its development is quite unknown but the plan form may be significant in the light of the fact that James I was entertained there in 1619 (Nichols 1821–3, Vol III, 534).

16 Summerson 1953, 40.

17 Hatfield House and Gardens (MS vol), 115.

18 Notes on Hatfield House.

19 de Sorbière 1709, 64–5.

20 Pepys Diary: 7 August 1661.

21 The Building of Hatfield House (MS vol), 53–6.

22 Bacon 1625 (essay entitled 'Of Building').

23 Extract from J Smyth, Lives of the Berkeleys (1618–28), quoted in Stone 1965, 158.

24 Bacon 1625, 133–6.

25 Stone 1965, 158.

26 Cobham Hall: Newman 1976, 231–7; Trefalun: Hubbard 1986, 287–9; also Girouard 1962.

Chapter 5

1 Evelyn Diary: 18 April 1680.

2 Girouard 1978, 123. For Coleshill, see Silcox-Crowe 1985, 5–7.

3 Gunther 1928, 166.

4 Although the example of Hatfield House shows that minor staircases used exclusively by servants might have disappeared without trace.

5 RCHME 1975, 7–12.

6 Salisbury Hall: for an apparently similar development, cf Little Warley Hall, RCHME 1923, 90; for 'alternate development', see Fox and Raglan 1951–4, Part II (1953), 72.

7 Clarendon 1702–4, Vol II (ii), 577. It was the seat of the lawyer Sir John Bennet (d. 1627; see DNB); the entry in RCHME 1937, 129, and the archive plan, do not elucidate the description.

8 Gunther 1928, 154, 160. Plan of Clarendon House: Keller 1986.

9 Begun in 1697; CL 24 August 1951, 572–6.

10 Fiennes Journeys, 117–18.

11 Colvin and Newman 1981, 15 and Plate 14.

12 Harris 1961, Plate 16.

13 Gunther 1928, 126.

14 Exceptionally, Great Hyde Hall, Sawbridgeworth (which was not a double-pile house), appears to have had, c.1700, a low gabled wing to the left of the frontage, but the perspective of the engraving is confusing and it may have been a stable block slightly to the rear.

15 Fiennes Journeys, 24.

16 See note 8 above. The fourth pavilion was occupied by the chapel.

17 Written c.1695–6; Colvin and Newman 1981, 129.

18 Pepys Diary: 17 March 1663 (Latham and Matthews 1970–83, Vol IV, 77, note 3).

19 For progresses by Charles II, see Heath 1676, 523, 581, 602; by Monmouth, Roberts 1844, Vol I, 88–105; Vol II, 132.

20 Evelyn Diary: 9/10 October 1671.

21 Clarendon 1702–4, Vol I (i), 78.

22 Dineley 1888.

23 Quoted in Ollard 1979, 110.

24 Luttrell 1857, Vol II, 52.

25 Summerson 1953, 96, 97; Colvin 1978, 551–3 (entry on Peter Mills).

26 Roger North, quoted in Girouard 1978 (page 122), citing BL Add MS 32540 fo 51v; a similar passage, lacking the words 'piece of state', occurs in Colvin and Newman 1981, 60.

27 Thomas Heywood The English Traveller, Act IV, Scene i.

28 For this interpretation of Hatfield House see Girouard 1978, 115.
29 Evelyn *Diary*: 9/10 October 1671.
30 See *DNB*.
31 RCHME 1987, 32–3, where the house is misinterpreted; Jackson 1875, 130–1, 134, 139.
32 Evelyn *Diary*: 1 January 1648/9; on 30 May 1648 he mentions 'my house at Says Court'.
33 Habakkuk 1955, 174.
34 Boswell 1785.

Chapter 6

1 Emery 1970.
2 Mercer 1975, index, under 'Smoke-bays'.
3 This may overstate the problem because recent work in Virginia has established that timber chimneys existed there in the first phase of settlement, but if the difficulties were real, and so far no comparable evidence is known in England, they formed an obstacle to adopting upper-class practice.
4 Mercer 1975, 170 .
5 See below, p 99; also, for example, Dorset (RCHME 1970, 87, 138, 181, 245).
6 RCHME 1968, *xlvii–xlix*. In Cambridgeshire, such houses appear to be designated Class I in the classification of plan types for the county.
7 Smith 1975, 203–4 and *passim*; Mercer 1975, 167–8; Jones 1971; also several important articles by N W Alcock in the *Transactions of the Devonshire Association*, listed in Hall 1972 and Michelmore 1979; RCHME 1987.
8 This also applies to a putative byre rebuilt as a kitchen, for example, Old Raisins Farm, Wheathampstead.
9 Jones and Smith 1960. For a classification of longhouse derivatives, see Jones and Smith 1963–72, Part I (1963), 5–34.
10 Fox and Raglan 1951–4, Part III (1954), 19–23.
11 Rouse forthcoming.
12 Jones and Smith 1963–72, Part VII (1972), 10–11.
13 Hemp and Gresham 1942–3.
14 Machin 1978, 117–24, and 1976, 26–37. These books are of far wider significance than their titles suggest.
15 Ambler 1913.
16 Cf the two doorways at Scout Hall, Northowram, dated 1681; their significance is unfortunately not revealed in RCHME 1986 (see page 210 and Plate 97).
17 Laslett 1965.
18 Machin as note 14, especially Machin 1978, 117–24.

Chapter 7

1 George Colman and David Garrick *The Clandestine Marriage* (1766), Act II, Scene ii.
2 Crabbe 1851, 40.
3 Pepys *Diary*: 14 July 1664; Gunther 1928, 158, 160.
4 Oldfield II, 30.
5 '. . . in the 18th century the word was never used with any *architectural* precision at all': Summerson 1958–9. The quotation (page 570) is followed by discussion of the various meanings. Cf Harris 1981, 129.
6 Summerson 1958–9, 578.
7 Plan numbers (6C) and (4B) respectively of those in the possession of Beechwood Park School.
8 Stone 1972, 77.
9 Girouard 1978, 234–5.
10 Ibid, 234.

11 Young 1770, Vol I, 13–19: 'a bedchamber opened off the waiting room'.
12 Cussans 1870–3, Vol I (i), 50.
13 Colvin and Newman 1981, 79.
14 Defoe *Tour*, Vol II, 200.
15 Colvin 1978, 69.
16 Gandon and Woolfe 1771, Plate 46.
17 Colvin and Newman 1981, 122. North required 'the entry to be fair from the staires into an antiroom . . . then 2 apartments from that, either way ranging in a line': ibid, 132.
18 Stapleton Park: Strong *et al* 1974, Plate 102, built mid 18th century; end-entrance probably created *c*.1820; Colvin 1978, 218. Tillmouth: Strong *et al* 1974, Plate 136, where no date is offered but the builder is said to be Sir Francis Blake, presumably the first baronet who died at Tillmouth in 1780 (see *DNB*). He or his successor must have altered the 'large new built house' acquired *c*.1740 (Raine 1882, 324, note (c)).
19 Defoe *Tour*, Vol II, 200. Some of the intended work may have been carried out and may survive, but it is difficult to know what date is referred to in the additions to the first edition of the *Tour*.
20 *Red Book* HRO, C2404.

Chapter 8

1 Conzen 1960; Slater 1980.
2 Reynolds 1977, *ix*.
3 Biddle 1976, 100.
4 Leland *Itinerary*, 98.
5 Ibid, 99.
6 Main streets appear to have served as markets even in large towns, for example, Winchester; Biddle 1976, 130.
7 Lobel 1969.
8 Page 1920. This article enlarges on many points made briefly in VCH 1902–14. Only for three towns can his views be questioned in the light of recent research. A fourth, St Albans, is a generally accepted early instance of town planning comparable to the larger and better known example of Bury St Edmunds, for which see Beresford and St Joseph 1979; Biddle 1976, 110–11.
9 Page 1920; Biddle says only: 'the medieval town grew up or was created at the abbey gates' (Biddle 1976, 110–11).
10 Known only from a later copy now in St Albans Public Library; redrawn, Page 1920, 50. For the occurrence and significance of such streets, see Biddle 1976, 130–1.
11 Romeland probably means 'empty, unoccupied land'; Gover *et al* 1938, 88.
12 Mr Gordon Davies, formerly of Hertford Museum, made available the conclusions of his study of this market-place, which require fuller publication than is possible here.
13 Information from Mr Philip Coverdale of Ashwell.
14 Plan in RCHME 1926, 174.
15 Testimony of Robert Sawcer of Hemel Hempstead, 50 yrs, gent., relating his great-grandfather's statements; Oxley *v* Partridge and others, 1677; PRO E 134/29 Charles II Mich 20; cited in Yaxley 1973, 59.
16 *Hertfordshire Genealogist and Antiquary* 1898, 114.
17 Smith 1953.
18 Although few shop fronts of this kind were found in Hertfordshire they were common throughout England and northern Europe in the Middle Ages. See Braudel 1981, 136, 194 and 441, for examples in Holland and Germany.
19 See Appendix, p 185.
20 See Chapter 1, note 6.
21 Eland 1947, 3.
22 RCHME 1980, monument no. 82.

23 VCH *Herts*, Vol II (1908), 162.

24 Ibid, 474.

25 In 1678, when it was referred to as 'a void piece of ground in Fishpool Street called Roome Land', encroachment was taking place (St Albans Public Library, lease no. 698).

26 PRO E 134/29.

27 VCH *Herts*, Vol II (1908), 470, note 19. Distinctions of this kind are implied by the request of John Goodes, brewer, to 'grunsell over' a piece of ground in St Peter's Street; Gibbs 1890, 51.

28 In Hitchin the tanners may have had a hall with a hammer-beam roof if it has been correctly located at 103/104 Queen Street, and The Cooper's Arms in Tilehouse Street has been claimed for another guild, but both identifications rest on slender evidence.

29 Defoe *Tour*, Vol II, 194.

30 RCHME 1987, 117–18, 139–45.

31 Pantin 1961.

32 VCH *Herts*, Vol III (1912), 141.

33 Nos 71–77 Stowe Street; Alcock 1981.

Chapter 9

1 Defoe *Tour*, Vol II, 474; Vol I, 49. In 1750 Shrewsbury had *c*.8,700 inhabitants. Hertford, Ware and St Albans differed little in size: 2,700, 2,600 and 2,500 respectively; Law 1972.

2 St Albans Public Library, Mayor's Book 1586–1634, MS no. 312, fo 15; lease, fo 60. Boards and finishing; Gibbs 1890, 39, 51 respectively.

3 PRO E 317/29.

4 St Albans Public Library, MS no. 736.

5 St Albans Public Library, MS no. 159, Mayor's Accounts, 1620–1.

6 An early example is the Corn Exchange in St Albans, of 1791: Oldfield, Vol VIII, fo 495; Gibbs 1890, 14. That at Royston was rebuilt in 1829: Cambridgeshire RO, 296/B113, 119. A wooden building 'of very light construction' was designed for Hitchin; *The Builder*, 28 February 1852.

7 Salmon 1728, 116.

8 Lincolnshire RO, Terr/22.

9 Built: VCH *Herts*, Vol II (1908), 219; repaired: Yaxley 1973, 125. The former is more likely. See Buckler, BL Add MS 32350.

10 VCH *Herts*, Vol II (1908), 219.

11 Ware Court Rolls 1665–1706, 2 April 1669, BL Add MS 27977. At St Albans a market house replaced the old Cross in 1703 and a shed was erected 'to shield the market people', in 1730; Gibbs 1890, 101, 110.

12 At Hitchin encroachments on the west side, shown in Drapentier's view (Chauncy 1826, Vol I, opposite page 160), were swept away between 1825 and 1856 (Hine 1927–9, Vol II, 425), a change dismissed by one inhabitant as 'a trifling improvement'; Lucas *Diary*.

13 Parker 1971, Figs 9, 20 and 21.

14 I am indebted to Professor M W Beresford for pointing out this distinction.

15 George 1931, 31–5; cf also Lloyd 1931, Figs 279 and 280.

16 By 1700, retailers were using inns as temporary shops, thereby foreshadowing the late 18th-century appearance of permanent shops in most provincial towns; Clark and Slack 1976, 21, but cf the references to shops at York (page 61) and, more generally, between 1500 and 1700 (page 1).

17 BM Department of Prints and Drawings, 1874/2/14/750. Until *c*.1975 an early Victorian flat canopy existed above the unglazed front of a butcher's shop in High Street, High (or Chipping) Barnet.

18 Now called Abbey Cottages, Nos 34–50 Church Street; Jones 1968, plan on page 129.

19 An early example, probably of the 1730s, is No. 9 Market Place, Blandford Forum; RCHME 1970, 34 (monument no. 56) and drawing opposite page 32.

20 Etching of 1783, *TSAAAS* 1895–1902, opposite page 280; cf lease of The Clock House Shop, St Albans Public Library, Mayor's Book 1586–1634, fo 50.

21 Narrow, encroaching shops of this kind in London were being removed by the Lord Mayor as early as 1663; Pepys *Diary*: 17 March 1663 (Latham and Matthews 1970–83, Vol IV, 77, note 3). The Hertfordshire towns did not secure Acts of Parliament for town improvements and the replacement of such shops by brick fronts was left to individuals.

22 Geoffrey Holmes: his *Augustan England: Professions, State and Society 1680–1730* (1982) appeared too late to be used here; Holmes 1979.

23 See plans of houses in Dorchester and Poole; RCHME 1970. In an old town, access, or the lack of it, to a back lane does not necessarily distinguish between these categories; a residence might well have a long garden with a coach house and stables facing a back lane.

24 Pepys *Diary*: 5 June 1661 and 25 April 1666; 'supped upon my leads', 29 April 1666.

25 PRO WO 30/48 (Abstract of particulars of Alehouses and Inns).

26 RCHME 1981, Introduction.

Appendix

1 Smith 1974.

2 The roofs over the nave of Lisieux Cathedral and the hospital of St John at Angers are more or less coeval with Burston Manor (Smith 1974).

3 Harding 1974.

4 Fletcher 1979, especially pages 186–7.

5 Roberts 1979.

6 Bailey and Hutton 1966.

7 Fletcher and Spokes 1964.

8 Smith 1960, especially pages 114–16.

9 This paragraph modifies Smith 1960, 112–13. For a different view of the function of the collar-purlin roof, see Charles 1967, 10–12.

10 Salzman 1952, 437–8.

11 Smith 1981, modifying Smith 1960 and 1974.

12 Charles 1967; drawings in Dollman and Jobbins 1861–3. This type is well illustrated in a 19th-century engraving of Wanswell Court (Glos), conveniently reproduced in Wood 1965, Plate 5B.

13 Rudimentary trusses in stables at the Bishop's Palace, Bishop's Waltham, Hants; Mercer 1975, 163; also Great Coxwell Barn, Berks: see Horn and Born 1965. Slight principals occur in a barn at Titchfield, Hants; Mercer 1975, 164.

14 Alcock 1981 provides the only guide to both controversies and evidence.

15 Mercer 1975, 115.

16 Mercer 1975, 118; Fig 77 on this page illustrates this technique.

17 St Albans Public Library, MS no. 118.

18 Colman and Colman 1964–6, 155–6; Baker 1980, 268.

19 For example, at South Witham: full report on the excavation of the preceptory forthcoming; interim report, Mayes 1967. Also a guest-house at Tintern Abbey; Courtney 1989.

20 Hence Rooks Hall, Cressing, Essex, is likely to be dated 1675 rather than 1575; Hewett 1980, 225–6.

21 As, for example, at Toft (6), RCHME 1968, Plate 107.

22 RCHME 1922, 195–204; Lloyd 1925, 81 and illustration on page 341; Lloyd 1931, Figs 330 and 563.

23 An explanation based on the conflict between Court sympathisers and Parliament may be possible; cf Mercer 1962, 10–11.

24 Clarkson 1887.
25 In two of the Warwickshire hundreds there were 52 cases of over-assessment by one hearth: Styles 1957, Introduction, *xlv*.
26 I owe this alternative suggestion to Mr A R Dufty.
27 Decoration of this kind is presumably referred to at Hatfield House in 1695 when a bricklayer was paid for 'Whiting and blacking several chimnys'; *Hatfield House and Gardens* (MS vol), 10.

28 Pepys was using them as early as 1663, commenting that his rich acquaintance Thomas Povey had the walls of the stable done with Dutch tiles, 'like my chimnies'; and at Hatfield House in 1700, payment was made for setting Dutch tiles. Pepys *Diary*: 19 January 1663. Hatfield House: *Hatfield House and Gardens* (MS vol), 10.
29 Smith 1978.
30 Pepys *Diary*: 13 January 1663.

Primary Sources

A Whitford Anderson, drawings in Hertford Museum (not numbered).

A Whitford Anderson, photographs in Watford Central Library. References to these are followed by date or number where known.

H C and R T Andrews, a collection of engravings, photographs, etc, in Hertford Museum. Cited only where ultimate source of illustration is not known.

Beechwood Park, Flamstead: a collection of plans and drawings dating from the late 17th to early 20th centuries and listed by H M Colvin and J Harris (unpublished MS). Most of the collection was still in the possession of Beechwood Park preparatory school when the house was visited in 1976.

John Hickman Binyon, MS book on Northaw, where he lived 1829–79; HRO D/P73 29/3.

Bosanquet family, members of, *Bosanquettina*, a small album of drawings by, *c.*1812, Ashmolean Museum, Oxford.

Charlotte Bosanquet, drawings by, 1842–3, Ashmolean Museum, Oxford.

John and John Chessell Buckler, drawings by, in HRO unless otherwise stated; references followed by volume and folio number.

John Charnock (1756–1807), drawings in National Maritime Museum.

W B Gerish Collection in HRO: mostly newspaper cuttings of the late 19th and early 20th centuries.

Richard Gough (1735–1809). Unpublished folio collection of engravings of British topography in forty-six volumes, Bodleian Library, Oxford. Hertfordshire is covered in Volume XI.

The Building of Hatfield House: MS volume of excerpts from the Hatfield MSS compiled in the early 20th century by R T Gunton, librarian to the 3rd Marquess of Salisbury.

Hatfield House and Gardens: MS volume of excerpts from the Hatfield MSS compiled in the early 20th century by R T Gunton, librarian to the 3rd Marquess of Salisbury.

J W Jones, collection of drawings, etc, to illustrate grangerized Clutterbuck; BL, 5 vols, Add MSS, 32348–52.

Luppino drawings, in the Lewis Evans Collection, St Albans Public Library; see Chapter 1, note 10.

Drawings in the collection of Godfrey Meynell.

G E Moodey, drawings deposited in HRO.

H G Oldfield, drawings in HRO.

James Wilcox, drawings in Hertford Museum; see Chapter 1, note 11.

Bibliography

Alcock, N W 1981. *Cruck Construction: An Introduction and Catalogue* (CBA Research Report 42).

Alcock, N W and Barley, M W 1972. 'Medieval roofs with base-crucks and short principals'. *Antiq J* **52**, 132–68.

Alcock, N W and Laithwaite, M 1973. 'Medieval houses in Devon and their modernisation'. *Medieval Archaeol* **17**, 100–25.

Ambler, L 1913. *The Old Halls and Manor Houses of Yorkshire, with some examples of other houses built before the year 1700*.

Bacon, Francis 1625. *Essays* (Everyman edition, 1973).

Bailey, G and Hutton, B 1966. *Crown-post Roofs in Hertfordshire*. Hitchin.

Baker, J L 1980. ' "Smoke deflectors" in hall houses'. *Surrey Archaeol Collect* **72**, 268–9.

Bedal, K 1978. *Historische Hausforschung*. Münster.

Beresford, G 1974. 'The medieval manor of Penhallam, Jacobstow, Cornwall'. *Medieval Archaeol* **18**, 90–145.

—— 1975. *The Medieval Clay Land Village: Excavations at Goltho and Barton Blount* (Society for Medieval Archaeology monograph 6).

—— 1978. 'Excavations at the deserted medieval village of Caldecote . . . an interim report'. *Hertfordshire's Past* No. 4 (Spring), 3–14.

Beresford, M W 1957. *New Towns of the Middle Ages*.

Beresford, M W and Finberg, H P R 1973. *English Medieval Boroughs: A Handlist*. Newton Abbot.

Beresford, M W and St Joseph, J K 1979. *Medieval England: An Aerial Survey*, 2nd edn. Cambridge.

Biddle, M 1976. 'Towns' in D M Wilson (ed) *The Archaeology of Anglo-Saxon England*, 99–150.

Biddle, M, Barfield, L and Millard, A 1959. 'The excavation of The More, Rickmansworth'. *Archaeol J* **116**, 136–99.

Blair, J 1987. 'The 12th-century Bishop's Palace at Hereford'. *Medieval Archaeol* **31**, 59–79.

Borenius, T and Charlton, J 1936. 'Clarendon Palace: an interim report'. *Antiq J* **16**, 55–84.

Boswell, J 1785. *Journal of a Tour to the Hebrides with Samuel Johnson* (Everyman edition, 1941).

Braudel, F 1981. *Civilization and Capitalism: Vol I The Structures of Everyday Life* (revised edn, Sian Reynolds).

Carson, C *et al* 1981. 'Impermanent architecture in the southern American colonies'. *Winterthur Portfolio* **16**, 135–96.

Castle, S A 1977. *Timber-Framed Buildings in Watford*. Chichester.

Charles, F W B 1967. *Medieval Cruck-Building and its Derivatives* (Society for Medieval Archaeology monograph 2).

Chauncy, Sir H 1826. *The Historical Antiquities of Hertfordshire*. (First published 1700. References are to the 2nd edn of 1826 (2 vols, London and Bishop's Stortford), reprinted 1975, Dorking, with Introduction by Carola Oman.)

Cherry, M forthcoming. 'Nurstead Court, Kent: a re-appraisal'. *Archaeol J* **146**.

Chronica Monastici S. Albani

    Annales Monastici. *Monasterii S. Albani* (ed H T Riley, 2 vols, 1870–1, Rolls Series).

    Gesta Abbatum Monasterii S. Albani (ed H T Riley, 3 vols, 1867–9, Rolls Series).

    Registrum Abbatiae Johannis Whethamstede (ed H T Riley, 2 vols, 1870–3, Rolls Series).

Clarendon, Lord 1702–4. *History of the Rebellion and Civil Wars in England* (ed Macray, 6 vols, 1888). Oxford.

Clark, P and Slack, P 1976. *English Towns in Transition*. Oxford.

Clarkson, S F 1887. 'The Saunders Almshouses at Flamstead...'. *Trans St Albans AAS* **1**, Part IV, 88–90.

Clutterbuck, R. *The Topography of Hertfordshire*: the author's grangerized copy (in HRO), in 6 vols, of his *The History and Antiquities of the County of Hertford* (3 vols, 1815–27).

Colman, G and Colman, S 1964–6. 'A thirteenth-century aisled house: Purton Green Farm, Stansfield'. *Proc Suffolk Inst Archaeol Hist* **30** (published 1967), 150–65.

Colvin, H M 1978. *A Biographical Dictionary of British Architects 1600–1840*, 2nd edn.

Colvin, H M and Newman, J (eds) 1981. *Of Building. Roger North's Writings on Architecture*.

Conzen, M R G 1960. 'Alnwick, Northumberland: a study of town-plan analysis'. *Trans Inst Brit Geogr* **27**, 1–127.

Courtney, P 1989. 'Excavation in the Outer Court of Tintern Abbey'. *Medieval Archaeol* **33**, 99–143.

Crabbe, G (ed) 1851. *The Poetical Works of the Rev. George Crabbe*, new edn.

Croft-Murray, E 1962–70. *Decorative Painting in England,* 2 vols.

Cussans, J P 1870–81. *History of Hertfordshire.*
    Volume I (1870–3):   (i) Braughing Hundred
                       (ii) Edwinstree Hundred
                       (iii) Odsey Hundred.
    Volume II (1874–8): (i) Hitchin Hundred
                       (ii) Hertford Hundred
                       (iii) Broadwater Hundred.
    Volume III (1879–81) (i) Dacorum Hundred
                       (ii) Cashio Hundred.
    (Reprinted 1972, Wakefield, with Introduction by W Branch Johnson.)

Defoe *Tour. A Tour Through the Whole Island of Great Britain,* 3rd edn, 4 vols, 1742.

Dineley, T. 1888. *Progress of the 1st Duke of Beaufort through Wales 1684.*

Dollman, F T and Jobbins, J R 1861–3. *Analysis of Ancient Domestic Architecture in Great Britain,* 2 vols.

Drinkwater, N 1964. 'The Old Deanery, Salisbury'. *Antiq J* **44,** 41–59.

Dury, A and Andrews, J 1766. *A Topographical Map of Hartford-Shire: from an actual survey* (9 sheets; facsimile published at a reduced scale by Hertfordshire Publications, 1980).

EHAST 1940–2. 'Henry George Oldfield and the Dimsdale Collection of Hertfordshire drawings'. *E Herts Archaeol Soc Trans* **11,** 212–24.

Eland, G (ed) 1947. *The Shardeloes Papers.*

Emery, A 1970. *Dartington Hall.* Oxford.

Evelyn *Diary. The Diary of John Evelyn* (ed E S de Beer, 6 vols, 1955).

Faull, M C and Moorhouse, S A (eds) 1981. *West Yorkshire: An Archaeological Survey to AD 1500,* 4 vols. Wakefield.

Fiennes *Journeys. The Journeys of Celia Fiennes* (ed C Morris, 1947).

Fitzherbert. *Booke of Husbandrie* (ed Revd Walter W Skeat, *The Book of Husbandry* by Master Fitzherbert, English Dialect Society, Series D, Miscellaneous, 1882).

Fletcher, J M 1965–6. 'Three medieval farmhouses in Harwell'. *Berkshire Archaeol J* **62,** 46–69.
    1979. 'The Bishop of Winchester's medieval manor house at Harwell, Berkshire, and its relevance in the evolution of timber-framed aisled halls'. *Archaeol J* **136,** 173–92.

Fletcher, J M and Spokes, P S 1964. 'The origin and development of crown-post roofs'. *Medieval Archaeol* **8,** 152–83.

Fox, Sir Cyril and Lord Raglan 1951–4. *Monmouthshire Houses,* 3 parts (Part I 1951; Part II 1953; Part III 1954). Cardiff.

Gandon, J and Woolfe, J (eds) 1771. *Vitruvius Britannicus,* Vol V.

George, D 1931. *England in Transition.*

Gibbs, A E 1890. *The Corporation Records of St Albans.* St Albans.

Gibbs, H C 1915. *The Parish Registers of Hunsdon 1546–1837.* St Albans.

Girouard, M 1962. 'Trevalyn Hall, Denbighshire'. *Country Life,* Vol **132,** 78–81.
    1978. *Life in the English Country House: A Social and Architectural History.* New Haven and London.

Gover, J E B, Mawer, A and Stenton, F N 1938. *The Place-Names of Hertfordshire* (English Place-Name Society). Cambridge.

Gravett, K 1981. 'The Clergy House, Alfriston: a re-appraisal'. *National Trust Studies,* 103–8.

Gunther, R T 1928. *The Architecture of Sir Roger Pratt...from his Note-books.* Oxford.

Habakkuk, H J 1955. 'Daniel Finch, 2nd Earl of Nottingham: his house and estate' in J H Plumb (ed) *Studies in Social History,* 139–78.

Hall, R de Z 1972. *A Bibliography on Vernacular Architecture.* Newton Abbot.

Harding, J 1974. 'Surrey, Dunsfold'. *Medieval Archaeol* **18,** 215.

le Hardy, W (ed) 1961. *Guide to the Hertfordshire Record Office,* Part 1. Hertford.

Harris, J H 1961. 'Raynham Hall, Norfolk'. *Archaeol J* **118,** 180–7.
    1981. *The Palladians.*
    (ed and transl) 1969. *William Worcestre Itineraries.* Oxford.

Hatfield and its People, Books 1–12 (by members of Hatfield WEA, 1959–64, Hatfield).

Heath, J 1676. *Chronicle of the Late Intestine War,* 2nd edn.

Hemp, W J and Gresham, C A 1942–3. 'Park, Llanfrothen, and the unit system'. *Archaeol Cambrensis* **97,** 98–112.

Hertfordshire Countryside Magazine (Hitchin, 1946–).

Hewett, C 1980. *English Historic Carpentry.* Chichester.

Hill, O and Cornforth, J 1966. *English Country Houses: Caroline 1625–1685.*

Hine, R L 1927–9. *The History of Hitchin,* 2 vols.

Holmes, G 1979. 'The professions and social change in England, 1680–1730' (The Raleigh Lecture on History). *Proc Brit Acad* **65,** 313–54.

Horn, W and Born, E 1965. *The Barns of...Great Coxwell and Beaulieu St Leonards.* Berkeley and Los Angeles.

Hubbard, E 1986. *Clwyd (Denbighshire and Flintshire)* (The *Buildings of Wales* series).

Hussey, C 1958. *English Country Houses: Late Georgian 1800–1840.*
    1963. *English Country Houses: Mid Georgian 1760–1800,* revised edn.
    1965. *English Country Houses: Early Georgian 1715–1760,* revised edn.

Jackson, C (ed) 1875. *The Autobiography of Mrs Alice Thornton... .* Surtees Society, Vol LXII.

James, T B and Robinson, A M 1988. *Clarendon Palace: The History and Archaeology of a Medieval Palace and Hunting Lodge near Salisbury, Wiltshire* (Society of Antiquaries of London Research Report XLV).

Johnson, W Branch 1962 and 1963. *Hertfordshire Inns*, 2 parts. Letchworth.

— (ed) 1973. *Memorandoms for .... :* the diary, 1798–1810, of John Carrington. Chichester.

Jones, S R 1968. 'Domestic buildings (in Tewkesbury Borough)' in VCH *A History of Gloucestershire*, Vol VIII, 110–69.

— 1971. 'Moorland and non-moorland long-houses'. *Trans Devonshire Assoc* **103**, 35–75.

Jones, S R and Smith, J T 1958. 'Manor House, Wasperton'. *Trans Birmingham and Warwickshire Archaeol Soc* **76**, 19–28.

— 1960. 'The Great Hall of the Bishop's Palace, Hereford'. *Medieval Archaeol* **4**, 69–80.

— 1963–72. 'The houses of Breconshire', Parts I–VII. *Brycheiniog* **9–16**.

    1963. Part I The Builth District. **9**, 1–77.

    1964. Part II The Hay and Talgarth District. **10**, 69–183.

    1965. Part III The Brecon District. **11**, 1–149.

    1966/7. Part IV The Crickhowell District. **12**, 1–91.

    1968/9. Part V The Defynnog District. **13**, 1–85.

    1972. Part VI The Faenor (Vaynor) and Penderyn District. **16**, 1–37.

    1972. Part VII The Ystradgynlais District. **16**, 39–78.

Jones, T 1809. *History of the County of Brecknock* (ed Baron Glanusk, 4 vols, 1911–30. Brecon).

Keller, F-E 1986. 'Christian Ellesten's drawings of Roger Pratt's Clarendon House and Robert Hookes' Montague House'. *Burlington Magazine* CXXVIII (October issue), 732–7.

Kelly's Directory of Hertfordshire.

Kingston, A 1894. *Hertfordshire during the Great Civil War and Long Parliament*. London and Hertford.

King's Works. The History of the King's Works (gen ed H M Colvin), Vols II (1963), III (1975), IV (1982).

Knowles, D and Hadcock, R N 1953. *Medieval Religious Houses: England and Wales*.

Laslett, P 1965. *The World We have Lost*.

Law, C M 1972. 'Some notes on the urban population of England and Wales in the 18th century'. *Local Hist* **10**, 13–16.

Lees-Milne, J 1970. *English Country Houses: Baroque 1685–1715*.

Leland *Itinerary. The Itinerary of John Leland* (ed L Toulmin Smith, 5 vols, 1907).

Lloyd, N 1925. *A History of English Brickwork from Medieval Times to the End of the Georgian Period*. London and New York.

— 1931. *A History of the English House from Primitive Times to the Victorian Period*. London and New York.

Lobel, M D (gen ed) 1969. *Historic Towns Vol I*. London and Oxford.

Lucas *Diary. A Quaker Journal...the Diary...of William Lucas of Hitchin (1804–61)* (ed G E Bryant and G P Baker, 2 vols, 1934).

Luttrell, N 1857. *A Brief Historical Relation of State Affairs*, 6 vols. Oxford.

Machin, R A 1976. *Probate Inventories and Manorial Excepts of...Yetminster*. Bristol.

— 1978. *The Houses of Yetminster*. Bristol.

Mayes, P 1967. 'Lincolnshire: South Witham'. *Medieval Archaeol* **11**, 274–5.

McFarlane, K B 1973. *The Nobility of Later Medieval England*. Oxford.

Mercer, E 1962. *English Art 1553–1625* (Oxford History of English Art, Vol V). Oxford.

— 1975. *English Vernacular Houses: A Study of Traditional Farmhouses and Cottages*.

Metcalf, W E (ed) 1886. *The Visitations of Hertfordshire* (Harleian Society).

Michelmore, D J H 1979. *A Current Bibliography of Vernacular Architecture* (Vernacular Architecture Group).

Munby, L M 1977. *The Hertfordshire Landscape*.

— (ed) 1963. *History of Kings Langley*.

Neale, J P 1819–29. *Views of the Seats of Noblemen and Gentlemen in England, Wales, Scotland and Ireland, from drawings by J P Neale*, 6 vols.

Newman, J 1976. *West Kent and the Weald* (The Buildings of England series), 2nd edn.

Newton, Frank, builders and decorators, of Hitchin; brochure (n d, c.1912), issued by, copy in NMR.

Nichols, J 1821–3. *Progresses of Queen Elizabeth*, 3 vols, 2nd edn (first published 1788–1805).

Notes on Hatfield House, dictated by James, 2nd Marquess of Salisbury, to Mary, Marchioness of Salisbury, in 1866–7 and edited by her; privately printed in 1886.

Oldfield. See EHAST 1940–2.

Ollard, R 1979. *The Image of the King*.

Page, W 1920. 'The origins and forms of Hertfordshire towns and villages'. *Archaeologia* **69**, 47–60.

Pantin, W A 1961. 'Medieval inns' in E M Jope (ed) *Studies in Building History*, 166–91.

Parker, V 1971. *The Making of King's Lynn*. Chichester.

Pepys *Diary. The Diary of Samuel Pepys* (ed R Latham and W Matthews, 11 vols, 1970–83).

Pevsner, Sir N and Cherry, B 1977. *Hertfordshire* (The Buildings of England series), 2nd edn.

Rahtz, P A 1979. *The Saxon and Medieval Palaces at Cheddar* (British Archaeological Reports: British Series **65**). Oxford.

Raine, J 1882. *History...of North Durham*.

RCAHM (Wales) 1988. *An Inventory of the Ancient Monuments in Glamorgan. Vol IV Domestic Architecture from the Reformation to the Industrial Revolution part II: Farmhouses and Cottages*.

RCHME. *An Inventory of the Historical Monuments in:* *Hertfordshire* (1910).
    Essex. Volume I. North-West Essex (1916).
            Volume III. North-East Essex (1922).
            Volume IV. South-East Essex (1923).
    Huntingdonshire (1926).
    Middlesex (1937).
    Dorset. Volume I. West Dorset (1952; reprinted with amendments in 1974).
            Volume II. South-East: Parts I and II; Central: Part 1 (1970, 3 vols, continuous pagination).
            Volume V. East Dorset (1975).
    Cambridge. Volume I. West Cambridgeshire (1968).
    The City of Salisbury. Volume I (1980).
    1962. *Monuments Threatened or Destroyed. A Select List: 1956–1962.*
    1981. *Hotels and Restaurants: 1830 to the Present Day* (by P Boniface).
    1986. *Rural Houses of West Yorkshire 1400–1830.*
    1987. *Houses of the North York Moors.*
Renn, D 1971. *Medieval Castles in Hertfordshire.* Chichester.
Reynolds, Susan 1977. *An Introduction to the History of English Medieval Towns.* Oxford.
Roberts, E 1974. 'Totternhoe stone and flint in Hertfordshire churches'. *Medieval Archaeol* **18**, 66–89.
Roberts, G 1844. *Life, Progresses and Rebellion of James, Duke of Monmouth,* 2 vols.
Roberts, J H 1979. 'Five medieval barns in Hertfordshire'. *Hertfordshire Archaeol* **7**, 159–80.
Rouse, E C forthcoming. 'Domestic wall and panel paintings in Hertfordshire'. *Archaeol J* **146**.

Salmon, N 1728. *The History of Hertfordshire.*
Salzman, L F 1952. *Building in England down to 1540.* Oxford.
Sandall, K 1975. 'Aisled halls in England and Wales'. *Vernacular Architect* **6**, 19–27.
    1986. 'Aisled halls in England and Wales'. *Vernacular Architect* **17**, 21–35.
Silcox-Crowe, N 1985. 'Sir Roger Pratt' in R Brown (ed) *The Architectural Outsiders*, 1–20.
Slater, T R 1980. *The Analysis of Burgages in Medieval Towns* (Department of Geography, University of Birmingham).
Smith, J T 1953. 'Shrewsbury: topography and architecture to the middle of the 17th century' (unpublished MA thesis, University of Birmingham).
    1955. 'Medieval aisled halls and their derivatives'. *Archaeol J* **112**, 76–94.
    1960. 'Medieval roofs: a classification'. *Archaeol J* **115**, 111–49.
    1971. 'Lancashire and Cheshire houses: some problems of architectural and social history'. *Archaeol J* **127**, 156–81.
    1974. 'The early development of timber buildings: the passing-brace and reversed assembly'. *Archaeol J* **131**, 238–63.
    1978. 'A clay fireback at Hitchin, Herts'. *Post-Medieval Archaeol* **12**, 127–8.

    1981. 'Mittelalterliche Dachkonstruktion in Nordwesteuropa' in Claus Ahrens (ed) *Frühe Holzkirchen im nordlichen Europa*, 379–90. Hamburg.
Smith, P 1975. *Houses of the Welsh Countryside: A Study in Historical Geography.*
de Sorbière, S 1709. *A Voyage to England, containing many things relating to the state of learning, religion and other curiosities of that Kingdom* (1st edn 1667, Cologne).
Steensberg, A 1952. *Bondehuse og Vandmøller i Danmark gennem 2000 år (Farms and Watermills in Denmark during 2000 Years).* Copenhagen.
Stone, L 1965. *Social Change and Revolution in England 1540–1640.*
Stone, L and Stone, J 1972. 'Country houses and their owners in Hertfordshire 1540–1879' in W O Aydelotte, A G Bogue and R W Fogel (eds) *The Dimensions of Quantitative Research in History*, 56–123.
Strong, R, Binney, M and Harris, J 1974. *The Destruction of the Country House 1875–1975.*
Styles, P 1957. 'Introduction' in M Walker (ed) *Warwick County Records XCVIII, Hearth Tax Returns 1.* Warwick.
Summerson, Sir J 1953. *Architecture in Britain 1530–1830.*
    1958–9. 'The idea of the villa'. *J Roy Soc Arts* **107**, 570–87.
    1959a. 'The building of Theobalds, 1504–1585'. *Archaeologia* **97**, 107–26.
    1959b. 'The classical country house in 18th-century England'. *Journal of the Royal Society of Arts*, July 1959 (reprinted in *The Unromantic Castle* (1990), 79–120).
    (ed) 1966. *The Book of Architecture of John Thorpe in the Soane Museum.* Walpole Society, Vol XL.

Tate, W E 1945–9. 'A hand list of Hertfordshire Enclosure Acts and Awards'. *E Herts Archaeol Soc Trans* **12**, 18–31.
TSAAAS 1895–1902. Transactions of the St Albans and Hertfordshire Architectural and Archaeological Society, New Series 1.
Thieme, U and Becker, F (1907–50). *Allgemeines Lexikon der bildenden Künstler*, 37 vols. Leipzig.
Turner, T H and Parker, J H (1851–9). *Domestic Architecture in England*, 3 vols. Oxford.
The Victoria History of the Counties of England.
    1902–14. *Hertfordshire*, 4 vols.
    1906. *Northants*, Vol II.
    1923. *Berkshire*, Vol III.
    1968. *Glos*, Vol VIII.
    1907. *Hertfordshire Families* (ed D Warrand).

Viney, E 1965. *Sheriffs of Bucks.* Aylesbury (privately printed).

Weinbaum, M 1937. *The Incorporation of Boroughs.* Manchester.
West, S E 1970. 'Brome, Suffolk. The excavation of a moated site, 1967'. *J Brit Archaeol Ass* 3 ser **33**, 80–121.
Wheathampstead and Harpenden 3 parts (by Harpenden and St Albans WEA, 1973–5).

Wood, M E 1948. 'Thirteenth-century domestic architecture in England'. *Archaeol J* **105** (Supplement), 1–150.
1951. 'Little Wenham Hall'. *Archaeol J* **108**, 190–1.
1965. *The English Medieval House*.

Yaxley, S (ed) 1973. *History of Hemel Hempstead*. Hemel Hempstead.

Young, A 1770. *A Six Months' Tour Through the North of England*, 4 vols.

Gazetteer

(A list of Hertfordshire houses discussed in the text: the name of each house is followed by its National Buildings Record number)

Abbots Langley

The Abbot's House	77178
Cecil Lodge	77179
Hyde Farm	77180
Kings Lodge	77182
Langleybury	77183
Manor House	77184
The Vicarage	79301
Yew Cottage	77185

Albury

Albury Hall	77186
Albury Lodge	77187
Kennel Farm	77191
Tudor Cottage	77192

Aldbury

The Old Manor House	77193
40 Stocks Road	77195
Town Farm	77197
Tudor Cottage	81908

Aldenham

Aldenham House	77200
Aldenham Social Club	79306

Ardeley

Ardeley Bury	39601
Chapel Farm	77392
The Cottage, Cromer	77393
Cromer Farm	77394
Cromer Hall	77395
High Tree Farm	79318
Moor Hall Cottage	77397
Peartrees	77398

Ashwell

29 High Street	77404
Bear House	77408
The Guild House	77405

Aspenden

Aspenden Hall	36946
The Old Rectory	77416

Aston

Aston Bury Manor	77417
Chells Manor	77420
Yew Tree Cottage	77422

Ayot St Lawrence

The Manor House	79341

Ayot St Peter

Ayot Place	77424

Baldock

'Ancient House'	77425
The Bury, 33/33A Hitchin Street	77435
Church Cottages	77426
16 High Street	77428
Holford House, 9 High Street	77427
Oak House, 22 Whitehorse Street	77437
3/5 Sun Street	77436

Barkway

Cokenach	77438
Newsells Park	77441
	77442

Barley

Lower Farm	77444
White Posts	79359

Bayford

Bayfordbury	77446

Benington

Cutting Hill Farm	77451

Berkhamsted

Ashlyns Hall	77453
Berkhamsted Place	29838
Dean Incent's House	77459
214 High Street	77461
The King's Arms	79377
Market House	77462
The Swan Hotel	77460

Bishop's Stortford

The Black Lion	77465
2/4 Bridge Street	77466
Church Manor House	77468
The George Hotel	77473
Guild House	77477
6 High Street	77469
8 High Street	77470
10 High Street	77470
17 North Street	77475
21 North Street	77476
Wickham Hall	77479

Bovingdon

6/8 Church Street (Bull Cottages)	77480
Water Lane Cottage	79376
Westbrook Hay	77482

Bramfield

Bramfield Bury	77483

Braughing

Causeway House	77487
The Gatehouse	77490
Hamels	77491
Old Rose and Crown	77492
Turk's Cottage	77493
Upp Hall	77494

Brent Pelham

Beeches	77495
Blackhall Cottage	79392
Brent Pelham Hall	77496
Church Cottage	77498

Brickendon Liberty

Brickendon Bury	77501

Buntingford

Little Court	77510

Bushey

Bushey Hall	77511

Oundle	77514
Patchetts Green Farm	77515

Bygrave
Manor House	77516

Cheshunt
Cheshunt Nunnery	79425
The Four Swans	77518
Cheshunt Great House	29842
Theobalds Manor	77520

Chorleywood
4/5 Chorleywood Bottom	77522
Dell Cottages	77523
King John's Farm	77524
The Retreat	77525

Clothall
Quickswood	77529
Walnut Tree Farm	77527

Codicote
Codicote Bury	77530

Cottered
Hall Farm	77535
The Lordship	77536
Rumbolds	77537
Throcking Hall	77538

Datchworth
Hawkins Hall Farm	77540
The Horns	77542

Elstree
Nicoll Farm	77545
The Holly Bush	78458

Essendon
Bedwell Park	39610

Flamstead
Beechwood Park	39611
Delmerend Farmhouse	77550
Saunders Almshouses	82043

Flaunden
Oak Cottage	77552

Furneux Pelham
Furneux Pelham Hall	77553

Great Gaddesden
Ballingdon Cottage	77559
Gaddesden Hall	77560

Glebe House	77561
Golden Parsonage	77562
Moor Cottage	77565

Great Munden
Old Farm	77572

Harpenden
Cross Farm	77573
Harpenden Hall	77574
The Old House, 27 Leyton Road	77575

Harpenden Rural
Rothamsted Manor	39613

Hatfield
Brocket Hall	33636
Great Nast Hyde	77578
Hatfield House	77579
Market House	79495
Old Palace	77580

Hemel Hempstead
Boxmoor Place	77584
33–39 High Street	77586
60 High Street	79514
63 High Street	77587
65/67 High Street	77588
75 High Street	29839
76 High Street	77590
81/83 High Street	77591
Market House	77594
Piccott's End Farm	77596

Hertford
3 St Andrew's Street	77622
21/23 St Andrew's Street	77625
22/24 St Andrew's Street	77624
28 St Andrew's Street	77626
40/42 St Andrew's Street	79525
43 St Andrew's Street	79526
51 St Andrew's Street	77627
Balls Park	39616
Bayley Hall	77601
Dimsdale House, 16 Bull Plain	77603
3–13 Fore Street	77608
The Salisbury Arms (formerly The Bell)	79519
28/30 Fore Street	79521
99/101 Fore Street	77612
130 Fore Street	77613
Goldings	39617
Hertingfordbury Park	79532
5 Old Cross	77617
19/21 West Street	77629
Bridgeman House, 37 West Street	77630

Hertingfordbury
Cole Green Park	79533

Hinxworth
Hinxworth Place	77637

Hitchin
34 Bancroft (Bancroft House)	77642
The Brotherhood	77638
The Hermitage	77639
31/33 Bancroft	77641
105 Bancroft	77644
15 Bucklersbury	77647
The George Inn	77646
4 High Street	77650
Hitchin Priory	39620
4 Market Place	77652
23 Market Place	77655
103/104 Queen Street	77656
7 Sun Street	77659
13 Tilehouse Street	77660
30 Tilehouse Street	79551
Lewesford House, 42 Tilehouse Street	77662

Hoddesdon
Broxbourne Bury	77503
The Grange	77505
Rawdon House	77504

Holwell
Church Farm	77667

Hormead
Great Hormead Dane	77671
Judd's Farm	77672
The Old Rectory	79554

Hunsdon
Briggens	77677
Briggens Home Farm	77678
Hunsdon House	77679

Ickleford
Old Ramerick Manor	77683
The Parsonage	77684

Ippollitts
Almshoe Bury	77685
Maydencroft Manor	79561

Kelshall
The Maltings	77686

Kimpton
Ballslough Cottage	79567
Kimpton Hall	79569
Ramridge Farmhouse	77690

Kings Langley
Langley Lodge	77692

Kings Walden		Shootersway Farm	77745	3/5 French Row	77793

Kings Walden

Kings Walden Bury	39628
Leggatt's Farm	77695

Knebworth

Knebworth House	79579

Letchworth

Letchworth Hall	77697

Little Gaddesden

Ashridge House	39612
John O'Gaddesden's House	77702

Little Hadham

Acremore Cottage	77705
Ashmeads	77706
Bridge End	77708
The Whare	77708
Bury Green Farm	77709
Clintons	77710
Gouldburns and May Cottage	77711
Green Street Cottage	77712
Hadham Hall	79598
2 Ford Hill	77713
Hollands Close	77713
Westfield	77715

London Colney

Colney Park	77721

Markyate

Markyate Cell	77723

Much Hadham

Green Tye Farmhouse	77727
Bull and Campden Cottages	77724
Gaytons	77726
The Hall	82650
Morris Cottage	77732
The Old Red Lion	79614
Mingers	77730
Moat Farmhouse	79620
Moor Place	77731
The Palace	77733
Yew Tree Farm	77734

Nettleden with Potten End

Corner Cottage	77737
Holly Bush Farm	77735
1–3 Frithsden Gardens	77736

Northaw

Nyn Hall	77742

Northchurch

Arne Cottage	77743

North Mymms

Brookmans	77746
Lower Farm	77748
North Mymms Park	61271

Offley

The Old Post Office (now The Court House)	77753
Offley Place	39632

Pirton

Hammond's Farm	77756
Pirton Grange	77758
Pirton Old Hall (now called Docwra Manor)	77759
Walnut Tree Farm	77761

Potters Bar

Clare Hall Manor	77763
62–68 Blanche Lane	77762
Salisbury House	77765
Wrotham Park	77766
Wyllyots Manor	32256

Preston

Temple Dinsley	77768

Redbourn

Beech Hyde	77770
Cumberland House	79657
Redbournbury	77772

Rickmansworth

The Bury	77774
Croxley Hall Farm	81779
Moor Park	79667
The More	77778
The Priory	77779

Ridge

Tyttenhanger House	77780

Royston

9 Kneesworth Street	77786
11 Kneesworth Street	77786
59 High Street	77784
61 High Street	77784
18 Melbourn Street	77787
Royston Priory	77788

Rushden

Julians	39634

St Albans

137 Fishpool Street	77792

3/5 French Row	77793
6 George Street	77794
12 George Street	77795
18/20 George Street, Tabard Inn	77796
22 George Street	79696
Clock Tower, High Street	81003
Barclays Bank, 3 High Street	77799
33 High Street	77802
37 Holywell Hill	77804
Holywell House	79693
18 Lower Dagnall Street	77805
2 Market Place	77806
The Old Boot, 4 Market Place	81843
Moot Hall, 25 Market Place	77807
New Barns	77808
61/63 Park Street	77809
St Julians	77811
33 St Michael's Street	79688
Mr Kentish's Mansion, 1 St Peter's Street	77812
6 St Peter's Street	77813
32 St Peter's Street	77815
53/55 Sopwell Lane	81005

St Michael

Childwick Bury	77817
Hill End Farm	81014
Gorhambury	39636
Verulam House	77818
Westwick Row Farm	77820

St Paul's Walden

The Hoo	32423
Hoo End Grange	77823
Stagenhoe Park	77824

St Stephen

Burston Manor	77825
Holt Farm	77826
Searches	77827
Tenements Farm	77828

Sandon

Hyde Hall	77829
Sandon Bury	77831

Sarratt

The Grove	77834

Sawbridgeworth

The Elms	77837
Great Hyde Hall	77838
Pishiobury Park	77840

Shenley

Salisbury Hall	77841

Standon

Standon Lordship	77850

Fabdens	77843	Grove Farm (Cottages)	77884	Woodhall Park	81144
59/61 Collier's End	77842	Pendley Manor	77885		
Rigery's Farm	77849	Tring Park	32409	*Welwyn*	
Great Barwick Farm	32424			Guessens	81145
Sutes	77851	*Tring Rural*		The Old Rectory	77929
Town Farm	77852	Betlow Farm	77886		
30/32 High Street	77855	Red House Farm	81108	*Welwyn Garden City*	
52 High Street	77856			Digswell House	60014
		Walkern		Ludwick Hall	77930
Stanstead Abbots		Rook's Nest Farm	77888		
Bonningtons	77858			*Westmill*	
Red Lion Inn	77859	*Ware*		The Dower House	81153
Stanstead Bury	77861	14–18 Baldock Street	77890	Wakeley	77931
Rye House	77860	20 Baldock Street	77891	Westmill Bury	77932
		The Old Bull's Head	77893		
Stevenage		45 Baldock Street	77894	*Weston*	
Stebbing Farm	77872	Place House	77895	Howell's Farm	77933
3 High Street	77865	The Manor House	77897		
The Grange, 5 High Street		The Priory	81117	*Wheathampstead*	
(formerly The Swan)	77864	French Horn Inn	77898	Bride Hall	77934
68 High Street	77867	94 High Street	77904	Bury Farm	77935
72 High Street	81071			Delaport Farm	77938
		Ware Rural		Mackerye End	77940
Tewin		Blakesware Manor	77907	Mackerye End Farm	77941
Marden Hill	77874	Fanhams Hall	77908	Old Raisins Farm	77942
Queen Hoo Hall	77875	New Hall	77911	Turners Hall Farm	77944
Tewin House	77876	New House Farm	77912		
Tewin Water	77877	Ware Park	77914	*Widford*	
				Goddards	77946
Therfield		*Watford*			
		Cassiobury Park	39642	*Wyddial*	
The Old Rectory	81094	The George Inn	81141	Beauchamps	77950
		Little Cassiobury	77921	Wyddial Hall	77953
Thorley		177/179 High Street	77919		
Thorley Hall	77879			*Wymondley*	
		Watford Rural		Manor House	77955
Thundridge		Oxhey Hall	77923	The Priory	77959
Thundridge Bury	77882	Oxhey Place	77924	Redcoats	77956
				Wymondley Bury	32405
Tring		*Watton-at-Stone*			
15 Akeman Street	81102	Watton Woodhall	77926		

Index

Figures in **bold** refer to the illustrations. Houses in Hertfordshire are listed under the parish name, while other houses referred to in the text are under the name of the house and county.